Debt Cures™

"They" Don't Want You to Know About

Debt Cures™

"They" Don't Want You to Know About

Kevin Trudeau

EQUITY
PRESS

Contents

Disclaimer

I am not a lawyer. That is no secret. I also am not an idiot. Some may like to debate me on that, but I know when people are being taken advantage of, and when it is happening by people that they think they can trust, something needs to be done about it.

Because of the success of my past books, I have been the subject of intense scrutiny. I have been called the "epitome of the snake oil salesman," a "quack," and a "flim-flam-man." One internet blogger has called me "Satan." Maybe that's why I can take the heat.

Think of me what you will, but the facts exposed here are what I believe to be the simple truth. The solutions are bona fide concepts that can get you out of debt and on your way to wealth. There is no hocus-pocus happening. This is not a shell game. The federal government and the banks and the credit card companies are ripping off the American public, plain and simple.

I tell you what I see happening and I tell you what you can do about it. These are easy techniques that anyone can do. I am not an attorney, a financial planner, or an accountant. You should check with those professionals before you take any of the steps outlined in this book. They will probably want a copy of this book for themselves.

As with everything in life, things change! The government, the credit agencies, the banks, the credit card issuers, they seem to always be making changes to laws and policies. You should be aware that information in this book may change, so you'll need to check for any updates!

Examples and stories are used to illustrate the methods available. Names, amounts and numbers are fictionalized, but the facts do not change: you can get out of debt and you can create wealth. It is my purpose to enlighten you and to provide you with an interesting book to read. Enjoy.

Acknowledgments

Getting a book written, proofed, and published is no small job. I want to thank the many people who helped bring this book from the idea stage into the final printed pages that you now hold in your hand.

I know that you too will be thankful for their hard work when you read about what goes on behind the closed doors of the banking and credit card industry. The powerful executives and their pals in Washington may be motivated by greed, but I am powered by need – the need to reveal what is happening, so you can get out from under their grip.

The facts and information have been gathered here for you. My sincere thanks to all who made this book what it is. The shared goal of all involved is to give you the information so that you have the power – the power to cure your debt, the power to create wealth, and the power to take back control of your life! That deserves a round of applause!

CHAPTER 1

A License to Steal

I go to my mailbox every day just like you, and nearly every day, no exaggeration, certainly at least four times a week, I receive a credit card offer beckoning me with "You're Pre-Approved!" "0% Interest Rate!" "Transfer all your balances!" Many of these companies have now gotten so bold that they even say in bright red ink printed across the envelope: "URGENT! Don't throw me away!" But I do throw them away, and you should too.

I'm not the only one getting inundated with credit card application offers. You get them. Your neighbor gets them. Your college-age child gets them. We all do. Even my dog has gotten one. Fortunately, Princess had the good sense to chew it up. The credit card companies send out four billion pieces of mail like this every year. That's right: 4 BILLION.

That's crazy.

And why do they bother with the time and expense of all those mailings? Because they are making billions of dollars by ripping off the American citizen! The credit card companies, the banks, the mortgage lenders, the payday loan companies, the debt consolidation agencies, the debt collectors, and the entire consumer lending industry are designed to screw the American consumer. That's me, that's you, that's our friends and family. And you know what? For lack of a better way of saying it, I'm mad as hell and I'm not going to take it anymore. And neither should you.

It wasn't always this way, but there is a problem in America that is not being talked about and the US government, that's right the federal government of this country, is partly to blame. Over the last three decades, the consumer lending industry has spiraled out of control. And the United States federal government has let it happen. In fact, they helped create the monster that is now eating the average American citizen alive. They're actually working with the banking industry, creating laws and regulations that allow the credit card companies to rip off the American citizen.

The system is geared to keep you in debt!

Are you in debt? I see you nodding your head. Again, you are not the only one. It's the American way. The system is made to keep Americans in debt. We as a nation are carrying a balance of consumer debt to the tune of 2.4 trillion dollars. I don't know if I can carry that tune, and I am not sure if I know how to write out that many zeroes. The amount is even more staggering when you realize that figure does not include our home mortgages. Based on the latest census statistics, that equates to $8,000 of debt for every man, woman, and child living here in the United States. Let's assume the kiddies are not charge card-carrying consumers, not yet anyway, so that means the figure per adult is even higher. The number is not per household; it is per person. That is a heavy weight to bear. It is too much to bear, and the scales are out of balance, completely lopsided. They are in fact tipping out of control, and in favor of the credit card companies.

Ordinary People

Let's take a look into the life of an ordinary couple. Ed and Sue have been married for several years. They have two kids, a dog, a minivan, and a small house, but no white picket fence. Ed and Sue both work to make ends meet, and they do not live an extravagant lifestyle. Their money is spent on groceries, daycare, and paying their credit card bills. Like the average family, they have almost $10,000 in credit card balances. Ed and Sue sat down together and looked at their bills. They knew they had to do something. Every month, they made payments, but the balances never seemed to get smaller. We'll be seeing a lot more of Ed and Sue in the coming pages.

We all have some amount of debt, but some of us are up to our eyeballs. I can reassure you, it is not your fault! The aggressive practices by the credit card companies, banks, mortgage lenders, department stores, corporations, lending institutions – the entire consumer lending industry – are criminal in my opinion and should be illegal, but in fact the federal government allows it to happen. These companies take advantage of the American citizen, and our government has already rubber stamped its approval of their treacherous ways. This deceitful abuse of the people of our country is the greatest rip-off in our nation's history.

Just what are these aggressive, underhanded tactics? In a nutshell, the system is geared to keep you in debt! The practices of the industry are designed to make sure you are late on your monthly payments, to make sure you go over the limit on your credit cards, and to make sure that the enormous fees and incredibly high interest rates continue to go up and up. Hang on and I will explain in detail, but first, notice the title of this book: *Debt Cures "They" Don't Want You to Know About.* Who is the "they" that I am referring to? The credit companies, the mortgage lenders, and the banks, of course. And the United States federal government.

Obscene Profits

Why should they care what I am telling you? The almighty dollar, of course. They want it, and they want it to come from you. All companies are out to make a profit, and I have no problem with that. I do have a problem with industry insiders confiding that the profits these companies make are not only astronomical, but are referred to as "*obscene profits,*" likened to those parties who are involved in oil cartels. They – these lending institutions – are predators, and they prey on the innocent hard working bill-paying individuals of the United States. It's like the American citizen doesn't have a prayer. And it's not me saying it. The government officials and the insiders call the profits that the banks and the credit card companies and the mortgage companies are making "obscene."

The American credit card industry alone earns a profit of $30 billion every year. Not $30 million; $30 billion. And they still want more.

In my first book series, *Natural Cures,* which sold over ten million copies, I exposed the pharmaceutical industry. Because of what I printed, the drug companies feared losing profits, and they lashed out at me with a vengeance. I have been the object of false accusations, of lawsuits, even death threats. I don't care. I will not back down. I know in my heart what is right. If you have not read any of my previous books, you need to know what I am all about.

> Credit card company profits are $30 BILLION every year!

Twenty years ago, I used to be an overly ambitious young man, desiring nothing more than wealth. And you know what? I achieved it. Now, because of all that I have been through in my life, and because of all the letters and testimonials from the thousands of readers who have been helped, I am on a mission, and my mission has nothing to do with making money. It is always easier for someone who has money to say that, I know, but wealth is not my objective. I have reached a point in my life that I need to do things that I believe have a positive impact on individuals and society. The mission of my books, newsletters, and website, my entire business enterprise, is simple: We positively impact the whole person. That includes doing things that I believe are beneficial to a person's physical health, emotional well-being, intellectual endeavors, personal fulfillment, and financial health. All aspects of our health are interrelated. I have spent years dealing with physical health, and now I feel compelled to focus on another aspect in society that needs the hot white light to be shined down upon it. Besides a person's physical health, what is usually our number one concern? That's right. Money. Our financial health.

Get Mama Happy Again

Everyone who has ever had financial problems knows what I am talking about. The old saying, "If mama ain't happy, ain't nobody happy," can be twisted to say, "If money is a problem, everything is a problem." The constant stress eats away at all areas of our life. We can't sleep. We are distracted at work, which can cause problems with our employers. We can't eat, or we eat too much and do harm to our bodies. We snap at our children and argue with our spouses. Because of our monetary situation, family and work are affected and everyone suffers. Pressures mount until we feel our whole life is a house of cards that is going to tumble to the floor at any second. Those who have a debt hanging over their heads know exactly what I am talking about.

Consumer debt is an epidemic in our country. Every one of us is affected by it. Anyone who has ever taken out a loan or opened a credit card account is affected. If you are holding this book, I imagine you fall into that category. The consumer lending industry is taking advantage of the American public, and it touches all of us, regardless of your gender, your race, your age, your status, your religion, or your income. This is one case where Uncle Sam is pointing his finger at all of us, and he is saying, "I want you." The banks and lenders are standing behind him, rubbing their hands together in greedy anticipation.

Government and business are in this together, and this is the one scam that affects every single person, every one of us. It does not matter if you are low income, middle class, or extremely affluent. It does not matter if you are black, white, or purple with pink polka dots. It does not matter if you are man, woman, or dog – considering my dog is receiving credit card offers too. Regardless of all these things, the rules are the same across the board. They, of course, don't want you to know the rules. That is why they hate it when I write books. So lenders, look out! The good news for you is that basically everything you need to know to get off the merry-go-round of credit card scams and lending industry abuse is right here in this book. This book is going to help millions of people lower their payments and get out of debt very, very quickly.

The banks are in bed with the feds, and we all know by now that politics, and the love of money, make for strange bedfellows. Bed hopping may make for an interesting daytime afternoon soap opera drama, but when it is your life or your wallet or your future that is affected, it is time to change the channel.

The Good Old Days

I remember the "good old days" of how business used to be handled. The days of a smile and simple handshake are long gone. A gentleman's agreement is a thing of the past, as today's lenders certainly do not act like gentlemen. They more likely resemble barracudas, who lie in wait and rely on surprise. Or perhaps Count Dracula, who will gladly suck you dry with nary a regret or backward glance. The days of trust have died, but we, the citizens, are the ones getting the stake pounded into our hearts.

It was not always this way. As recently as the 1970s, the American working citizen was treated with respect. Fair lending practices existed, and a banker was a trusted partner. A person could be granted overdraft protection on a checking account, simply by asking. It was a free courtesy granted to a good customer. A thirty-day free grace period to pay the balance was standard. But somewhere along the way, fairness went out of fashion. The terms "free" and "courtesy" have fallen out of the lending lexicon. Along came the 1980s, and the famous movie line from Gordon Gekko in *Wall Street*, "Greed is good," announced the mindset of banks, corporations, and lending institutions. Greed became rampant and once it reared its ugly head, it became a wild beast to tame.

In the early days of loans and lending, the bank or mortgage company would give money in return for simple interest. Here's my collateral; here's my signature; and I received a loan. I repaid it within a certain timeframe, plus I paid a stated amount of interest. There were no hidden surprises and creatively-named fees. Then the annual percentage rate entered the picture. The scene then ushered in loan sharks and shylocks right out of Shakespeare's *Merchant of Venice*, wanting to extract a pound of flesh and charging usury interest at exorbitant rates. The way some institutions deal with their customers today, a loan shark is a much better way to go.

The current method of fees on top of fees to keep a person tied up in debt their whole life, a prisoner to that debt, conjures up the days of the Dickens' era debtor prisons. However, today's lenders do not want us going to jail for not being able to pay our bills. They want us to keep working and therefore able to keep paying them month after month after month, while not reducing our debt at all. It truly is a crime.

Some states placed caps on the amount of interest that lenders could charge, but the banks and the credit card companies didn't miss a beat. A new world of possibilities was born; for the rest of us, a new four-letter word had arrived: fees.

Fees, Fees, Fees

Fees and points have no limits. They are the fine print, the nitty gritty, the name of the game, the bread and butter of the consumer lending industry. Basically, interest rates may be limited, but the fees are carte blanche, and credit card companies take full advantage in every way possible. Let's call a spade a spade, and let's call these fees what they really are: interest.

> One banker said, "The trick is charging a lot, repeatedly..."

The banks and the credit card companies can charge any number of fees, in any amount, and call them anything they want – activation fee, annual fee, monthly maintenance fee, sign-up fee, credit protection fee, late fee, over-limit fee, we-are-greedy-fee – and the net effect is that we, the "consumer," could end up paying 50%, 60%, 70% in "interest." The banks are allowed to be legal loan sharks.

They have gone mad with greed. We the people are no longer human beings, fellow citizens of America; these companies see us as nothing more than numbers consuming products. All we are now in their eyes are "consumers." If we are not a consumer, we are not important. We are merely a country of consumers, not individuals, not living, breathing, human beings. This is an element in our society that needs to be changed. Who resists change the most? The ones making the money off of those of us who once were blind. But now we see! It is my job to open your eyes to the scams going on in the credit card industry, the student loan industry, and the debt collection industry. Once you know, you will never fall into their traps again. Just because they give you money, they do not own you forever. You don't have to be a slave to them. Stop thinking that you don't have options. You do!

A Tangled Web

The stories of their power and corruption are endless. The following pages are chock full of them. Maybe the name Providian does not ring a bell, but this credit card company was one of the largest credit card issuers in the country, and you probably have received an offer from them just like I have in my mailbox. They have sent over one billion offers in the mail, so it is a good bet that you have been targeted by them.

What most people don't know is that this company was investigated for fraud and ended up paying $300 million to settle the allegations of unfair and deceptive business practices. $300 million. Six months after that, Providian paid an additional $105 million to settle the same allegations in a class-action suit, filed on behalf of the customers. The California District attorney involved in the case stated that Providian's way of treating their customers was a "web of deceptive and misleading business practices."

> It's a web of deceptive and misleading practices.

The San Francisco Chronicle reported that Providian founder Andrew Kahr wrote in an internal memo about their customers, the "problem is to squeeze out enough revenue and get customers to sit still for the squeeze." *The Chronicle* also obtained a separate memo that Kahr wrote to the executive vice president that stated, "Making people pay for access to credit is a lucrative business wherever it is practiced....The trick is charging a lot, repeatedly, for small doses of incremental credit."

What makes my head spin even more is that the director of this bank was then hired by the federal government to be the new ethics czar for businesses! "The man President Bush tapped to lead his corporate crime watchdog team was a director of a San Francisco credit-card firm that just two years ago paid more than $400 million to settle charges that it cheated consumers." That actual statement taken from the San Francisco *Chronicle* sounds like a bit from the fake newscasts on *Saturday Night Live*.

A credit card issuer, unrelated to Providian, was alleged to have committed even more egregious deceptive practices. The employees of this credit card issuer have anonymously come forward under the shadow of darkness for fear of losing their jobs to confess that they were told to hold customers' payment checks for a few days and not post them to the accounts, so that the payments would be deemed late and they then could charge a late fee. People paid on time and then still got dinged a $25, $35, or $45 late fee! Because the company was not posting their payments! This company allegedly even had employees shred checks so no payment at all was recorded! That didn't make front page news, did it? It's like some sort of secret society from the dark ages still exists.

Legal scams in the lending industry happen every day, ripping off the American citizen. You sign up for a credit card with a credit limit of $1000. The credit card company allows you to charge over the limit; they don't tell you that you have gone over your limit because they want you to do it so they can then slap you with an over-limit fee. You may pay timely every month, but if one time, for whatever circumstance, you pay a day late, you could be hit with a $29, $39, or $49 late payment fee. The credit card companies structure your minimum payment amount so if that is all you ever pay, you will be paying forever. They don't want you to pay it off. They want you to pay a little every month so they can keep their hand in your wallet. The interest will continue to accrue faster than you can pay down the balance. You make the minimum monthly payment, month after month, and yet the balance never seems to get smaller. You begin to feel like the proverbial hamster on the wheel, working up a sweat and going nowhere.

I Like This Guy

Let me tell you a story, a true story that was printed in the *Houston Chronicle* about one ordinary man, just like you and me, who used his credit card to pay for his lunch one day. Hale Hilsabeck owns a karate school in Denver. He is an average tax paying citizen who pays his bills timely. In March 2005, his $12 charge for his lunch unwittingly put him over his credit limit on his MasterCard by $1.91. His monthly billing statement showed up a couple weeks later, and they had hit him with a $35 charge for going over the credit limit. He paid the minimum payment and did not use that card again. However, his minimum payment did not bring him below his credit limit so the next month he was again charged an over-limit fee.

He called the credit card issuer to complain about the second fee and was told nothing could be done and that he should apply for a higher credit limit. When the next bill arrived, there was yet a third over-limit fee due to the fact that he did not pay the second fee, which kept him over the credit limit. Tired of the game, and the $105 in over-limit fees, he paid off the entire balance, $799.19, by writing a check for $800, and he closed the account.

Now what he did next is why I really like this guy. He treated them like they treat us. He then wrote the credit card company a letter, requesting a refund of the eighty-one cents he overpaid. "I'd prefer that you send a certified check or money order, since you have no credit history with me and I have no information in regard to your references," he wrote.

If they did not pay him within 25 days, he told them that they would be subject to the $105 late fee. He was informed that they would refund his overpayment and $70 of the over-limit fees he paid. They, however, did not make payment to him in the 25-day timeframe that they allow for their customers to pay their bills, so Mr. Hilsabeck stated he would assess additional late fees and finance charges of 20% for every month that they were delinquent. He maintained that he would continue to send them statements each month even though they said they would not pay. This article ran in October 2005. I do not know if he is still persisting, but I like his gumption. He is only treating them the exact way they treat their customers.

It's Where You Live

It happens every day, in every city, town, and borough. Men and women; low income and high income; less educated and highly educated; every color, every creed; every "consumer" is at risk for these scams. Albert Einstein is attributed as saying something to the effect that "compound interest is the most powerful force in the universe." I don't disagree. I also believe that knowledge is the most powerful force in the universe.

As with all my books, I tell you that knowledge is power, and by reading this book cover to cover, you will be armed with the ammunition that you need to know so that you will never be taken advantage of again by the banks and credit card companies.

Take the time to read this book through, chapter by chapter, in order. I don't talk in financial jargon or legalese. I speak the plain truth in plain English. You will understand every word, and the techniques outlined and the steps to follow are not difficult. I guide you every step of the way.

It is outrageous and ridiculous what the lenders and banks and corporations are getting away with, and it is mind-boggling that the US government slaps them heartily on the back and allows them to make their money by screwing the American citizen. Banks and lenders and credit card companies are taking advantage of people. I say, enough is enough. Let's expose the industry, and let's take control of our debt and our lives again.

> Knowledge is power – use it!

The credit card issuers are playing a numbers game. They could issue you one credit card with a $10,000 limit, but they don't. They don't make their money that way. The same bank will offer you ten cards with a $1,000 limit on each card so it can hit each card with fees. They hate people who have just one card, and they hate people who pay their bill each month. Sure, the credit card company gets a small fee for each purchase you make with the card, but that is not enough for them. They have succumbed to the green monster called greed.

It is not a fabrication that a person with a balance of $1000 can go over their limit by $1 or pay one day late and be buried with fees. By making the minimum monthly payment alone, the balance will grow like a snowball rolling down the mountain, and the individual is hit with an avalanche of a huge bill. That $1000 can become $2000, $3000, $4000, even $5000. But wait a minute, all that person really owes is the $1000 – the rest is industry-created FEES!

It happens to all of us. My friend Kelly only uses a Visa card and pays the balance each month. She was shopping at the mall one afternoon and was enticed to open a department store credit card in order to save 15% that day. She charged $65. Kelly did not receive the first bill timely in the mail, and paid one day late, but that does not matter. She received a late charge assessment of $29. That's 45% of the balance she owed. A bank or credit card issuer is not allowed to charge 45% interest, but by calling it a "fee," it is fair game. A telephone call to the company received no sympathy, no "sorry," and no solution. A hit of 45% certainly washes out any savings of 15% on the $65 purchase. Opening a new credit card to save money obviously did not turn out that way. That's how they make their money – being able to hit you with fees. $29 from customers month after month adds up to a lot of money.

Personal Slaves

Just like casinos are in business to make money, credit card companies are in business to make money. They are not offering a service out of the kindness of their hearts. They are bloodsuckers looking for patsies. A major senior official of one of the largest banking groups in the world allegedly said that they make most of their money off the lower and middle class because they are, and I quote, the "easiest to rob." They have no shame in stating that they make their profits off those people who are most desperately in need of credit cards and loans. I sat in a meeting once with high-level bankers and I was told, "We love consumer lending. We want them to be late; we want them to just make their minimum monthly payments. We virtually are in their wallets for the rest of their lives."

> Another banker said: "Slavery is alive and well in America."

Aghast, I declared, "It sounds like they are your personal slaves."

Without missing a beat, this banker replied with a grin, "Slavery is alive and well in America."

Well, I beg to differ. These bankers and corporate executives may think that they are the Goliaths, but they have forgotten that David was victorious, and Goliath fell and he fell hard. It is time that we revoke their license to steal.

If you are one of the millions of Americans who have some debt, and I'm not talking about a home mortgage necessarily, but a car loan, a student loan, a personal loan for a boat or a vacation, credit card debt, whatever the case may be – don't think you are stuck forever. They want you to feel like you have no options, but you do. They don't have to own you forever. They don't have to own you at all. You can get control of your debts, and you can get control of your life.

Many television commercials and internet ads tout that debt consolidation is the way to go or that even bankruptcy is a good alternative. Don't do it. I have the insider secrets, and I am ready to share them with you. No longer will the banks and the credit card issuers and the lending companies make obscene profits off the backs of the American citizen. The consumer lending industry really has become like the Wild West where anything goes. They act as if they're above the law. I'm the most hated guy in corporate America for good reason. I hurt their profits. I am not against profit, but rape is against the law. They are not satisfied with healthy profits. They have risen to the level of outrageous and egregious fees, and we can fight back.

Freedom from Bondage

People like Ed and Sue, and me and you, we can fight back and take control. Take control of your debt and you take control of your life. It really is that simple. I'm going to show you how. Don't think that they hold invisible power over you. And don't think that debt is a four-letter word. Once you pay off your bad debt, you will learn how to use good debt to create wealth. Once the insider secrets are exposed, you will learn how to play their games and reduce your "bad" debt very, very quickly. Just about every millionaire in this country will tell you that using credit, good debt, helped them get rich. Not only do I want you to cure your debt, I want you to learn the secrets of good debt. You could become the next millionaire to tell your story.

The federal government is allowing the credit card companies and big banks to enslave people, but we don't have to live in bondage. We are now aware that trust is a thing of the past. The Enron scandal certainly taught us that. Big business only looks out for big business. Corporate greed and accounting games seem to be the norm, instead of the exception. Providian, the credit card company that paid millions to settle fraud charges, didn't even make headline news. I'm not sure exactly what *cahoots* smells like, but when the government and the consumer lending industry are in *cahoots*, I know that it stinks.

We have a lot to cover in this book, but rest assured, curing your debt will cure your life. Let me show you the way out of the trap and the path to freedom. The following pages will show you how to eliminate the fees, the penalties, the interest – the rip-off money. I can show you how you can, virtually overnight, take your monthly payments (credit card bills, personal loans, etc.) and, with techniques outlined in the upcoming chapters, reduce the total by one-half or even two-thirds. We will talk about credit scores and credit reports, and how to get yours, and how to fix yours in 30 days. This is critical. Your score is how you are judged and determines the amount of interest you will be charged.

> Get rid of "bad" debt and move on to "good" credit!

I will show you how to reduce the amount you owe, be it $5K, $10K, $20K, or even $30K of debt, in 30 days, or perhaps even eliminate it, just by following some simple steps. Can you imagine that? Totally eliminating your debt! You can, and the consumer lending industry does not want you to know about it! This book will show you how you can reduce the amount of your student loans and pay them off. The whole student loan industry is a scandal unto itself and the biggest rip-off game in town!

Free Money?

Best of all, I will turn you on to free money! There is a whole chapter on free money programs that nearly anyone can get just by making phone calls, filling out simple applications and following the requirements. You can get $5K, $10K, $30K, and in some cases $50K and more. The beauty of these programs is that they are grants and you do not have to repay them!

I will explain the difference between good credit and bad credit, and how credit can be used to create wealth. I will tell you how, no matter your current credit situation, whether you have so-so credit, bad credit, or no credit, you can improve and start with a clean slate. I will tell you how to get corporate credit of up to $1 million, which will send you on your way to creating wealth, not debt. I will also expose the debt collection scams and how the debt collectors are trained to lie and harass. They allegedly even told one nine-year-old girl that they could take her mommy away for the rest of her life. You will learn how you could stop debt collectors cold, and I will tell you how two magic words turned one person's nightmare story into a platinum card.

Ignorance is not bliss. In fact, it can be a nightmare. I don't want you to end up like Abby, who was heavily marketed to by credit card companies at age 18. By the time she reached age 21, she had her car repossessed, had 8 credit cards, defaulted on two loans, and was unable to even open a savings account in her own name alone. All this credit was given to her while she was earning minimum wage at a part-time job. It should be obvious by now that the credit lenders do not have your best interests at heart. They don't have a heart.

Read and You Will Be Rewarded

As with all my books, I ask that you read through all the chapters in order and don't skip around looking for a certain issue. Topics are explained as we go, and I want you to understand the whole picture. I am really proud of you for taking this journey and breaking free from the invisible ties that have you all wrapped up. You are in bondage no more!

This book explains how all these legal scams work in the so-called prestigious firms of consumer lending and how the government allows them to do it. We can turn the tables on them. Instead of paying them billions of dollars, this book tells you where to find the billions of dollars that are available to you.

The miserly profit-hoarding consumer lending industry will be exposed for what it is. When you learn the nuts and bolts of the industry, they will no longer be able to put the screws to you. I know the rules, and now you will too. Together we can stop the insanity. For everyone who is sick and tired of the money games and wants relief, *Debt Cures* is the answer. The consumer lending industry profit is obscene, and basically every single person is paying too much. That is the point of this book. We no longer have to be victimized by big corporations and the government. We can stop being slaves to the banks. We can stop being owned by the credit card companies. Their license to steal is being put through the shredder. It is time we simply say, "No more." It is time we become, once again, free.

CHAPTER 2

The Credit Shakedown

"She works hard for the money, so hard for it, honey. She works hard for the money so you better treat her right."
~ Donna Summer

Let me give you some interesting big number statistics to throw out at your next neighborhood barbecue:

- ✔ By the end of 2003, there were nearly 1.3 billion credit cards in circulation in the United States.
- ✔ We Americans spend approximately $1.5 trillion using our credit cards.
- ✔ America's credit card use is greater than the rest of the entire world combined.
- ✔ Among U.S. industries, none draws higher profits than the credit card industry.
- ✔ Credit card banks were top contributors to President Bush's 2000 election campaign. MBNA ranked #1, the largest donor; Citigroup, #10, and Bank of America, #13.
- ✔ The MBNA president personally gave $100,000 to the Bush fund.
- ✔ MBNA dropped to #6 for the 2004 Bush campaign, but gave more money – more than $350,000.

Billions in Profits

Credit card companies here in the land of the red, white, and blue spend $5 billion a year marketing their credit cards to us. That's a lot of greenback. If they weren't making any money they would not be able to spend so much in offers and advertising, so obviously the credit card industry is a lucrative endeavor. And they're making it off the back of the American citizen. The average American carries about $8,000 in credit card debt, and the credit card companies are making record profits, roughly $30 billion before taxes. There are nine zeros in a billion, so let me draw you a picture: $30,000,000,000.

Deep in debt? It's not your fault!

Now we understand why the insiders called the profits obscene.

The offers that show up daily in our mailboxes promise us: Rewards! Privileges! Cash Back! A couple years ago, one major credit card company even had a promotion that offered the chance to win a private tropical island! Eventually the credit card representatives may show up at your door with a pony for your kids and a complete three-ring circus if you open a credit card account.

The major credit cards all have expensive ad campaigns. Most of them are clever and stick with us. Just saying the word "priceless" probably makes you think of a television commercial, and you may even have your personal favorite from that ad series. The marketers are aggressive, as the credit card industry is a very competitive business. The competing credit card companies are getting more and more creative in their rebate and reward schemes. They are also getting more and more creative in their fees and hidden costs.

The credit card companies will attack me for that statement, and they will have a valid point. The costs are not exactly hidden; they are disclosed in the fine print. The disclosure statements that accompany our credit cards require a law degree and a magnifying glass to read. I don't have either, nor do many of you.

Telling Stories

The credit card companies epitomize "big business," giving big business a bad name. They try to convince the world that Americans are spending recklessly and that is why the credit balances are out of control and so many are in need of debt cures. That is not the case. Most people today are using their credit cards to bridge the gap between paychecks. They are not buying expensive cars, lots of jewelry, and throwing fabulous parties like the celebrities we see on *Lifestyles of the Rich and Famous*. They are buying groceries, gas, and paying the dentist for their kid's broken tooth.

Adam was getting by, check to check, working for a small company. Then the company went under, and Adam was out of a job. He was forced to cover his car payment, his rent, and other basic expenses using his credit cards. Adam found a job four weeks later, but in that short amount of time, he racked up almost $5000 in credit card debt.

Peter has four kids and currently has $100,000 in credit card debt. He can't afford to pay rent and basic needs, let alone tuition. He has borrowed money from friends and struggles to pay back all his debts. Creditors are hounding him. All day long, Peter's wife receives calls from credit card companies, collection agencies, and the landlord. They are constantly playing the shuffle game with their balances, shifting from credit card to credit card to try to minimize the fees and penalties. The financial stress is putting a severe strain on their marriage. The entire family is under extreme pressure day and night. Peter's doctor has warned him that he could have a heart attack in the near future unless he reduces his stress.

Greg, a painter and handyman, was celebrating his recent engagement by going on a vacation with his bride-to-be. While he was away, he didn't get the bill for his medical coverage and missed the payment. He unexpectedly had to undergo surgery for an emergency appendicitis, but his medical coverage had lapsed. Now Greg has an $18,000 bill for the surgery and no means to pay it.

If you do not have a similar story, odds are that you immediately can think of someone you know who does.

Reality Check

There are a million stories like this in the naked city, in the small town, and in your neighborhood. The image that every credit card user is shopping on Rodeo Drive, buying diamond-encrusted designer handbags for their dogs, is not the real story. There certainly is an occasional debt situation where someone is needlessly purchasing clothes, shoes, vacations, what have you; but take a look at the credit card statements of most Americans. You will see charges for school supplies, cough syrup, and toilet paper.

Most credit card debt accumulates when there is a job loss, a medical illness, a divorce, or a death in the family. People turn to their credit cards when they are in a crisis mode, to simply help them get by. When the crisis passes and they want to pay off their debts, they find that the balance they owe has exponentially increased over what they originally charged. No one argues that a reasonable amount of interest is inherent in the use of credit. What is an outrage are the shocking fees, penalties, and increases of the interest rate, and the insinuation that the fault lies with the card holder.

The consumer lending industry wants to avoid the reality, and the culpability, and place the blame on the struggling citizen. You will hear the spokespeople of the mega-corporations make statements to the effect that if the credit card holder can't be "responsible enough" to pay off their bill, then they should not be using their credit cards.

If they want to debate responsible, let me take the podium.

Who's Scamming Whom?

Where do I begin? The credit card industry has an unbridled sense of entitlement. They receive a small percentage fee of each single transaction made with a credit card, and most anything these days can be paid for with plastic. It was not so long ago that grocery stores, fast food restaurants, and some Mom and Pop joints did not accept credit cards. Now, anything, anywhere, can be paid for with your credit card. Gone are the days when you could tell your children, "No, we can't stop at McDonald's. I do not have any cash." Even a four-year old today knows that all we need to buy anything is a small but powerful rectangular object that fits in our jeans pocket.

We rarely have to carry cash, if ever. Buy your gas by paying at the pump with a card. Forgot your checkbook and you want to buy fruit at the market? No problem. All major credit cards are accepted now. And McDonald's? They'll let you swipe your card for an eighty-six cent soft drink. Kids' toys today may or may not come with play money, but the pretend grocery store has a price scanner and credit card swipe machine. Credit may not be the way of the world, but it is the way of America. We are a convenience-oriented society, and credit cards are convenient. It is very fitting that our government, the IRS, allows people the "convenience" of paying their taxes with their credit cards today.

The credit card companies bombard us with advertisements, offers, and competitive terms. We can personalize our cards with our favorite charity logo, a scenic picture, or if we so desire, our baby's first birthday smile can be emblazoned on our plastic of choice. And if we have a standard issue card, we can now buy a "credit cover" to dress it up and make it reflect our personality, just like we can buy a funky cover for our cell phone or iPod. A young entrepreneur has started a company selling "skins" for credit cards for five bucks a pop, and business is booming. So when you tire of a certain design, for another five dollars, you can spruce up the wardrobe of your constant companion. And how do you pay that five dollars? With your credit card, of course.

The consumer lending industry desires that credit purchases be easy in order to eventually become a habit. They want you to make that first purchase, and then they start cranking the reel, drawing you in with the hook attached to your wallet. The aggressive practices of the credit card companies, the banks, and the lenders take advantage of the American public. It's the greatest rip-off of American citizens in our nation's history. They rip us off and then they turn up their noses and say credit card customers need to be more "responsible." Let's see who the conscientious party is in the credit card world.

Piling It On

The tactics that the banks and credit card companies use affect every single person in America, regardless of your income or education. What you don't know does hurt you. The credit card companies can steal you blind, and the government lets them.

For example, Sharon paid off her credit card balance in full every month for two years. She had a medical emergency, missed work, and incurred some unexpected bills. Sharon, unable to pay off the balance in full, made the minimum monthly payment, but she paid one day late. She was charged a $45 late payment fee. Sharon was also then hit with an over-the-limit fee because that late charge, plus her medical bills, exceeded her credit limit. Her credit card company then raised her interest rate because she made a late payment and exceeded her credit limit. Most people are not aware of it, but some credit card institutions can increase fees and interest rates basically at any time. A single debt incurred by a person in a jam can double or triple because of the fees and penalties that can get heaped on. Quite often the credit card companies send checks, telling the card holder "just deposit" for whatever you need, and in doing so, it could take the consumer over their credit limit. The result? More fees.

"Charge a little, owe us a lot..."

Why do the credit card companies spend so much on ads and mailings? To get you to open an account with them, so they can be "partners" with you for life. They're leeches. They purport that they are providing a service when they in fact are constantly creating new ways to extract fees. There is typically no government regulation on fees. "Charge a little, owe us a lot" should be their new industry slogan. The average American has eight credit cards. Ed and Sue have nine each. How many do you have?

Yes, It Is Legal

The credit card companies do have the legal right to review your credit report. They want to know your spending habits and paying habits. That is legitimate business practice. But here comes the unjustifiable part...

Even if you make your credit card payments on time, Credit Card Company #1 could raise your interest rate, based solely on the fact that you messed up with Credit Card Company #2. By messing up, all I mean is that you paid late once or missed one payment. If you are late to your car loan company, your mortgage loan broker, other credit cards, or any other creditor, just one of them, just once, they could have the legal right to raise your interest rate. They do it quietly and hope you won't notice. Most of the time, you don't.

But every debt you have now has just gone up. The increase in interest rates means thousands of dollars over the life of the loans. Thousands of dollars that you originally did not owe! Creditors may have the legal right, granted to them by their pals in Congress, to raise your interest rate merely because they see fit. The act of opening a new account can make them decide that you have now taken on too much credit so WHAM – with a review of your credit report, they have decided it is time to raise your interest rate. This is the one instance in the consumer lending industry where it is all for one, and one for all.

Remember the term I'm about to tell you: *universal default*. Not all banks and credit card companies use universal default, but quite a few do! When universal default is applied – and believe me, it is commonly applied – the bank is essentially saying, "We have the full right to raise our rates if the customer *might not* repay us."

So goes their infallible logic. Even though they reviewed your credit report and credit score when you opened your credit card account, they continue to look at your credit report, looking for ways to weasel more money out of you.

Because of "universal default" (which you will hear about plenty), you can be charged the highest interest rate, up to 29%, even if you have never made a late payment on that card with their company or any other credit card. How outrageous is that! A late payment to another type of creditor, whether it's a personal loan, car loan, or mortgage loan, sets the guillotine in motion.

In addition to being able to jack up your interest rate, the credit card issuer can reduce or cancel your credit limit at any time. With no warning. Read the fine print of the disclosure statement for your credit card account; it is a real eye-opener. Any charge can be rejected *for any reason,* including default. You may be in the check-out line, buying diapers and formula, only to be sent home empty-handed after having your card rejected. When you call the credit card company to ask why they rejected the card, they can offer up just about any reason, and the sad part is: they are allowed to do so.

Spin City

They like to put their own spin on the matter. I hold in my hand a mailing that I have just received, offering me yet another card. The fine print insert of the four-page solicitation gives me "important information about procedures for applying for a new account." The credit card company has every right to review my credit history before they give me a credit card, but now they want me to fall under the spell that they are patriots as well. This is the first paragraph of the disclosure statement:

"To help the government fight the funding of terrorism and money laundering activities, Federal law requires all financial institutions to obtain, verify, and record information that identifies each person who opens an account. What this means for you: When you apply for or open an account, we will ask for your name, address, date of birth, and other information that will allow us to identify you."

The waters get murkier and murkier. They will check you out to see if you are a terrorist, and while they are at it, they will look to see if you have paid late to any of your other lenders recently. Once you have a credit card account with a company, they continue to monitor your credit report, even if you are an excellent customer. In fact, if you are an excellent customer who pays timely, universal default may be the only way they can squeeze more money out of you.

Get Out Your Reading Glasses

Study that fine print. If there is more than one interest rate on the account, for example, because of a limited time offer on purchases or on balance transfers, any payment made will be applied to balances with the lower interest rate first. Meanwhile, interest continues to compound on the balance with the higher rate. A great and fully legal gimmick. It pays to have friends in high places. The credit card companies and their government pals have it all worked out.

Rolling balances are another hidden trick that the credit card gurus love. If you start with a zero balance, make purchases during the month, and pay the entire balance off timely each month, there is no finance charge. That is how it happens in a perfect world. Most of us cannot pay off in full each month. If you do not pay the balance in full and have an amount carrying over to the next bill, any subsequent purchases that month get interest accrued from the date of purchase. As in the minute it hits your statement. There is no grace period. You do not have a 30-day period of no interest for new purchases. That's a hidden whammy few people are aware of and one that the lenders don't advertise in large bold type.

> Terms can change, at any time for any reason.

Kathy started out with a shiny brand new card and shiny zero balance. The first two months, she paid off her balance in full. Then the next month, she only paid the minimum payment and made several purchases. Those purchases hit the card and started tallying up the interest immediately. She could not pay off the balance in full the next month, and those balances carried over. She had to use her credit card when her car broke down the next month, so that expense started racking up interest the minute it hit her account. She went from being able to pay off her balance to being buried in three short months.

Looking Out for #1

As I have said time and time again, fees are the heartbeat of the consumer lending industry, and they are out for blood. In addition to an "annual fee," you can be charged a late fee, usually around $35. If you know your payment won't arrive in time by mail and want to avoid a late fee, you can make a telephone payment – but, you could be charged another fee of $14.95 or more by some banks. If you want a copy of your statement, there is no courtesy; there's very likely another fee. If your payment check bounces, there is a fee. If you forget to sign your check, they can hit you with a $35 fee. The creditors and the lenders make no apologies for their business practices of fees, fees, fees. They say that they disclose their fees and that it is *buyer beware*.

Pam likes to pay her bills online to save time and postage. Her credit card company very often says that their online payment service is "down."

It can be down for several days. Hmm, a convenience for customers that is not convenient at all if it does not work. But if it doesn't work, they end up with a late payment. Anyone smell something fishy? Recently, Pam had 48 hours left before her payment would be considered late. It was too late to mail a check to arrive on time. She kept waiting for the online payment option to work. She had the option to pay by phone, but they would charge her another fee of $14.95, and frankly that's plain stupid. So she waited and hoped that the online payment service would magically get fixed. If not, she could mail and have a late fee, or she could pay by phone and have a "convenience" fee. This is modern day customer service?

It is probably true that most of us don't read the disclosure statements that come with our credit cards. The print is purposely too small and the language purposely confusing. Somewhere in the disclosure, it states that merely by using the card, you are indicating that you accept their terms. The real kicker is that the terms can change at any time for any reason, affecting current balances in the process. Occasionally you will get a mailing of a new disclosure statement all by itself with no explanation. That means your terms have changed.

They can do that. Whenever they want.

Nobody else is allowed to do that. The credit card companies are the only ones who can pull the switch-a-roo. Imagine this scene played out at the dinner of a married couple: The husband arrives home with a blonde on one arm, and a redhead on the other. The wife is appropriately stunned. The husband innocently says, "Honey, the terms of our agreement have changed. Didn't you read the fine print of that notice I left on your pillow?"

The credit card banks are a world unto themselves. The more cards you have, the more the banks can make. And the more opportunities they have to change your rates and terms. That is exactly why you will get ten offers from the same bank for cards with low limits, instead of an offer for one card with a higher limit. In my mind, that conjures up the image of the big, bad wolf in granny's head scarf, saying, "All the better to eat you up with."

I'm ready to switch fairy tales, but still want one with the big, bad wolf. Instead, in this version, we are the ones equipped to huff and puff and blow his house down.

CHAPTER 3

Hanky Panky

"I have not yet begun to fight!"
~ John Paul Jones

Not all statements are universally true, but there is one statement I think is: Most Americans want true financial independence. We do not want to be slaves to our debt, and we desire to be financially wealthy. Those two goals can go hand in hand. The beauty of the *Debt Cures* methods is that they will show you ways to do just that.

Another statement that I believe to be fair: Most people of this grand United States of America have no idea that the federal government is getting in the way of their financial independence.

Trust Is Dead

In general, we Americans are too trusting. People of other countries often view Americans as naïve and childlike. It is time we grow up. We are buried deep in debt, and hindered from achieving wealth, because the government allows it! The feds are aware of the games being played by the banking industry and the credit card companies. The boys in Washington aren't doing anything to halt the nefarious practices of the financial power brokers because the Big Money Guys give big money to their election campaign collection baskets. It's politics, it's a big game, and the only loser is the American citizen.

The Debt Epidemic

The United States takes pride in breaking records. Here's one we should not be proud of: American household debt – our credit cards, our mortgage loans, our student loans, our car loans – is at an all-time high. We are $6.7 trillion in debt and it is increasing by $2 billion each day! That statistic alone should make someone in Washington take notice!

> **Debt is epidemic, but the government ignores it!**

Credit card issuers, banks, and mortgage companies have no trouble sleeping at night while the average U.S. citizen lies awake, worrying about bills. The average college graduate now enters the workforce already behind the eight ball, with more than $2000 racked up in credit card debt alone, not including their student loans. I've heard that the average working person spends 90% of their disposable income toward paying off their debts. The average bank executive drives a Mercedes and drops $1000 per plate on a campaign fundraiser dinner.

Debt in this country is an epidemic; it is like a disease that is spreading out of control, and even taking innocent lives. Instead of trying to find a cure, the government looks the other way and ignores the problems of the ordinary working person. The people in Washington make excuses to protect their banking buddies, whose banks are setting record profits, by the way. What is worse, they try to point the finger of blame at me and you.

Many of the ails that we experience in life are brought on by the burden of our debt. The debt bears a much heavier weight than we realize. The ugly feeling of helplessness creeps in and we feel stressed out all the time and we get anxious over every little thing. We can't sleep or we don't want to get out of bed; we may experience any number of personal issues. It should not be happening. We should not have to live our lives under such oppression. People look to the government in times of crisis. In this case, the government is part of the cause of the crisis.

"A government of the people, by the people, for the people" – not anymore; unless, of course, the people referred to are the consumer lending industry. It's all about them. Abe Lincoln may be rolling around in his grave, but we do not need to roll over. We need to remind the government who they really work for.

Partners in Crime

There are many infuriating examples of how the American citizen is being taken advantage of by the partnership of big business and big government. I'll hit on some of these deceitful practices a bit more in depth as we go, but let me mention just a few of these offensive acts that immediately come to mind.

1. Bankruptcies are at an all-time high. It makes sense. The debt is rampant. People are out of work or have medical emergencies or a death in the family, and they can't pay off their debt; they assume that bankruptcy is the only way out. Nearly one out of every fifty households in the United States files bankruptcy. Instead of trying to treat the root cause of the problem and address the real issue – why the debt is so high that people are forced to such extreme measures – the government tightened up the bankruptcy laws.

    In 2005, the feds made it harder for people to file bankruptcy. Does this help the individual citizen? Not at all. Who does it help? The banks and the credit card companies. If a person files bankruptcy, the banker boys don't get paid. So the bankers went to their buddies in Washington and got them to change the law. For some people, bankruptcy was their only protection from the predatory practices of the lenders, and now that protection is much less. How I see it: I give a guy some money, and then he does a favor for me. In some circles, that could be called a bribe.

2. Who is in control? You need to know up front that the number one reason that debt is out of control in America is because the lenders are out of control, NOT the spenders. Do you have high credit card debt? Most of us carry some debt. If you are among the millions of hard working bill-paying people who cannot pay off the balance each month, that is where they get you. Their devilish ploy is to keep you trapped so you *cannot* pay off your debt in full. The fees ring up when you have a balance, and that is music to their ears.

The real punch – the banks argue that they are not doing anything wrong by charging all their outrageous fees and secret interest rate increases. They are abiding by all the existing government regulations. That should tell you right there that the regulations are pretty loose. It is pretty easy to stay within the lines if there are no lines. And if there is a law that the credit card companies and banking industry do not want to comply with, they just ask their pals in Congress to change the law!

3. Subprime mortgage defaults and home foreclosures are at an all-time high. A subprime mortgage is the term for a mortgage loan given to someone with a bad credit history. The lender often tries to imply that they are doing a favor by providing a loan at all. It is a self-serving favor, and now has become a nightmare.

Several years ago, the government launched a joint effort with the banks to make home buying "easier." Loans with low interest rates and longer terms appeared. The banks and the government considered it a great success. Many people were able to become homeowners. Then after the first year or two, the low interest rates skyrocketed – an easy tactic to get the mortgage holder to refinance again. That means more closing costs for the bank to collect, along with the chance of raising the interest rate again.

Borrowers were often talked into an increased mortgage amount as well, and with dropping home prices in some areas, they owe more on the loan than their home is now worth. Recently there were an unprecedented number of homes that rolled over into the higher rate of their adjustable rate mortgage and people simply could not make the higher payments. They owe more than the value of their homes and they bailed. A record number of foreclosures rocked the financial world. In a nutshell, the mortgage companies had given loans to people they never should have given loans to and then they feigned surprise when the bottom fell out. Hard working American citizens are losing their homes every day while the fat cats are buying up vacation properties. We'll delve more into this later.

4. Three little words: Student loan scandal. The student loan industry is huge. $85 billion huge. So I guess these lenders had enough cash sitting around to pay off college officials to

send students in their direction. The financial aid director at John Hopkins University is alleged to have received $60,000 in exchange for sending students needing loans to a lender called Student Loan Xpress. The financial aid director at Columbia University also allegedly had $100,000 of stock in this same company. Guess where he directed students?

The New York attorney general led the investigation into the abusive practices. According to a May 7, 2007 article in the *New York Times,* the Education Secretary tried to defend the government by stating that she "lacked the legal authority to clamp down on the many abuses." Lacking integrity, perhaps. Lacking authority? Now the federal government is saying it does not have authority? Give me a break.

It gets my ire up when I think of all the outrageous, abusive, and predatory practices that these big corporations and lending institutions get away with. It is not the small-time local banker on the corner, it is the largest banks and credit card companies in our nation pulling these stunts. They need to be stopped, and it is time to blow the lid off how they do their business. The inner workings of the entire consumer lending industry are one of the greatest travesties that this country has ever seen. The money that they are making off me and you and just about every single one of us who has a car loan, a student loan, a home mortgage loan, a credit card, or any kind of bank loan is a crime. In my opinion, their methods should be illegal. They get away with their transgressions because they are the ones pulling the puppet strings on the guys who control the laws.

The License to Steal Is Government Issued

The student loan lenders gave pay offs and gifts to financial aid directors at various colleges and universities. In return, the financial aid folks advised their students to use their loan services. One director allegedly owned a huge chunk of stock in the student loan company that he sent his students to. Talk about looking out for #1.

It gets worse. A Department of Education official was also discovered to hold a large amount of shares in the same student loan company, and somehow he just forgot to disclose this fact to his employer, the federal government. His position? General manager of federal student aid! When the allegations came to light, he was put on administrative leave, which means he still received his paycheck. The April 2007 News Blog of the *Chronicle of Higher Education* stated that this discovery was just one more incident in "a series of 'disturbing findings of improper relationships' between lenders in the federal guaranteed-student-loan program and the government officials charged with overseeing them." Amen to that.

In a press release issued by one senator addressing the situation, it states, "We need to ensure that those charged with administering federal student loan programs put the interests of students first. It is inexcusable for students to be paying the price for backroom deals in the student loan industry."

Lenders + Government = Improper Relationships!

We all are paying for these types of backroom deals between the consumer lending industry and the federal government. And it is inexcusable. It's beyond inexcusable. There has been a serious breach of trust. Moral code seems to have vanished. If we cannot have faith in our government and our big business bankers, who can we have faith in? Ourselves.

We can learn how to circumvent the problems when we know what they are up to. The best defense is a good offense. We can learn how they play the game so we can beat them at it.

These are all examples of the enormous problem of greed in our country. Many colleges and universities have a required ethics course, but obviously it was not part of the graduation credits when the current bank executives and people in high financial places were in school. Maybe they just forgot what they were taught; or perhaps the golden rule of "treat others as you would like to be treated" was not part of the curriculum in their kindergarten class. There is a basic element in our society that we need to get back, a sense of honor and a backbone of integrity. We need to teach future generations that human beings can succeed without greed. Striving for wealth and stability is not the same as indecency and gluttony.

And while we work toward that, we will fight back.

CHAPTER 4

Eliminate Your Debt!

"Nothing gives a person so much advantage over another as to remain always cool and unruffled under all circumstances."
~ Thomas Jefferson

Thomas Jefferson was a great leader, a great visionary, and a great president. And he left us with some pretty great advice. Remaining cool and unruffled in the face of your debt struggles will serve you well.

I don't know about you, but talking about all the injustices heaped on the American people by the federal government and the big banks and the credit card companies makes my blood boil. I could go on and on, and maybe I will later, but for now the best tonic for anger is action.

I will bring out more "sins" of the government against its citizens, and I will talk about credit scores and easy strategies to boost that credit score. I will cover how to get a credit line and start building your wealth. We have a lot of material to get to, and we will, in good time. I could spend the next two hundred pages just exposing the government and their illicit ways. But *Debt Cures* is not just about whistle blowing, although it is crucial that we all become aware of what is going on around us. It's all about knowing. Knowing what they are doing, and how they are taking advantage. What the government and the credit card companies and the banks are doing is just plain wrong. We need to tackle that.

Solutions!

And we need to realize that the information packed in *Debt Cures* is also about solutions. It's about knowledge. If people know what to do, they can reverse the roles, they can get control. Like salve to an open wound, the methods found in *Debt Cures* can ease the pain of debt, relieve the burden you bear, and put a little spring back into your step. When you are feeling bouncy, you are more apt to feel like you can take on the so-called powers that can control us and our financial situations. So let's bounce.

What I am about to tell you might get you a little ruffled, but in a good way, and that is okay.

Since you are reading a book, I will assume that you are sitting down, but if you are not, then I will ask you to please take a seat. I don't want you passing out and falling down when you read what I am about to say next.

One of the best-kept secrets of the consumer lending industry is the fact – yes, I said *fact* – that you – yes, I said *you* – may be able to eliminate 100% of your debt! The whole lump sum, *poof*, gone! That is worth getting excited about. Now you may put the book down for a moment and jump up and down like the people who have just won a car on *The Price Is Right*!

Better Than a Game Show

Eliminating the whole sh-bang of your debt is better than winning a car. It is like getting the keys to your life back. Of course, not everyone will be able to get rid of the entire 100% of debt, but some of you will. Are you still jumping around? I would be! For those of you who don't qualify for this top-secret strategy, do not despair! We will soon get to the next chapter in which there's a technique that I believe virtually every person who has credit card debt can use to cut their payments in half – virtually overnight! I repeat *anyone* can successfully reduce their debt by up to half or even up to 75%!

But first, without any further delay, let's discuss the secrets, and the debt cures, that they don't want you to know. With this technique, amounts don't matter. If you have ten or twenty or thirty thousand dollars in credit card debt, you can completely wipe out that debt.

Statute of Limitations on Debt

The secret technique to completely wipe out debt

Once upon a time, you had debt that you could not pay. The creditor wrote it off as uncollectible. Now, out of the blue, you are being harassed for that debt. It is bad enough to be bothered by a debt collector, but to be hounded for something that you believed to be ancient history is doubly annoying. If you are being pestered by someone for old debts, then more than likely you have come across what is called a scavenger debt collector. Or actually, they have come across you.

Scavenger debt collectors purchase bundles of dated debt (which probably can't be collected on) for incredibly low prices. These collectors buy low and hope to collect high. They have very little invested; therefore, they have the opportunity to make big profits. And they will do basically whatever it takes to get those profits. They don't care if their method is unethical or something that would make their dear old granny cry or give 'em a swat with the broom. In the scum-filled pond of bottom dwellers, these guys are even lower than the regular debt collectors. Who knew?

You can tell the debt collector to get lost!

Pay attention to the next sentence: Paying a debt that is too old is NOT required of you. How old is too old? That depends upon your state's statute of limitations period, or "expiration date." I'll list them later in this chapter so you know what your state enforces. Every state has different laws, but it can be as early as three years!

If you have a debt that was written off six years ago and there has been no activity on your credit report for the debt since then, you are probably free of that debt forever.

You can find out the statute of limitations on debt for your state (listed below) so if a scavenger comes around, you can tell him to bug off. These guys will be very surprised to hear you say that because they are assuming that you have never heard about these laws.

Debt Relief

The statute of limitations on debt is there as a protective measure for you. It may be one of the only things that I can think of that the government has done in the interest of fairness to the consumer. It certainly would not be fair for a lender or credit card company to sit around and not enforce collection action at the time the debt incurred, and then, thirty years later, come knocking on your door with brass knuckles. A person should not have to live a life of anxious stress, wringing their hands, harboring a worry about an old debt for the next 60 or 70 years. Imagine if your best friend from sixth grade showed up and started putting the squeeze on you for the $10 you borrowed at the movies many years ago. My reaction would most likely be, "Are you nuts?" Allowing debt collectors to come after you forever would be nuts too, which is why the statute of limitations exists to create an expiration date.

> Your debts have an expiration date!

Sometimes creditors ignore the expiration date, and may decide to sue you for an old debt even if the statute of limitations has run out. Don't worry! All you have to do is go to the judge and request that the case be dismissed because the statute of limitations has run out. That is why the financial lending industry does not want you to know what they are up to! If you know their dirty secrets, you will be able to escape their grimy grasp. In fact, very often the creditor or collection agency will contact you near the end of the statute period. They know that time is ticking so they get very adamant with you, saying that unless you pay right away, you'll be slammed with a lawsuit. They hope the fear factor works; they want to get a buck out of you before the hourglass runs out.

Your Strategy

If this is the case for you, and you are being threatened by a creditor or a collection agency for old debts, or debts very near the end of the statute of limitations period, sit tight and zip your lip. You may be able to eliminate 100% of your debt by following Thomas Jefferson's words of wisdom: Remain always cool and unruffled under all circumstances.

When the telephone rings, many people who are being bothered by debt collectors stare at the phone with a fear in their eyes, afraid to pick it up. You don't have to be like that. This is not a horror movie. The boogie man is not going to reach through the phone and strangle you.

The debt collector wants you to think that he has that kind of power over you, but he does not. This is not a movie; this is your life, and you have the starring role. The debt collector does not even get a mention in the footnotes of your life. Do not let the collection agencies rule your life. Remember when you were a small toddler, you would march around and say, "I am the boss of me"? Well, you still are the boss of you, so when the telephone rings, remember that you have the upper hand.

Fear Not

Ring. There it is. The telephone. You, without a quiver of fear in your voice, say a very strong "hello." Tell yourself that the debt collector is just a scavenger who bought your debt for a pittance, sometimes as little as three cents on the dollar! He knows your debt is old. He is hoping that you don't have a clue.

But you do have a clue. You have a book of knowledge. You know the debt is old, that the statue of limitations has passed, so all you have to do is tell the collector that the account is no longer collectible. Click. That was you, hanging up.

Even if you are not sure if the debt is "time-barred," which means the statute has passed and they cannot collect, you need to remember that the collectors are foragers, scrounging around for a crumb, and they lie, cheat, and steal to get it. They may be trying to collect on an account that is indeed too old. You are now smart enough to know that you should not admit to owing that debt, or the statute could start up again. Silence is golden, and that silence can be a silver lining.

No Admission

Do not admit to owing any alleged debt, and sure as heck, don't send them any money. Remember what your mother told you way back when: If you can't say anything nice, don't say anything at all.

If the collector is persistent, and that is a quality inherent to their job, they may keep calling. Don't cave in. You tell them that it is not collectible and hang up; or you say that you don't remember anything about the alleged debt and hang up.

Then you send off a letter, telling them to stop calling you. A sample letter for you to use as a guideline is included in the Appendix.

Be Smart

If you were to admit to the debt, then the statute of limitations might start running all over again, because the debt has become "active" again, giving them the legal right to pursue their collections or sue you. You don't want to be close to eliminating all your debt, only to blow it by saying too much! Remember: all you have to do is tell them that the time to collect this debt has expired. End of discussion.

Be bold and be firm. These scavenger debt collectors are feeding off the waste droppings of the bottom feeders, so they stoop low. They will be aggressive and will probably identify themselves as a law firm in an effort to intimidate you. Don't be thrown off your course. Stand your ground and firmly state that the debt is beyond the statute of limitations and is not collectible.

It is a very simple strategy. Wait them out and the debt can disappear! Your credit card company wrote off your account a long time ago as uncollectible, and got a tax deduction for it! There is no right that these scavenger debt collectors have to try to collect on that old debt now.

Their scare tactics are working though, and some people pay off a debt that has passed the statute of limitations timeframe. The scoundrel scavengers, of course, will not tell you this. They want your money! Even if they have no legal right to collect it!

Tell your friends! Tell your family! Tell your neighbors, your aunts, your uncles, your cousins! Tell the babysitter, and tell your co-workers! Don't be duped! These scavenger debt collectors are getting rich off of unsuspecting citizens. They buy up these old debts for close to nothing and are trying to get people to pay in full, plus interest! It is a highly profitable business and growing. Two of these "investment companies" have even made the Fortune 500 list.

What to Expect

Miranda had an old credit card debt of $3000. She had gone through some trying times and simply did not have the money to pay it. Miranda's husband had left her. Not only that, but she had a new baby, along with a part-time job that just wasn't cutting it. Times were tough. She had no means to pay back that $3000, which accumulated due to purchases her husband made and stuck her with. He had used a lot of her credit cards without her knowing, but that is another story. When the credit card company could not collect from her way back when, they turned it over to collections, which also could not collect. The

> Miranda did not have to pay her debt!

credit card company wrote off the account. Now fast forward a few years. Miranda has forgotten all about it, but the credit card company has sold this $3000 debt to a scavenger debt collection firm for about $200. The aptly named scavenger will now, after all this time, put the squeeze on Miranda for the whole $3000, along with the interest too! If greed handed out prizes, the scavenger debt collectors would win the blue ribbon.

Lucky for Miranda, she knows the *Debt Cures* methods and knows exactly what to expect and how to avoid the trap. The scavengers know these old debts are the hardest debts to collect, so accordingly, they play hardball. Don't let them scare you!

If you get a call from one of these scavenger debt collectors, they will try to buffalo you into believing that they are a lawyer or work for a law firm. They often use the term "litigation firm" and tell you that they are in the process of drawing up the paperwork for a lawsuit against you on such-and-such debt. They are now giving you a "courtesy call" and a chance to pay it off or work out a settlement deal. Of course, if you don't work out a deal or agree to send in your hard earned cash, they say that you will be slapped with a lawsuit.

If they are pretending to be an attorney, you can pretend to be Thomas Jefferson, cool and unruffled. Let them know that you're onto them. The person on the other end of the phone is not used to people talking back. They are used to being the intimidator, and they expect you to be quaking in your boots. But now that you know what the score is, you won't be.

"I Don't Owe"

If you know that it is an old debt and the statute has expired, remember what I just told you a few paragraphs ago: You don't owe them any explanation. You don't owe them one thin dime. You don't owe them anything.

This is your movie, and you have one line: "That debt is not collectible." However dramatic you want to be as you slam down the phone is up to you.

These guys bluff better than the poker players in Vegas, and will use every intimidation trick in the book to try to collect as much as they can out of you. They want to get you to send them as much money as you can, as quickly as you can. That is their job and these "professionals" take a twisted pride in doing their job well. They will say anything because they know they will probably get away with it. Most people simply don't know about debt collection laws.

Even for those of us who do know the law, it's very difficult to go after them when they do cross the line, and they know it. There is a ridiculous loophole in our current consumer law that allows these bozo collection agencies a "get out of jail free" card, if they do get tangled up in a case against them. They simply shut down their current business and start a new one. They may change their name, but they do not change their ways. They go on their merry way, operating in the same outrageous manner. I know, I know. It is just one more thing that makes us smack our foreheads and wonder what in the world the federal government is doing, or not doing, by letting them get away with such conduct.

Shake your fists and rail against the system if that makes you feel any better. The system is far from perfect, and the creatures who make their living off the system are not saints. I do not have to tell you who the villains are in our story or that it is unwise to trust them. The important thing is that we know how to defeat the villains. We can fight fire with fire. Or better said, you can arm yourself with a little bit of knowledge and watch your debts disappear!

Repeat After Me

Being a guy that likes to write books, I know that words matter. What we say or don't say is vital. When it comes to your debt elimination strategy, what you say or don't say is critical. Follow the *Debt Cures* advice, and when you find out that it really works, you will be telling everyone you know what to say and what not to say!

For old debt: Sorry, Charlie. The statute of limitations has run out on this debt. Stop all contact with me. This debt has expired. You can't touch it. You can't touch me. Leave me alone.

For any other debt: We'll give this a little more attention later, but you need to know that even if the debt is not expired, it could still be wiped off your record. There are many times debt is reported in error. So absolutely any time that you get a call from any creditor, or any collector, follow these guidelines…

> *Tip #1* – Never admit that you owe the debt. You might not and with the *Debt Cures* methods, you may be able to eliminate or greatly reduce your debt, so always be smart and always be vague. This tactic is NOT a debt cure: Hello, Mr. Mean Collection Agent. You say I owe $10,000? Well, gee, you must be right. Let me send you a check right away.

> *Tip #2* – The debt collectors hone their skills and sharpen their claws on the naïve and unsuspecting citizen. The easiest way to avoid entrapment is to not agree, and when talking about the

debt, do not claim it as yours. Instead, use the word "alleged." It is simple. You do not think that it could be your debt, so by using the word "alleged," you never admit that it is yours. Ask the collection agent to send you all their information on the "alleged" debt because it does not sound at all familiar to you. When did the "alleged" debt occur? What was purchased? The collector gets the point that you do not think it is yours, and you are allowed to ask questions without placing the debt on you. You can ask all the questions you want about something that doesn't exist!

Tip #3 – A reinforcement of Tip #2. This is a two-part tip.

The first in rhyme: When a debt is old, you can be bold.

However you want to say it, just point blank tell the debt collector that the statute of limitations is expired. They can't collect. Then you hang up. How simple is that?

The second part of the tip: Don't ever agree, and you can set yourself free.

It can be as easy as that!

Tip #4 – Be confident that the *Debt Cures* methods work! It is 100% possible to eliminate 100% of your debt! That is 100% encouraging. Know your financial situation, and know your rights. With this technique, you can eliminate your debt, no matter how much you previously owed!

It is always a power struggle, so the more you know, the more power you have over them. Know if your debt is expired. And remember, you can always ask point blank, "How old is this alleged debt?" Find your state below and know the time period it takes for debts to disappear. Financial freedom starts right here.

Find Your State

Miranda's credit card company wrote off her $3000 account five years ago. Miranda lives in California, where the statute of limitations is four years, so she can tell the debt collector these beautiful words, the debt elimination sentence, "The statute of limitations is gone, baby! Do not contact me again! Good bye!" If Miranda lived in Alaska, where the statute of limitations is six years, she would not admit that she owed such a debt; she would not agree to pay such a debt; and she would not agree to send the debt collector any money at all. Calm, cool, and unruffled is the tactic of a debt eliminator!

> You may be able to totally ELIMINATE your debt!

I've included a table below so you can find your state and determine when your old debt officially becomes a time-barred debt, and the collection folks will have to leave you alone forever!

In this table, the term "open accounts" includes revolving accounts, like your credit cards. This statute of limitations information is correct to the best of my knowledge as we go to print. Be sure to check with an attorney or a friend or someone else in your state who is knowledgeable in these areas, in case the number of years for expiry of your debt has changed, and for any other relevant information.

State	Open Accounts (e.g., credit cards)	Written Contracts
Alabama	3	6
Alaska	6	6
Arizona	3	6
Arkansas	3	5
California	4	4
Colorado	6	6
Connecticut	6	6
Delaware	3	3
Washington, DC	3	3
Florida	4	5
Georgia	4	6
Hawaii	6	6
Idaho	4	5
Illinois	5	10

State	Open Accounts (e.g., credit cards)	Written Contracts
Indiana	6	10
Iowa	5	10
Kansas	3	5
Kentucky	5	15
Louisiana	3	10
Maine	6	6
Maryland	3	3
Massachusetts	6	6
Michigan	6	6
Minnesota	6	6
Mississippi	3	3
Missouri	5	10
Montana	5	8
Nebraska	4	5
Nevada	4	6
New Hampshire	3	3
New Jersey	6	6
New Mexico	4	6
New York	6	6
North Carolina	3	3
North Dakota	6	6
Ohio	4	15
Oklahoma	3	5
Oregon	6	6
Pennsylvania	4	4
Rhode Island	10	15
South Carolina	3	10
South Dakota	6	6

State	Open Accounts (e.g., credit cards)	Written Contracts
Tennessee	6	6
Texas	4	4
Utah	4	6
Vermont	6	6
Virginia	3	5
Washington	3	6
West Virginia	5	10
Wisconsin	6	6
Wyoming	8	10

Debt Be Gone!

Now this is what I call exciting news! If you live in Alabama, Arizona, Arkansas, Delaware, Washington, D.C., Kansas, Louisiana, Maryland, Mississippi, New Hampshire, North Carolina, Oklahoma, South Carolina, Virginia, or Washington state, your credit card debt is untouchable after just three short years!

With this little known method, you can wipe out 100% of your debts! Uncollectible accounts that have been written off cannot come back to haunt you. Do not own up to a debt that you don't own! When Miranda got the call from the debt collector, she did not fret. She knew her rights, and she knew that the $3000 debt was beyond the reach of any collection effort. If you have been victimized with debt that ballooned beyond belief and now the collection hounds are after you, you can throw water on them and burst their bubble. The statute of limitations on debt exists to keep creditors from ceaselessly harassing you. They must stop forevermore.

There is no quicker path to wealth than the elimination of bad debt! In the immortal words of Dr. Seuss, "Congratulations! Today is your day. You're off to Great Places, you're off and away. You have brains in your head. You have feet in your shoes. You can steer yourself any direction you choose."

I am confident that you will steer yourself in the direction away from old debts, and the debt collection piranhas, and instead move toward the direction of magnificent wealth. You do not have to be wracked with fear, guilt, stress, anxiety, eating distress, weight gain, weight loss, thinning hair…well, actually, maybe thinning hair is something you have to live with, but you can see what I am trying to say. Eliminating your debt lifts the heaviness that can hold you down. Eliminating your debt lifts your spirits! The collection trolls can go back to living under the bridge or wherever it is that they came from. You can start living with a new confidence, refreshed and untouched by the worries of bad debt.

If you live in a state where the number of years for the statute of limitations on debt is not an immediate debt elimination strategy for you, don't be dismayed! There are *Debt Cures* methods with which I believe virtually everyone holding this book can reduce their debt significantly. No matter how much debt you have, or how long you have had it, you could cut your total debt payments in half! Maybe even two-thirds, or perhaps even 75%!

Straightforward techniques. No complicated statutes or tables. No smoke and mirrors. These solutions are so easy that every person in America who has debt can and should use these simple strategies.

This is not the point in the book where you go for a snack. This is the point where you turn the page and discover how you can get out of debt!

CHAPTER 5

Negotiate!

"A penny saved is a penny earned."
~ Benjamin Franklin

Every penny you earn adds up to a dollar eventually. Your hard earned dollars can stay with you, where they belong. If you have just eliminated your debt because of the last chapter, hurray! That is a lot of pennies that you have earned! And you have *earned* them. Taking on the giants of the consumer lending industry is no small feat, so be proud! Getting out of debt and getting to where you can start creating wealth takes effort, so congratulate yourself. And send your success stories to success@debtcures.com!

Simply Amazing – A Technique to Cut Your Payments in Half or More

Three very simple, yet amazingly effective steps among the *Debt Cures* methods are: Eliminate, Negotiate, and Cut Your Rate.

You have just learned a major solution – how to eliminate your debt! Maybe your debts are not old enough to be beyond the reach of the statute of limitations. Not everyone is able to totally eliminate debt with this method, but I believe that virtually *all of us can reduce our debt*! Some people have nearly wiped out their debt, to the tune of 75%, and many have cut out 50% of what they used to owe before learning these methods.

I think that you can see that sitting home and worrying does nothing. The absolute worse thing for you to do about your debt is *to do nothing*. Wishing debt away never works. It takes a simple action.

Financial Statements

One of the most amazing tricks is not a trick at all, and to my knowledge, there's nowhere else but *Debt Cures* that will teach you this technique, this pearl of wisdom, to reduce your debt and get you on your way toward financial freedom. It's a piece of paper!

One piece of financial data that people in debt often ignore is financial statements. Perhaps you are familiar with the terms *balance sheet* and *income statement*; if you're not, don't be intimidated. They are two very simple documents that present an easy-to-understand picture of your financial situation. It is "this is what I got" – a paint by numbers showing how much you do – or do not – have.

You need to know your current situation in order to move forward. Some people wrongly assume that they don't need a balance sheet or an income statement. They think they are only for people with lots of money. No matter your financial position, these statements can be key to the end of your debt troubles.

Balance Sheet

The balance sheet shows your financial situation at one moment in time. As of this particular date, you have *this much in Assets* (things of value that you own) and you have *this much in Liabilities* (debts that you owe). Your assets include your house; any other real estate you own, such as rental properties; cars; boats; any other vehicles; stocks; bonds; 401K investments; jewelry; art; business ownership; cash in the bank, etc. Your liabilities are what you owe on all those assets: your home mortgage balance; car loans or leases; lines of credit; credit card balances; personal loans, etc.

Individuals tend to have very simple balance sheets. Your "assets" are your stuff; your "liabilities" are your debt. Stuff minus debt equals your net worth. A lot of us have more debt than stuff. That means a negative net worth, or "in the hole," so to speak. Individuals with a lot of debt have such a simple balance sheet that it may not even be necessary. If there is nothing to show, you can't really show it, right?

Simply put, a balance sheet is a financial snapshot that shows your current financial health. You need to know what you have. It is essential in forecasting your financial health for the future. If the picture right now is nothing but zeros, you may not need to do a formal balance sheet. The point is to show your creditors that you're in the hole. You can accomplish the same thing with a two-sentence letter. We'll get to that in a couple paragraphs.

Income Statement

The other financial statement is the income statement. The balance sheet applies to a single point in time, i.e., as of today's date, I am broke. The income statement covers a particular period of time, i.e., for the entire month of June, I was broke.

The income statement shows what you made and what you spent for any given amount of time, one month, one quarter, or one year. It is a tracking of your cash flow – what came in and what went out. An income statement is also called a profit and loss statement.

For an individual, the income statement is very simple as well: What are all your sources of revenue? What are all your expenses?

Simply put: What came in? What went out?

With one glance at an income statement, you can see if you are spending more than you are making, and many of us do. Maybe you made $40,000 and spent $45,000. This obviously has you $5000 in the red. Reverse it. You took in $45,000 and outgoing cash flow was $40,000. Now you are $5000 in the black. Putting it down on paper is the key to understanding the spending path that you are on. These two simple financial statements are a great technique to show your financial situation.

Assets – Liabilities = No Money Left

A sample Balance Sheet and a sample Income Statement are included for you in the Appendix. These statements are vital for you to understand what is going on, but more importantly, they show your creditors your financial picture. They are important and simple tools to cut your debt. If there is no money, there is no money; plain and simple.

Neal was in debt for $50,000. He had two credit cards. The amounts that he spent, plus all the accrued interest and penalties, had him so deep in debt that he would never be able to pay it off. So that is exactly what he showed his creditors. Neal was being hounded by a collection agency, so he got his friend, an accountant, to draft his personal financial statements. In black and white, on only one page, the balance sheet and income statement clearly showed that he had nothing, so he was able to pay nothing. Nothing from nothing leaves nothing.

Neal reduced his debt by nearly 75%!

He sent the statements and a letter to the collection agency, telling them that they were wasting their time, because he absolutely could not pay the $50,000. The collection agency had bought the debt for pennies on the dollar, so by giving them a penny more, they make a profit. Neal's phone calls and letters, along with the hard facts on his financial statements, convinced the collection agency to negotiate. Neal settled for $14,000 on his $50,000 debt. That is nearly a 75% reduction!

Financial statements are a great technique for reducing debt with credit card companies, too. Show that you have no net worth, or a negative net worth. If the creditor can clearly see that you have nothing, they may be willing to settle. You don't need an attorney to do this. You can do this yourself. Take a look at the statements in the appendix and fill in your numbers. This is a technique that can work for virtually anyone!

A Simple Letter

In addition to the financial statements, or sometimes, instead of the financial statements, a brief letter may be all you need. A sample form letter is also included in the Appendix.

It is straightforward: Here are my assets; here are my liabilities; I have nothing left to pay you.

It seems so simple because it is. The creditors are "numbers" people. They don't care much for your stories. Cry all you want; they want to see the cold hard figures.

In general, it is wise to be brief. State the facts, and that is all. Trying to say too much really ends up not being helpful. If you have nothing, state that simple fact. Maybe you do not need an income statement or a balance sheet. A piece of paper with a bunch of zeros won't do any more than a simple letter.

Ask a friend who is an accountant, or the person who has done your taxes all these years, to draft a simple letter on their letterhead. All it has to say is something to the effect: "I have been doing Mary's taxes for years. Her liabilities exceed her assets and she has a negative net worth. Mary has no resources." Signed off by MR. CPA.

Telling them any more is not necessary, and it is not advisable. You can use this method to cut your debts in as much as half or 75%, even 100%!

We will revisit the topic later, but now you know: Everything is open to negotiation and financial statements are a technique to get you there!

CHAPTER 6

Cut Your Rate!

"You never know unless you ask!"
~ Kevin Trudeau

I may get harassed, and be the subject of occasional verbal abuse, but I am a simple guy. I like to tell it like it is, in simple language, so that other guys and gals, like me, understand what is going on.

Other people, like the big corporate moneybags, might have a problem with that. And that is exactly what it is – their problem.

It always amazes me that the whistleblower is the one that catches the most heat. The guys doing the dirty deeds want to cast suspicion away from their wrongdoings. They are pretty good at it. The credit card companies have mastered the technique of bait-and-switch. They bait you with a low teaser interest rate and then switch your rate to double or triple that, without you knowing.

Isn't that "Special"?

Their excuse? "We can." They are not breaking any laws. Their reason? "We're special." And actually, right there, they are telling the truth. They are special. The laws and regulations are tied up in a pretty green bow with dollar signs, just for them. When the president of a major credit card company, which is a profit leader of the big credit card companies, has a little party at his house for a few hundred of his closest friends, and they all just happen to bring their checkbooks and leave little love gifts for George Bush, then I guess you can say that you are indeed special.

America is the land of the free and the home of the brave; unfortunately, it is also the home of the advantaged and spoiled and "special." Do I want to put the kibosh on their deceptive practices? Yes, I do. And I state that up front and honestly. I don't hide in the fine print and legalese.

The credit card companies are in a class by themselves when it comes to manipulating the terms of their contracts. In an interview for the PBS documentary, *Secret History of Credit Cards,* Harvard law professor, Elizabeth Warren, has pointed out that the credit card industry is the only one able to run a business like this. "Nobody signs contracts to buy things that say, 'I'm going to pay you $1,200 for the big-screen TV unless you decide, in another month or two months, that it should really be $3,600 or $4,200 or $4,800.' But that's precisely how credit card contracts are written today."

Crazy contracts, yes. Crazy consumer, no. It's time to play a new game called, "Let's Get a Better Rate."

Rate Switch

If you want to get better telephone rates, you call them up and ask. If you don't like their deal, you switch providers. You are not afraid to call your cable company and ask if HBO is on special this month. You know to never ever take the first offer that the car salesman gives you, so why are we all so intimidated by the credit card companies?

Maybe many of us had no idea what they were really up to. Blind trust is now shattered. Maybe we feel it is futile. They have gotten away with it for so long, it is all we know. We have taken our beatings and have decided to stay down on the mat. One thing that I have learned in my life is that staying down, or remaining quiet, only leads them to believe that they are in control, and then they will only try to get away with more. They think their tricks are top-secret or untouchable. Wrong.

We can pull the plug on the runaway interest rates and fees. We can cut our debt in up to half by doing so! And it all starts with a simple phone call.

Another Technique for Anyone & Everyone –
Cut Your Payments in Half!

Phone Calls Can Save You Thousands!

Phone calls are usually easy, time efficient, and believe it or not, effective. Most people assume that a phone call is a waste of their time, so they don't make them. Nothing is further from the truth. Pick up the phone and dial. Don't let your nerves get the best of you. Why in the world should you be concerned with what the person on the other end of the line thinks of you? Make the call. It is the most valuable thing you can do with your next five minutes, and it can save you thousands.

Interest Rates

Call up your credit card companies. Their phone number is right on the back of your card. Ask what your current interest rate is, then ask them to lower it. If the first person you speak to doesn't help you, ask to speak to a supervisor. If they say "no," call back. Keep trying. Don't give up. It may take seven calls, but I believe that the vast majority of the time, they will lower your rate, simply because you asked.

It really is that simple. Take Vendel and Gwen – they had a whopping 29.75% interest rate on their Bank of America card. After calling up their credit representative, their rate was lowered to 5.75%, and they get to keep that rate for 5 years! They used the same technique to lower the rates on their three other cards.

Hang on to all those credit card offers you get in the mail today. (If you don't get one today, bet you do tomorrow.) When the customer service person tries to give you the brush-off, you can say, "I'm holding an offer that I got yesterday in the mail from Super Credit Card Bank. I will transfer my balance over to them today if you do not give me a better rate." I kid you not, you should get results. Lowering your interest rate instantly lowers your payments. You have just lowered your debt! Immediate results like that are very empowering!

As long as you carry a balance on any card, it's possible that your credit card company could raise your rates, without you knowing, so it is up to you to make a periodic phone call and check on your rate. You can explain that you have been a long-time, good paying customer. If they don't lower your rate, you will drop them. Simple as that.

Ask and you shall receive. Be persistent if you have to, but a small investment of your time on the phone can save you thousands of dollars. Seriously, I believe this is a surprisingly effective technique that very few people know about. Even more surprising, it often works!

A lower rate can dramatically lower your debt!

Credit card companies love to raise your rates, but they won't lower them, unless you ask. How about reducing a 20% interest rate to 10.5%? Cutting a high rate like that, in half, is impressive. One follower of these methods had his rate of 9.99% dropped all the way to nothing! 0% for six months! Ask! You never know what they might do! Find out what rate you are paying now. One gal had been paying an outrageous 28% for the last six months, and she didn't even know it until she called. She is now paying a much more reasonable rate of 12.8%! Want to feel great? Call and ask to cut your rate! You never know unless you ask.

Spend a Minute, Save a Lot!

You only have to spend a few minutes of your time and you literally can save hundreds or thousands of dollars. Write a simple script for yourself if that makes you feel more comfortable. *Hello, my name is Ed Jones. I need to know what my current interest rate is with you.* This is the part where you pause and they tell you. If it is not a good rate, you say: *Wow, that seems high. I have a bunch of offers from other companies who will give me a lower rate. Could you match the rates being offered by your competitors?*

Even the most phone-shy person can handle that script. Some people get the hang of it after a few calls and get really brazen. I have heard of one guy who likes to play his own version of *Deal or No Deal*. He'll ask for his rate to be cut in half, or he will ask for it to be knocked down by 10%. He has even asked for 0% APR! You've got nothing to lose, and who knows, they could say "yes." This simple phone call technique works. Keep it polite. The key is to kill these fat-cat credit card companies with kindness! If the person you are talking with will not work with you, ask to speak to a supervisor, or hang up and try again later.

Let's Make a Deal

Being polite does not mean that you cannot be persistent. I have a friend Eric who always gets the best hotel rate, simply by asking: "Is that the best you can do for me?" So you can be direct and bold, and ask if that is, in fact, the absolute best rate that they can offer you at the present time. Ask if any special offers are coming up.

Even if you don't have huge debt on each card, the compounding of interest is frightening. Let's show an example of my friend Rhoda. She only had five credit cards. Most people have many more! On one card, she had an outrageous 22% interest rate on a balance of $2000. Credit card minimum payments are usually 2% or 4% of the entire balance. We'll say Rhoda paid 2% of her balance each month. She thought she was doing a good thing by making her minimum payment. She didn't realize that by sticking to the minimum payment it would take almost ten years to pay off that balance! Ten years!

The interest that would pile up over the course of these months would grow to over $3900! She would end up paying more than double the original balance of $2000. How crazy is that! Do you think that whatever she bought for $2000 is still going to be around in ten years? That is longer than a car loan time period. Some people can pay off their houses in ten years. Interest may be the 8th wonder of the world, but we don't need to be its shining examples.

Don't Throw Your Money Away!

Imagine how much greater the numbers in this example for Rhoda would be if the balance were higher than $2000; and many of us carry balances that are indeed more than that. The national average is at $8000 per person. The interest on that could fund a vacation or a retirement plan. I guess it is – only not *your* vacation or *your* retirement plan. Your money is going to the bankers and the credit card company folks instead of into your worthwhile endeavors. Not anymore!

Any reduction in rate is better than staying where it was before you made a simple phone call. Let's use Rhoda as an example. These days, when calling your credit card, your first lesson in patience is punching in enough numbers to get a real person on the line.

> Credit Card Company: Thank you for calling Outrageous Credit Card Company; this is customer service. How can I help you today?
>
> Rhoda: I'd like to find out my interest rate on my account.
>
> CCC: Yes, ma'am.
>
> Rhoda: Can you tell me what interest rate I'm paying right now?
>
> CCC: Yes, ma'am. That would be a rate of 22%.
>
> Rhoda: That is rather steep. I would like to request that my rate be lowered. Can you do that or do I need to talk to somebody else?
>
> CCC: Yes, ma'am. I can lower the rate to 19% for you today.
>
> Rhoda: 19%, is that the best you can do? I really need for a lower rate.
>
> CCC: Yes, ma'am. Let's see. I can lower that rate to 17% today.
>
> Rhoda: I was really hoping for better than that. I have an offer from Carefree Credit right now for 0% APR for balance transfers. Is there a promotion you are having right now for 0%?
>
> CCC: No, ma'am.
>
> Rhoda: If you can't give me better than 17%, I need to talk to a supervisor or a manager or somebody who has that authority.
>
> CCC: Yes, ma'am. Please hold.

Rhoda stayed cool and patient, no matter how times she heard "yes ma'am," and after a few minutes a supervisor came on the line and asked what she could do for Rhoda.

> Rhoda: I've been a customer for a long time and I usually pay my bill on time, but right now things have gotten tight and

with that high interest rate of 22%, my monthly payment is too high. I really want to stay with your company and if you look at my record, you'll see I've been a pretty good customer. I have an offer right now to switch my balance to Carefree Credit and if you can't give me a more reasonable interest rate, that's what I'm going to have to do. I have to lower my payments and this interest is ridiculous.

CCC manager: Yes, ma'am. What is it that you're asking me to do?

Rhoda: I'd like 0% interest rate right now for six months.

CCC manager: Yes, ma'am, I understand, but I cannot do that at this time. We do not have that product available right now. I see from your history with us that you are a long-standing customer, but there have been a few late payments here and there. The best I can do for you today is an interest rate of 12%.

Rhoda: Interest rate of 12%? Okay, I'll take it. Thank you.

Let's run the numbers for Rhoda after she made the call and was able to get an interest rate of 12%. A new rate would knock down the overall interest she pays over the life of the loan to about $1200. That is two-thirds less than what it was before!

Reducing the interest rate reduces the monthly payment and the overall debt. Cutting the interest on a loan is a tremendous thing! Paying $1200 instead of $3900 is a great improvement. Rhoda is going to make on-time payments for a few months and call back again to ask for a lower rate. You never know unless you ask!

Calling all your credit card banks and credit card issuers is worth the small amount of time, and it can save you thousands! Just like that!

Simple, fast, and effective. It's a beautiful thing.

Balances

The same tactic mentioned above about reducing interest applies to your credit card balances as well. Yes, I said balances. The credit card companies really do not want to turn your account over to a collection agency. Of course, their objective is to squash every penny possible out of you, but if that is not possible – you are squashed flat broke – they would rather that they are paid something up front from you, instead of giving it to collection for pennies. So call them up and negotiate.

That's Right

The secret is out! That's right, you can negotiate with the credit card companies. Keep in mind that department store cards usually will not, but the large card issuers will, and no one knows it! That is another reason to not get a department store card – you don't need it. It really won't save you anything in the long run.

You never know unless you ask!

Look at your statements and determine the debt that you have incurred. The actual debt, your purchases, the amounts you personally charged. Now take a look at all the fees, interest rates, and penalties that have accumulated. Sickening, yes, I understand. We have seen how fast interest grows. This total could be three or four times the original amount of debt that you started off with!

You can negotiate a better payment arrangement: pay just the balance that was charged, without all the other garbage. And while you are paying it off, make sure that you will not be charged with fees or interest. This deal gives you the ability to make your payment over time with a payment that you can now afford.

Go Straight to the Top

Talk to a manager. The first customer service person that you speak with on the phone will have to get a supervisor anyway, so ask for one up front. Explain that you are trying to avoid bankruptcy, in which case they would not get a dime. That will get their attention. Usually, they understand that something is better than nothing.

You are offering them money up front, and a chance for both of you to avoid the collection route. A bird in the hand is worth more than not knowing if you will ever catch the bird. Well, you know what I mean.

If the credit card company decides to sell your account balance to a collection agency, they may not recover your full original balance. It is highly unlikely that they would get that much, probably just a portion of it. You could be offering them the best deal that they are going to get out of you. It doesn't hurt to ask, so you have to give it a try. It can help you save thousands of dollars of unnecessary debt!

Actually, this exact situation just happened to one of our loyal readers, Jocelyn. She was deep in debt, to the tune of $33,800. Her husband saw the infomercial late one night and wanted to give *Debt Cures* a try. Jocelyn was a bit skeptical, but bought *Debt Cures* to appease her husband, and she admits that she was curious.

Jocelyn read the book and put it to use right away. Armed with these tips, she picked up the phone, took a deep breath, and demanded (very politely, of course) to speak to a manager. She explained that she could not ever pay the whole balance, but before they transferred her to debt collectors, she wanted to work with the creditor directly. She offered to pay a portion of her debt, the only amount she truly could pay. Much of the total was interest and fees that had accumulated.

The manager did not immediately say yes, but after some back-and-forth, Jocelyn whittled her monster debt of $33,800 to three miniscule payments of $1,800! One phone call saved her close to $29,000! She got a return on her investment in *Debt Cures* almost a thousand times over! Those are the success stories I love to hear!

Jocelyn, like most of us, used to be scared stiff of debt collectors. But after reading *Debt Cures*, she now realizes how she can work the system to her benefit. She shared her story and states, "It allows me to talk with creditors and not allow them to harass me. They don't even call me anymore!"

It Works

Kendra had a credit card bill of $3000 that she simply could not pay. She was a single mother, working as a waitress to take care of her sick mother and her own two kids. After paying her rent and car payment, and food and the bare basics, she was tapped out. With credit card bills skyrocketing every month, due to the interest and late fees,

Kendra was starting to feel a little panicked. She did not want to be bothered by a collection agent, and she knew her account was severely delinquent. Her children and her mom needed a peaceful home, so Kendra took a deep breath and picked up the phone.

She explained her situation to the customer service rep and had to repeat it all again to a manager. She offered to pay the balance, without all the extra charges that had accrued. Her next-door neighbor, who is an accountant, wrote a short two-line letter on his stationery, stating Kendra's facts. Her net worth showed that she would not be able to pay off the interest and fees that had piled up. She barely was able to pay the original debt of about $900. Kendra was shocked when her offer was accepted! Kendra now tells everyone that the methods that *Debt Cures* prescribes really are a prescription for success!

Another reader, Sam, got into serious debt when a friend borrowed money on his credit line to open a flower shop. His interest rate sky-rocketed to an out-of-control 27%. After a few phone calls, he got his rate down to – wait for it – 0% for 5 months! And after that, his rate only rose to 10%. After all was said and done, Sam used *Debt Cures* to pay only 20 cents on each dollar he owed!

Another reader wrote in to say that *Debt Cures* was one of the most useful books she has ever read, and she was able to get her credit card rates knocked down from 31% to 10% and helped her friend make the call to get a 15% rate down to 1%. She states, "It is amazing. I now have a mission to accomplish."

You too can join this mission. You never know until you try, and you have absolutely nothing to lose. So make some calls and let me know what happens! It could go something like this:

> Credit Card Company: Thank you for calling Outrageous Credit Card Company; this is customer service. How can I help you today?
>
> You: I need to talk to someone, maybe the manager, about my credit card balance. There is no way that I can pay it and my amount due has doubled because of all the fees you guys have piled on. I really need to discuss it.
>
> CCC: This is the manager, and what are you suggesting?

You: I am suggesting that we work together to keep me out of bankruptcy and you not have to turn my account over to collections. If you look at my history, you'll see that I am a good customer. I've had your card a long time. I used the card to do my holiday shopping last December and then I lost my job so I was not able to pay off the balance in full. I have made a payment every month, but the interest and the fees are adding up quicker than I can pay it down. I suggest that we just look at what I originally owed and let me pay that off. The rest is just fees that are extra and I do not have the money to pay for anything more than what I bought. Sound fair?

You'll be amazed to learn that credit card companies will in fact negotiate with you. Most people don't know to ask, and the credit card companies sure are not going to tell you! What a great technique to knock down your debt!

Three Incredible Techniques

All too often a person stuck in debt trouble feels like their life is stalled. They want to get back on track, but don't know how. Now you can see that anything is possible! Amazing results happen for people every day because they took that first step!

Don't ever think that you can't get out of debt. Yes, you can!

YOU CAN:

- ✔ Eliminate your debt! 100% purged!
- ✔ Negotiate your debt! Cut your debt by up to 50%, 75%, or more!!
- ✔ Cut your rate! Reduce your rates and cut your payments and your debt by up to one-half, two-thirds or more!

Success begets success. Just get that one small victory, and you are on your way!

What Not to Do

Equally important to knowing what to do, is knowing what not to do.

One misperception people often have when they are drowning in their debt is that they think bankruptcy is the only lifesaver. Everywhere you turn you see an ad for a bankruptcy law firm, begging you to come to them; on television, on the radio, on the internet. They are everywhere. No wonder people have bankruptcy on the brain. These lawyers are planting the seed.

Avoid Bankruptcy

We will dive into bankruptcy concerns later in the book, but please be aware that to keep your credit report and credit score in good standing, you should avoid the bankruptcy route. With *Debt Cures,* you typically don't have to file for bankruptcy. You're not Cinderella, so don't look to bankruptcy as the fairy-godmother solution to end all your problems. It is not a cure-all by any means. Your student loans, your alimony, and your child support won't be going anywhere.

Be wary of debt consolidation and bankruptcy.

But I know bankruptcy happens. Especially when medical bills are involved. The medical practices usually are very aggressive in their collection tactics. Medical bills can be a double or triple whammy, encompassing emotional trauma, physical health issues, and financial concerns.

Tina's son was born with what appeared to be a blockage in his throat. He unexpectedly had to stay in the intensive care unit for three days. Tina received a bill for $35,000. Her savings account was wiped out and she just didn't have the money to pay it off. Tina was forced into bankruptcy. Making matters worse, a collection agency was hired to collect this debt, saying that the bankruptcy didn't cover it. For Tina and all the others who find themselves in the same sinking ship, *Debt Cures* is the lifeboat you have been waiting for.

Bankruptcy is not the quick fix that some shady lawyers make it out to be. You won't be barred from obtaining credit ever again, but you will be targeted for astronomical fees. If you have already filed for bankruptcy, don't wallow in despair. I will show you ways in which you can rebuild your credit.

Beware of "Credit Repair"

While we are on that subject, you need to understand that you can rebuild your credit, but you generally do not need a "credit repair" service. Stay away from these types of ventures – or should I say "scams." Here's a profession that takes money from your wallet in return for *pretending* to edit your report so it's entirely positive. Impossible.

As you will learn, if the information is accurate, albeit negative, it stays on the credit report. If the information is not accurate, you do not need to pay somebody to dispute it. You can do that yourself! Credit repair services typically target those who are in financial crisis and are desperate for a way out. This is not the way.

Don't Consolidate – Eliminate or Negotiate or Cut Your Rate!

Debt consolidation agencies by and large are not the way either. Many people think this is a wonder cure-all, but what they do is take all your existing debt and lump it into a new loan, in theory with a better interest rate than what you were paying on all the other balances. You can get better rates all by yourself! You do not need to pay an agency; and some debt consolidation agencies charge outrageous fees and sky-high interest rates. With the *Debt Cures* methods, I will teach you how you can reduce or even completely eliminate debt – not merely consolidate it!

Another highly advertised option is credit counseling. Using this kind of service to "help" you actually used to hurt your credit report! The credit reporting agencies now recognize that trying to improve your credit is a good thing, and your credit score is not affected. Basically, a credit counselor is supposed to teach you how to handle your debt, like offering you the worn-out advice of "cut up your credit cards." They will also negotiate with your creditors for you, but now you know that you are able to do that yourself!

Credit counseling companies are often nonprofit organizations, but they charge a fee. Why should you have to pay a fee? You don't! If you have already gotten involved with an agency, you can check with the

National Foundation for Consumer Credit Counseling (www.nfcc.org or 800-388-2227) to make sure that they are reputable.

Break Free

We all have heard the FDR presidential inaugural address sound bite, "We have nothing to fear but fear itself." When most people find themselves tangled up in a web of debt, that is the emotion that takes control of them – fear. They fear collection agencies hounding them day and night, they fear losing their house or having their car repossessed, and they fear losing their job. It is an awful way to live. Fear makes some people take rash action, like filing for bankruptcy; for others, fear paralyzes them. They do nothing, and they let the predators sweep in, killing them with interest rate increases and outrageous fees.

Being in debt can be overwhelming. Getting it under control merely requires taking a deep breath and taking a step-by-step process. Most of the time, when people are feeling stress, it is because they don't know what to do. *Debt Cures* shows you what to do.

The banks and credit card companies and financial institutions do not own you. Follow the steps previously outlined. Make the calls. Negotiate. They will take you from fear to control. The greatest of all fears is the fear of the unknown, and we have dispelled that fear.

Remember Jocelyn, our reader who took a $33,800 debt and negotiated it to less than $6,000? She states that all she did was use the proven techniques in this book, and it saved her financial life: "If you work the book, it will work for you."

Another satisfied reader, Dave, wrote in, "Knowledge isn't power, only APPLIED knowledge is power." He has a delightful way of stating what I believe: "If you want to stay in debt…and want to stay fat, cranky and in generally poor health, then don't read books." A man after my own heart, and I'm glad he is a reader of my books. Dave adds: "Apply what you learn. You won't be sorry."

I couldn't have said it better myself!

CHAPTER 7

Fighting Back

"Truth is generally the best vindication against slander."
~ Abraham Lincoln

Abraham Lincoln also said, "How many legs does a dog have if you call the tail a leg? Four; calling the tail a leg doesn't make it a leg."

The whole purpose of my life is enlightenment. I live to enlighten people and expose the truth. Why should telling the truth be any cause for alarm? There is no valid reason why I should be lambasted for explaining how the consumer lending industry really works. When there are good things to expose, I do so gladly. I find that wonderful, and I am over the moon. I delight in sharing good news. On the other side of the coin, when things are not so good, I believe that it is my mission to reveal the situation for what it really is.

And yes, I admit, fighting back feels good.

They Fight Dirty

Sometimes it is mind-boggling what the credit card companies, the banks, the payday loan companies, the mortgage brokers, and the lending institutions will do. A very poor woman and her mentally-handicapped son had trouble making their house payment. The lender allegedly convinced them to sign the papers on a new loan that they could not afford and now they may lose their house. The fully-grown son did not have the ability to sign his name, but the lender had him copy block letters to spell out his name for his signature on the contract. Truth is stranger than fiction. I hate to see people being taken advantage of, and it is now my mission and life goal to bring the truth to the light of day.

Duncan McDonald, former Citibank General Counsel, has gone on television, stating that fees have become a profit stream for the credit card companies, and that fee income has gone up much faster than interest. Fees and penalties are three and four times higher than they were even less than ten years ago. So the debt that is crushing you is a relatively new monster. In fact, McDonald has overtly implied that we've created a Frankenstein.

Shine the Light

Ed and Sue, their neighbors, and so many others have debt that feels like a ball and chain. If your money burdens keep you awake at night worrying, you are not alone. The need to ease your burden is what keeps me awake at night, fueling my desire to take on the predators. Anyone who knows the secrets, anyone who has the insider knowledge, has the obligation to share that knowledge. What is that warm, fuzzy saying? *A candle loses nothing by lighting another candle.* Once you have finished reading this book, you will be a source of light, of knowledge, of life, and be able to illuminate the lives of your friends and family with this information as well. Knowledge is power, and it is exactly the power that they don't want you to have.

They want you to be afraid. They want you to be intimidated. That's how the system works. Debt collectors are trained to harass and to lay on the scare tactics. You don't have to carry this yoke of debt forever. In fact, you can have a fresh start and be on your way to wealth by the time you finish this book. You can create a brand new credit profile. You can start from scratch and build a whole new financial personality.

You Can Take Them On

You can do it yourself. You do not have to be a legal or financial whiz at all. Just follow the steps I've laid out, and you will succeed. There are two parts to the process: 1.Get out of bad debt; and 2. use good debt to build wealth.

No, that is not a contradictory statement. Hang with me for the duration of these chapters, and you will be on your path toward financial freedom. If you are currently dealing with collection agencies or credit card companies, you now know a few unique techniques that can literally save you thousands. Honestly, a few phone calls can save you thousands of dollars. And for some of you, you should be able to eliminate your entire debt completely! 100% of your debt gone!

These simple techniques are not common knowledge. After this book spreads the word, they will be! The best way to get someone's attention is through their pocketbook. If enough people start applying these techniques, the industry will take notice. The only way credit card reform will happen is if we do something about it.

Be a Success Story

My pal, Paul, was $80,000 in debt and forced into bankruptcy. Of the $80,000 that had snowed him under, $50,000 was credit card interest, fees, and penalties! Only $30,000 was actually spent by Paul, and if the amount had stayed that way, he could have managed to repay it. His debt nearly tripled because of the down-and-dirty methods of the credit card companies. The industry forced him into bankruptcy. He had his moments of despair and panic, but fortunately, he learned debt reduction methods and how to create wealth. Now it's Paul's turn to laugh all the way to the bank. His credit is superior, to the extent that he lives in a million-dollar-plus home, and he has the income and credit to support his $1.2 million mortgage. Paul is not the only success story. There are thousands of people who, in following these methods, have overcome what they thought was debt for life.

> Paul went from bankruptcy to a million-dollar-plus home!

Bill had a difficult time getting up and running in business. He was forced into bankruptcy – not once, not twice, but three times! Talk about perseverance! Bill learned how to once and for all take care of the bad debt. He turned his life around completely. Reducing debt and using credit in the right ways made all the difference. Now a multimillionaire with a number of profitable and successful businesses, Bill is also a well-known philanthropist who gives significant amounts of money to charity.

Andrew had $40,000 of debt that he owed to one credit card company. They had sold the debt for pennies on the dollar to a collection agency, which runs a very profitable business, buying delinquent loans and forcing people into settlements that they can't afford. Using *Debt Cures* methods, Andrew was able to successfully settle his $40,000 debt for just $14,000. He got rid of 65% of his debt. That made a tremendous difference in cleaning up his credit report and increasing his credit score.

That is what you can do. Clean up your debt, increase your credit score. Out with the old, in with the new. Bye-bye bad debt, hello wealth. One of the best investments you ever made is this *Debt Cures* book. I cannot wait to hear your success story.

Ready, Set, Go!

When we were in grammar school, our parents and our teachers taught us to be honest and fair, and that cheaters never prosper, but sadly, as we became adults, we saw that sometimes those who don't "play nice" still end up with all the marbles. Instead of saying, "I'll meet you in the playground after school at 3:00" and duking it out with our fists, we have more mature tactics, but we definitely can stand up to the cheaters and the bullies. We don't have to be pushed around.

I know that there are a lot of debt books out there in the libraries and on the bookstore shelves. They generally all say the same thing: cut up your credit cards; keep one for emergency use only and keep it in the freezer; save up for a major purchase and buy it with cash. There is nothing wrong with this advice, but they are operating under the premise that you are in debt over your head because of your spending habits. We have been led down the path to believe that it is the person's irresponsible behavior creating the situation of the ballooning balances. I'm here to tell you that the real problem lies in the habits of the lending industry and calling their behavior irresponsible would be a gross understatement.

If Ed and Sue, along with their neighbors who are facing bank-ruptcy, and the rest of us, the average hard-working citizens, only had to pay back the principle of the debt we incurred, plus a bit of fair interest, there would be no debt epidemic in this country. Ed and Sue studied their credit card bills and realized that what they originally had charged was only about half of the total amount they now owed. They were paying on a balance that was twice as much as when they started. Their next-door neighbors had gotten in over their heads with credit card debt when the company that they both worked for moved its operations out of the country. They both lost their jobs. The bills piled up, and they felt that they had no other option…except to file bankruptcy. It happens every day to people we know – our friends, our families, our neighbors.

Beating the Bully

There are a record number of bankruptcies filed every year. Every year since 2003, there have been more bankruptcies than people graduating college and more Americans going bankrupt than getting divorced. The number of bankruptcies is on the rise each year. Why? The nasty truth is that the banks and the credit card companies set their customers up to fail.

They want us in perpetual debt because that is how they make their money. That is how they make, in an insider's own words, their *obscene* profits. My Encarta dictionary defines obscene as "offensive to conventional standards of decency" and "morally offensive." I have to say that their practices are indeed offensive to my own standards of decency, and personally, I am morally offended.

> Take control of your debt, take control of your life!

Instead of just being offended and wanting to punch somebody out, we can do something about it. We can learn their secrets and their traps, and how to avoid them. Then we can tell everyone we know what we have learned and teach them the secrets as well. That is how to really hit them where it hurts.

Where to Start

Before you can do anything to get out of the debt quagmire that you are in, you have to know your current financial situation. The place where the credit companies start is where we should start also, and that is with your credit score and your credit report.

A physician or medical doctor first makes an analysis of your medical condition by checking out your symptoms. He then figures out where the problems are, and then gives you options or solutions to treat those problems. If you walk in with a bleeding ulcer, he'd better not say, "Take two aspirin, and call me in the morning." You have to take the same logical step-by-step approach with your financial health.

Imagine you enter your doctor's office and said, "Hey, doc, I have chest pains." Your doctor barely glances up and says, "Lie down on the table, let me do open heart surgery on you." Would you then simply nod, say "okay," and lie down on the table? No way. That would never happen. You expect the doctor to check you out and do a thorough exam before suggesting what may be wrong and how to solve your ailments.

The same rationale applies to your money and to your debt as well. Many people walk into a credit counselor's office and say, "Help! I'm buried alive with my debt." They receive the counselor's suggestion to file bankruptcy or to do a debt consolidation plan, and they blindly say: "Okay, sure, whatever you say."

We need to give our financial health the same thorough care that we give our physical health. You need to do an exam of your current financial well-being to determine where the problems are and how to proceed with solving them. It is amazing how many people naively believe that bankruptcy is the only solution to their debt troubles. Don't get me wrong. There may be occasions when bankruptcy is the way to go, but there are far too many folks filing for bankruptcy, and it does not necessarily end their nightmare. We'll talk more about that later.

In order to take control of your debt, and in doing so, take control of your life again, you first need to realize that it can be done. You don't have to live your life as a slave to the deep pockets of corporate America. Your situation is not hopeless. No situation is hopeless. Don't ever let that thought creep into your head. No matter how deep the hole you are in, there is a pole long enough to pull you out. It really is not that difficult, and I will map out the game plan for you.

The First Step

The potential lender or credit card company or bank does not look at you, the person, in your dapper new suit, all clean shaven with a fresh hair cut. You may go to your house of worship every weekend, volunteer at the charity pancake breakfast, and be a fine, upstanding, model citizen in every way, shape, and form. Maybe you can even do a handstand and walk it the length of Main Street. Impressive as that might be, they, the lenders, only look at your credit report and your credit score. You need to get a copy for yourself so you know what they are looking at and how they are judging you. Most importantly, you need to make sure that what is on the report is accurate.

What exactly is the credit report and credit score? The short answer is that these are the tools that the creditor or lender uses to assess your creditworthiness. Are you a good risk? Will you pay on time? An exact score is calculated, landing at a result between 300 and 850. How and why it is this range, I do not know. Rating on a scale of one to ten would be too easy, I guess.

Simply put, the credit report and credit score make up your financial reputation, in black and white, on a piece of paper. If your score is considered too low, a credit card company can deny you. With the way that they operate today, more than likely, they will be happy that you have a low score so they can give you a credit card and charge you a higher interest rate. They want you to have a lower score so that they can get more fees out of you. In fact, the system is designed so that you continue to have a lower credit score. Frightening, but true. We will go over all these details so you understand exactly what is happening, what the lenders are up to, and what you can do about it.

Credit Reporting Agencies

There are three national bureaus that keep credit reports on the good people of America. If you have any credit transaction at all, in any state, you have a credit history, and they have a credit report on you. The agencies are Experian, TransUnion, and Equifax. Their addresses and contact information will be provided later. The credit reporting agencies merely supply your information to the creditors; the banks are in charge of deciding whether you're qualified for credit. The banks and the credit card companies pay the agencies a fee to get the scoop on you and how you are with your money. The credit reporting agencies compile and update your credit information and provide it to the creditors – and you, but only if you ask for it.

The Credit Report

The credit report includes all your standard personal information, plus it lists all the credit card companies and banks that you have transactions with. It can be many pages since it lists all your credit cards, mortgages, student loans, car loans, home equity loans, etc. Basically, the credit report is a detailed history of the life of you and your money, showing whether or not you pay your bills on time. Each of the three major credit reporting agencies has their own separate report, but they contain pretty much the same information.

The Credit Score

A "secret" mathematical formula is used to calculate your credit score. A higher score means you are more likely to pay your debts. The credit score system gets fairly complicated, and I'll go into more detail soon. In fact, I will probably go into more detail than you may expect, but it is important information for you to know.

According to TransUnion, an individual's credit score is a "mathematical calculation that reflects a consumer's credit worthiness. The score is an assessment of how likely a consumer is to pay his or her debts." In the world of make-believe, a creditor could ask a person, "Will you repay this debt?" The person taking the loan would respond, "I solemnly swear that I will." And the person giving the money would say, "Good enough for me!"

But we don't live in a fantasy world. Maybe the lenders can trust us, but we cannot trust them.

It's a Numbers Game

The banks and credit card companies like the idea of using a credit score because it is designed to keep us paying them as much as possible, for as long as possible. They try to make the scoring system sound official, and complicated, and try to indicate that the credit score is used in order for them to be "fair."

In some regards it is. Using numbers and data to evaluate if a person should get a loan or not was the original intent of credit reports and credit scores. It was supposed to be an objective way that every lender could have the same information to make a decision on whether or not they should give you a loan or a credit card. The credit report is like a big report card of every credit test you have ever taken. For most of us, we didn't even know we were taking a test. Every month, our paying habits are turned over to the watchdogs. Having a way to track a person's credit record is a good tool for the lenders. It is not a good system for the consumer.

The system has morphed over time. What they don't want you to know is that credit score system is rigged *against* the consumer. The banks like the credit score's way of doing business because the score calculation is devised to keep you in their vise grip for a long, long time.

Not for Your Eyes Only

We will delve more into credit scores, credit reports, and credit reporting agencies, but for now, it is important for you to be familiar with the words they use. A credit report is a veritable treasure trove of information about you and your money. That information is no one's business but yours. And the government's. And the credit card companies'. And the bank's. And the mortgage broker's. And….

If you are wondering if anyone but the banks and lenders can look at your credit report, the answer is a definitive "yes." Who all is allowed to take a gander? A whole gaggle of people. Any business, individual, or government agency may request a credit report for its legitimate business needs involving a transaction with the consumer. Valid reasons for a company to review your credit report and credit score could include: credit granting considerations; review or collection on an account; employment considerations; insurance underwriting; a potential partnership; security clearance; or lease. Reports may also be issued at the written request of the consumer or a court.

| How private is your private information? | Basically, the feds say it is okay for lots of people to be taking a peek at your credit report. They are only supposed to do so in order to make a determination regarding you and your creditworthiness. The usual suspects are: landlords, current and potential; employers, current and potential; insurance companies; child support enforcement agencies; government agencies (because they are |

the government); an identity theft monitoring company (obviously – only if you hired them to do it); and of course, any potential lenders. And your mama.

Wow, that is quite a list; and that last listed item is just to see if you were paying attention. Your private information has the ability to be seen by a lot of eyes, but your mother has no legal right to it, unless you give her written permission.

Every time someone inquires about your credit, it impacts your credit score. That is unless a soft inquiry is made – like by a credit card company targeting you for business. If the number of credit card offers that arrive in our mailboxes every day are any indication, these kinds of soft inquiries are happening very frequently!

Got All That?

Every single thing you do with your credit cards, your car loans, your student loans, your home mortgage loans, any bank loans, is all reported by the credit companies to the credit reporting agencies. They do just that – report your credit.

It seems like everybody is able to see your credit report, but most of us have not seen our own. If the banks and the credit card companies are looking at your credit report every day in order to mess with your interest rate, it is important for you to understand your credit report too.

What if I told you that the difference between a person with a good credit score and a person with a bad credit score can add up to a million dollars? Got your attention? I thought so. It makes sense that the better our credit score, the better rates we get and the better our financial situation. Just how much better? According to TheStreet. com, a million bucks.

The article posted at http://www.thestreet.com/newsanalysis/ opinion/10371800.html will tell you. A guy with bad credit pays more for his car, his house, his insurance, everything. Over the span of thirty years, the difference of what he pays versus what a guy with good credit pays is huge. And if you figure in the money lost on interest that could have been earning interest, the total could equal one million dollars – or even more. Can you imagine blowing your shot at being a millionaire merely because you had bad credit!

The author of this article, Jeffrey Strain, runs some figures. The national average cost of a house is over $300,000. The guy with good credit gets a 30-year $300,000 mortgage for less than 6.5%. A guy with bad credit has an interest rate of over 10%. Over the life of that 30-year loan, he pays $288,000 more.

Then both of these two gentlemen purchase a new car. Mr. Good Credit gets a rate just over 7% on a $25,000 loan. Mr. Bad Credit's rate is doubled to 14.9%. He pays about $3200 more over the 3-year loan period for the same car. And the thing about cars, we don't keep them forever. So every time Mr. Bad Credit finances a new car, he pays more, which adds up to about $19,000 more than Mr. Good Credit over the course of thirty years.

Mr. Bad Credit has higher interest rates on his credit cards. The average credit card debt is $2200; compare a 9% good credit rate to a 20% bad credit rate and the difference is more than $7200.

Imagine Mr. Good Credit, who is not paying that extra interest, invests $800 a month (the difference between his house payment and that of Mr. Bad Credit). At 8% compounded annually for 30 years, Mr. Good Credit has earned $1.2 million. If that doesn't make you sit up and take notice, nothing will!

So never doubt that credit scores matter, and always keep in mind that you want to be Mr. or Ms. Good Credit. So if this credit report mumbo-jumbo bores you, just think "one million smackers" and your attention span will perk right back up again!

CHAPTER 8

Highest Points Wins

"Every win feels great, but there always are some that are going to stick out from others."
~ Michael Andretti

As with most sports and games in life, golf being the one exception that comes to mind, people with the highest scores win. With a credit score, individuals with the highest scores get the best interest rates and the credit offers with the lowest fees. It would seem logical, to Spock and to me, that the lenders would be most interested in those folks who have proven to be a good credit risk – the ones who pay their bills on time each month and the ones who pay off their balances with every statement. Surprisingly, the people with average or below average credit scores are the ones that the credit card companies salivate over like a big, juicy steak.

This midrange group is what puts the twinkle in the banker's eye and the fat in his wallet. These are the people who use credit, make late payments from time to time, go over the limit every now and then, and essentially give the lender every opportunity to stick the borrower with fees, fees, and more fees.

That is the ultimate goal of the credit card companies; they don't ideally want the excellent credit risk person who pays off the balance every month. They really want those who carry a balance and those who they can nickel and dime with fees until death do they part. It would not be so bad if the fees were only nickels and dimes, but the late fees, and the over-limit fees, and the fees simply for having the privilege to carry a credit card, can be $50, $75, or even $100 a pop.

For the person barely able to make their monthly payment, like Ed and Sue, and many other Americans who fall into this pool, the endless vicious cycle of fees keeps them paying, and playing catch up, until they die. The greedy bankers and lenders are fully aware of this, and this is exactly the type of borrower that has become the flesh of the credit lending business, and the creditors take their pound of flesh every month. When the consumer lenders look at such credit reports and credit scores, they don't see a bad credit risk – they see *dollar signs*.

Who Is a Deadbeat?

In a documentary that aired on PBS called *Secret History of the Credit Card*, author and actor, and former host of *Win Ben Stein's Money*, Ben Stein shows his four-inch stack of credit cards that he carries as he travels around the world. He claims the wallet that he carries in his suit jacket pocket is so thick, due to all those cards, that it gives him the appearance of having a third breast. Ben uses his credit cards, charging thousands of dollars every month. A rich man, spending lots and lots of money on credit – that is a banker's dream, right? Wrong. Ben pays off his balances in their entirety each and every month, and he pays on time. He says the credit card industry hates people like him. Verifying his claim, Ben ran into a high school acquaintance who works for a major credit card company and this man specifically stated, "We hate people like you. We call you the deadbeats."

> Are the credit card companies calling you a "deadbeat"?

How backwards is that? Doing what is right and what is responsible, and being dubbed by the insiders as a deadbeat for it. Talk about slanderous. That only shows how twisted the consumer lending industry has become and how inflated their sense of entitlement has become as well. They expect and want heinous profits, but they don't want to earn their money through honest efforts; they want to trick the American public, and then sit back and count their stacks of coins like Ebenezer Scrooge.

The big profits for the credit card companies come from the 90 million people who do not pay off their credit card debt each month. These people are labeled by the industry as the "revolvers," and this is the target group, the ones that the banks and the lenders and the credit card companies want to keep corralled. Edward Yingling, president of the American Bankers Association, called the revolvers the "sweet spot." They, the bankers, have a lot of tactics, deliberately misleading practices, to keep the revolvers right where they want them, continually going around and around the revolving door of credit. Revolving doors make me dizzy, and the lending industry makes me angry. The best way to get revenge is to get even. How do we go about that? We get our credit reports and our credit scores, and we take control. We don't have to be the pawns in their big bucks games. Once we learn what they do and how they do it, we are no longer under their thumb. We start where they start – with the credit report.

What Is on Your Credit Report

Call me crazy, but I think Ed and Sue, and you, should throw a credit report party. Invite a group of people in and share your *Debt Cures* know-how. If you learn of a good restaurant, you tell all your friends, don't you? So if you learn the way out of debt and the way to wealth, you should tell all your friends as well. Fire up the computer and play credit report poker. Whoever has the highest score wins. Some folks may want to keep their private information private and may prefer not to divulge their score. They still can take part and get their online report, and learn what to do to improve the score. When you are all out of debt and have become millionaires, they will thank you for sharing your tips. I am not joking. Later on, I will cover how you could get a line of credit of up to $1 million.

It all starts with the credit report. The format may vary depending upon which credit bureau is providing the credit report, but the data should be basically the same. There are four main categories of information included on every credit report: your credit information; public record information; inquiries by others to view your credit history; and your personal information.

#1 Personal Information

The obvious: your name, social security number, date of birth, current and previous addresses, telephone numbers, and current and previous employers. When the government starts handing out serial numbers to consumers, I'm sure that will be on there too. Your checking and savings account balances are NOT included on your credit report, nor is info involving your personal affiliations and background, from religious leanings to doctors' records to past legal problems.

#2 Credit Information

It is all here – the good, the bad, and the ugly…and the boring. The details of all your loans and credit cards are listed with the specific information for each one: the date you opened the account; your credit limit; your balance; your monthly payments, etc. It shows the positive credit information, and of course, it shows the negative information.

#3 Public Record Information

This section is exactly what the name suggests. If there is something on you on public record, it's here. This can run the gamut from legal judgments to tax liens, and don't think the information simply goes away, as it often lingers for years. You may want your past to stay in the past, but your credit report can sometimes be a glaring reminder.

#4 Inquiries

The credit report lists everybody who is checking you out. You need to check it out. Make sure that people are not inquiring into your personal affairs that have no right to be doing so. As I stated earlier, only those with a legitimate purpose – like those who are thinking about giving you money or a credit card – are allowed to see your credit report. Whoever is taking a peek stays listed on your credit report for two years.

I mentioned earlier that "soft" inquiries do not affect the calculation of the credit score. "Hard" inquiries do. When you apply for a mortgage, a loan, or a credit card, they will inquire to get your credit report. These hard inquiries stay listed on the credit report for two years, but for one year, they will negatively impact your credit score. How harebrained is that? A company needs to verify your credit score before giving you a loan, but the act of them requesting your information adversely affects your credit score for that year. That is unfair.

TMI ~ Too Much Information

Although it may seem that all your private details are laid bare for the world to see, your private information should indeed only be accessed by those with a legal right to see your credit report. When you are reviewing your credit report, make sure you read through the list of inquiries to verify that no one is viewing your information that has no right to do so. Your busybody neighbor, your nosy ex-mother-in-law, and your barber have no justifiable reasons for checking out your credit history.

> Most Americans – 75% – do not know their credit score.

In the next chapter, I'll tell you how to get your credit report and credit score, and what to do with it once you have it. For now, we should simply try to understand what the darn thing is. The credit report information is compiled by the big three credit reporting agencies – Experian, TransUnion, and Equifax – and it is ongoing. Every month, each creditor, bank, and collection agency that you are actively dealing with reports your payments, or lack of payment, to these agencies. They can report to one, two, or all three. They are only required to report to one. Your credit report and your credit score are thus continually updated.

FYI

In general, your medical bills and your utility bills are not considered credit, so they do not show up on your credit report. If you pay these bills timely every month, you will not get the benefit of it affecting your credit score in a positive way. However, if you do not pay these bills, and the company or the doctor or the hospital turns you over to a collection agency, your credit score will take a negative hit. Medical bills are aggressively pursued, and many doctors will not hesitate to turn you over to collections if you do not pay. This could bring down your credit score in a big way.

Believe me, when the topic of credit reports and credit scores comes up, I know some people are, shall we say, less than interested. Please remember that the lenders see you as a number, so you want to show the very best number possible. We have to get through this stuff before we can move on to the really good part. Your credit history is like the golden ticket that gets you into the candy factory. In this case, it is more like the money factory. Getting you out of debt and into wealth – I hope that holds your interest!

Most Americans don't know about this stuff, and that is why they fall victim to the system. It is up to us to spread the word. According to a July 2003 survey by the Consumer Federation of America, only two percent of Americans said they knew their credit score. And only three percent could name the three main credit bureaus.

Martin Luther King, Jr. once said, "The ultimate measure of a man is not where he stands in moments of comfort and convenience, but where he stands at times of challenge and controversy." Certainly facing a mountain of debt is a time of challenge. You and I may realize that the measure of a man, or a woman, can entail many facets, but as far as the lending industry is concerned, the only measure that matters to them is the credit score.

CHAPTER 9

The Report

Whenever you are asked if you can do a job, tell 'em,
"Certainly I can!" Then get busy and find out how to do it.
~ Theodore Roosevelt

Now that you are starting to understand the big picture of the credit lending industry and beginning to see that there can be a light at the end of your tunnel of debt, if someone asks you, "Do you think you can cure your debt?," you will respond, "Certainly I can!"

With this book in hand, you are taking the first step to getting busy and finding out how to do it. You are taking control. That is real power.

As we discussed in the previous chapter, you need to learn about your credit report and your credit score because that is your ticket to good credit. It makes you or breaks you. Your score determines if they will give you a loan or a credit card. Well, that is how it used to be in the good old days. Today, hardly anyone gets denied. Nearly everyone can get a credit card, but the fees and interest rates vary depending upon your credit score.

Your Report Card

Many Americans have never seen their credit report or credit score. Information is power, and you need to know the information that they have and are quite possibly using against you. When you were a student in school, you did your homework assignments, wrote essays, and took exams. All these things were graded and counted toward your final grade at the end of the semester. You received your graded papers back as you went along, so you knew where you stood. You knew if you were passing or if you were failing. You did not wait until the end of the year to receive your final report card with no prior feedback along the way to give you an indication of how you were doing. The letter grade that would be staring back at you as you read your report card was not a total surprise.

> **The first step in curing your debt – get your credit report!**

Can you imagine enduring an entire year of school, not knowing how you did on any of your homework or papers or tests? You just sat there, doodling on your desk, waiting in ignorance for the final grade to be delivered. Those final grades determined what college you went to or what profession you entered, but you just blindly accepted whatever your final grade card said. That kind of scenario does not make much sense, does it? And think of the times when the teacher graded something wrong that you, in fact, had correct. You were able to call it to his or her attention so the grade could be fixed. If you operated under a system where you did not get your homework back, you could not have known that there were errors that you needed to correct that affected your final grade and your future.

With any area of life, be it our education, our career, or our marriage, we need to know our progress and where we stand so we can take corrective action, if necessary. Our credit report is no exception.

What You Do First

Get your credit report. Check for any inaccuracies. Ninety percent of all credit reports have something wrong on them. If you don't ever get it and look at it, how will you ever know if something needs to be corrected? The first step to creating wealth is getting your credit report!

And once you get the report, it is critical, crucial, mega-important that you review it! Can I be any more clear? The credit score is the magic number that dictates your interest rate, your fees, your financial everything; and the credit score is the direct result of whatever is on that credit report.

Before we go any further, let me give you the contact information for what the industry calls the "big three":

- ✔ Equifax
  P.O. Box 740241
  Atlanta, GA 30374
  1-800-685-1111
  www.equifax.com

- ✔ TransUnion
  P.O. Box 2000
  Chester, PA 19022-2000
  1-800-916-8800
  www.transunion.com

- ✔ Experian
  P.O. Box 2104
  Allen, TX 75013
  1-888-397-3742
  www.experian.com

Just Get It

Each agency gives one freebie credit report per year. Get yours. Order online, by mail, or request it over the phone. Or you can order them all at once with the "Annual Credit Report Request Form." The name is self-explanatory, and it is free. Using the annual request also allows them all to know that you have gotten your one free report for the year, and now you will have to wait twelve months to use the annual service again.

The form is available on http://ftc.gov/credit and www.annualcreditreport.com or by mail at Annual Credit Report Request Service, P.O. Box 105281, Atlanta, GA 30348-5281. Or give them a ring at their toll-free number: (877) 322-8228.

Simple

The form itself is simple. All you need is your basic personal information, nothing you need to dig around for. For the last item, you need to check the boxes for Experian, TransUnion, Equifax. The whole point is to get all three at once. Check, check, check.

If you go through the internet to the Annual Credit Report site, it guides you to each of the three individual sites. It is one-stop shopping, with three separate stops. Follow the prompts, and you will get around and back again.

Easy

Go to their website (www.AnnualCreditReport.com) and select your state. Fill in the personal information. Click the boxes for Experian, Equifax, and TransUnion.

This Annual Credit Report website is linked to each of the three agencies. It takes you to every agency, one at a time, to get your free credit report from each of them. By using the annual request site, you only have to type in your main information once. AnnualCreditReport.com works as the middleman to get you what you need from all three sources. It sounds complicated and tedious, but it moves fairly quickly.

Security

When you are on the website of each credit reporting agency, you may be asked to create a free account. Enter a user name and a password. They may ask you a "secret" security question, and it is not, "What is your mother's maiden name?" That one is too common these days. They will ask for your mother or father's middle name or the name of your first grade teacher. These answers are not the stuff an internet hacker would readily know.

In order to proceed, the website will need to verify your identity. The TransUnion site says: "We want to ensure that you really are you." The website will match your birth date and address records automatically, but be prepared to have account numbers handy.

TransUnion may ask for verification of loan numbers and credit card account numbers, so be a good scout and be prepared. They may also want you to confirm employment information during a certain timeframe. Experian and Equifax may ask questions about your personal financial information, so you need to know who you have your mortgage with and what county you live in.

After you have answered the questions satisfactorily, your credit report pops up. Print it. Read it. There can be a lot of pages. We'll get to the nitty gritty on this in a moment.

Some sites may ask if you want to pay to get your FICO score. (We'll talk more about FICO scores in a second.) It usually is a good idea to get your FICO score.

What You Do Now

If you are like most people, what you want to do now is take a break. What you should do is look yourself in the eye and feel good about the knowledge you are acquiring. You are well on your way to getting out of the financial hole, and if you stick with me long enough, you will soon ascend to the financial mountaintop. Trust me, you will never regret it.

Okay, you have your credit reports in hand. Now you need to take the time to review all the information reported there. I know how tempting it can be to set paperwork aside, with very good intentions to get to it after more "pressing matters" like dinner, the laundry, or hmm…paying bills. Nothing is more pressing than making sure your credit report is up-to-date and accurate. That is the information that is used to determine your credit score, and the credit score is what is used to determine your interest rates on all your loans and credit cards. All your bills and financial bottom line depend on it!

Read the Lines

Take the time to read it through. Most items are obvious; a few need explanation.

- ✔ The creditor's name
- ✔ The creditor's address

✔ The creditor's phone number

✔ Your account number with that creditor

✔ The date the account was opened

✔ The type of account (auto, mortgage, etc.; credit cards = "revolving")

✔ The credit limit/original amount

✔ Reported since (date account started being reported)

✔ Terms (length of the mortgage; if a credit card, NA for Not Applicable)

✔ Monthly payment (credit cards may show $0)

✔ High balance (highest balance to date or original loan amount)

✔ Recent balance

✔ Status/remark (Open/Current; Paid/Closed; Never Late; etc. Open/Current = good standing)

✔ Date of status (date that the Status section was last updated)

✔ Last reported (date creditor last reported any information)

✔ Responsibility (joint or individual account; spouse's name may be listed)

✔ Recent payment (last payment received)

✔ Account history (sometimes the balance history just lists a lot of zeros)

Check, Check, Double Check

If you have a lot of financial activity, your credit report can be quite lengthy. If you do not have your own credit reports to look at right now while we are talking about this stuff, get a sample report to use as a guide. You can view one at the websites of the credit reporting agencies.

First, the easy part. Check your personal information: your name, your middle initial, etc. If you come across any mistakes in this section – and you might – notify that credit reporting agency directly.

You would be amazed how often someone else's information turns up on your credit report, simply for having the same name as you, the only difference being the middle initial. I was in line behind a man at the airport last week who was being delayed at passport control because of a similar situation. He even shared the same middle name, not just the initial, as this other person. My gentleman knew the other man's name, address, and details, even his hair color, because he has run into problems for the last several years, due to having the same name as some other guy. I imagine there are many John Smiths out there, but don't be so sure that no one else has your name, even if you do have an uncommon name. Or maybe you are John Smith Sr., and John Smith Jr. has lousy credit. You want to be sure only your information is showing on your report.

> You want 100% accuracy.

Verification in Progress...

So take a red pen, grab a cup of coffee, and have a seat. Today is the day you review your credit report. Verify that your social security number is correct. Confirm every detail of your personal information. Then look at all the rest.

As you go down the form, line by line, make sure that loans and debts listed are actually yours. If you find a twenty dollar bill on the street that isn't yours, great. If you find items on your credit report that are not yours, not good at all.

If there are any judgments on the credit report, verify that they are indeed against you. You should know if you have had a judgment against you. Check for closed accounts. Maybe you had a car lease that was closed three years ago and it still shows as an open account. Perhaps there is a credit card listed, and you know that you never had a Diner's Club card. These are the types of things to be on the lookout for.

If you find an error reported by a creditor, contact that creditor directly. If they do not give you the time of day to attempt to resolve your issue, or even pretend to care, you can contact the credit reporting agency. Each of the three credit bureaus has ways to submit your dispute online, which you may recall seeing when you were on their websites, getting your credit report.

Potentially Negative Items

Sounds dreadful, doesn't it? The reality is that sometimes there are negatives on your credit report that you cannot do anything about. Those are the buggers that are damaging your credit score. If it happened, it happened, and there it is. The credit report is supposed to be a truthful portrayal of your credit history. Incidents that you would rather forget are there, staring at you. If you paid late, or missed payments, or have a judgment against you, it will be there.

This "negative items" section is what the creditors focus on. They scrutinize it carefully, so you better as well. The information here is the "meat and potatoes": how often you have made late payments and how late those payments have been. Pay late a lot? Whammy. Balances too high? Double whammy.

Don't get too upset if you have a lot in this category. Often the case turns out that the negative item is there in error, so you can correct it. Sit tight and you will learn how to improve your credit report!

And look at the section of your positive credit information – Accounts in Good Standing. That is your goal!

Scrutinize

Who among us has never made a late payment or racked up a high balance? We all have. Whatever actual information you have could probably be enough to hurt your score, simply because the formula is rigged against you. But there very well could be a mistake on your credit report. You absolutely do not need false information bringing down your credit score. If you notice any error, jump on it right away.

Errors and Disputes

Over a billion credit reports are generated each year, with billions and billions of bits and pieces of information. Humans are reporting the information, and humans are entering the information. That means there is good chance of human error. Mistakes happen. Isn't that what we say when we mess up: I'm only human!

Review your three credit reports with a fine-tooth comb! Are there accounts you have never heard of? Are there amounts or information that appear incorrect? Compare the information on the credit report against your records. All it takes is a little bit of your time to make sure that the information is really yours and that it is accurate. And don't forget, time is money. Your money.

Check it!

Correct it!

Dispute it!

Errors in your personal information don't affect your credit score, but still need to be corrected. Errors, or strange information, like an oddball address, especially a P.O. Box that isn't yours, could be an indication someone else has access to your accounts. Identity theft is a very real threat and is becoming increasingly more and more common. Be vigilant in your efforts to protect yourself from identity theft. One of those efforts is to monitor your credit report. Do it at least once a year. Every few months is even better.

Initiate a Dispute

Errors are all over the credit reports, so be diligent in your search for mistakes. Find an error? File a dispute immediately!

The credit repair people try to make you believe that this is their area of expertise, and they will charge you to file a dispute. You don't have to pay anyone to do this for you! File a dispute, for free, online, over the phone, or by snail mail. Once you file a dispute, the credit reporting agency contacts the lender or the creditor or the credit card company.

If you file by writing a letter, make a copy of the current credit report. Highlight the credit report number, the date, and the actual error. Your letter needs to include your basic information, plus a copy of a current utility bill, showing your name and address, and a copy of your picture ID (passport or driver's license). Include a detailed explanation of each error, along with your statements, or whatever else you have to prove your dispute. Keep a copy of everything for your records.

The credit reporting agency has 30 days to resolve the dispute. If they cannot prove the error one way or another, the item you are questioning has to be taken off your credit report until they can prove that it belongs there.

If you have errors bringing down your score, in 30 days they're gone and your credit has gone from bad to good! In 30 days!

Ed Did

Ed's credit report showed that he had an Old Navy credit card, yet never in his life did he ever have an Old Navy credit card account. Sue closed her Discover card three years ago, and it still showed as an open account. Perhaps when you review yours, you will find that there is a judgment listed against you that simply does not belong to you. These are the types of items to get corrected.

Ed discovered the same error on all three credit reports, so he initiated a dispute with all three credit reporting agencies. He also could have contacted the creditor directly to make the correction and report it to the credit reporting agencies. Ed initiated the disputes online, the most time-efficient way to go. Each credit reporting agency website had prompts to follow that easily guided Ed through the process.

Personal Statement

If you want to explain negative information on your credit report that is legit, and not an error, you can add a "Personal Statement" to your credit reports. Your comments don't impact your credit score, but will be read by anyone reviewing your credit. Whether it will affect the interest rate they give you is highly doubtful.

Ed and Sue used this opportunity to explain that their house payments had been late because they had paid for their son's medical bills. As soon as that debt was taken care of, the house payments were timely again. Perhaps you were late on your car payment because you lost your job. Or you had collection action taken against you on an account because you were unable to pay when you had a medical emergency or a sudden illness.

The Personal Statement has to be short – 100 words or less. If the negative item is later removed, your Personal Statement does not automatically fall off with it. So when you review your credit report from time to time, make sure personal statements get removed, or it could become very confusing.

Somebody Is Watching You

As you can easily see, the credit report has all your secrets. It also includes all your past residences and all your past employers. It is almost like watching an episode of *This Is Your Life,* except there are no surprise reunions or hugs or tears. The credit report is a powerful piece of paper, and it was created by the financial industry for their benefit, not yours. It sort of has that "Big Brother" feel – they know where you work and how long you have worked there, where you live and how long you have lived there. And, of course, they know how much you pay and owe on all your bills.

A monitoring service (www.debtcures.com) is a smart idea.

Your credit information is your track to wealth. Since you cannot stop the train, you have to at least make sure that you are on the right train. You do so by making sure that every bit of information that is reported on the credit report is accurate. The first step to taking control of your credit and your life is to take control of your credit report. It is absolutely critical.

More Than Once a Year

You can, and should, get your credit report more often than once a year. It just won't be free. The Annual Credit Report Request Service is allowed only once a year, just like your birthday. Instead, contact each agency directly. I suggest a credit monitoring service that includes unlimited access to your credit report. You won't have to worry about it again. Peace of mind is worth a few dollars and is a good investment.

You Are in Control

All this information about credit reports may have you feeling a little overwhelmed. Don't be. The point of the information I am giving you has one primary purpose: now that you have the same information that they do, you are not powerless. You can take control of your credit. Knowledge is power!

The credit report is a tool that you now know how to use. There is no point in having a tool that you do not use, so do what they do. Monitor your own credit activity. Review your accounts and make sure they are yours and that it all makes sense.

Make it a habit to review your credit report regularly. When you take control of your financial health, every area of your life improves. You can sleep better at night, you feel less stressed at work, you are not so tense with your significant other, and you are not biting the heads off of your family. Curing your debt really does help cure your whole overall life.

Many people experience various emotions in their life and think it is just a part of the rat race (or is it the rate race?) that we live in. You do not have to go through life as one tightly wound ball of stress! Do you ever feel anxious about:

- ✔ The credit card balances that never go away?
- ✔ The fear of being turned over to a collection agency?
- ✔ The fear of being forced into bankruptcy?

Are you sick and tired of:

- ✔ Living paycheck to paycheck?
- ✔ Having no retirement fund?
- ✔ Having no emergency nest egg?
- ✔ Having no savings account?
- ✔ Having no money to invest?
- ✔ Feeling sick and tired?

Do you feel anxious about feeling anxious?!

All the unnecessary extra stress in your life can melt away. If you are feeling bogged down because of your debt, know that you are not stuck forever. They don't own you and they can't run your life. The ties that bind, the financial purse strings of the lenders and the government, are loosening. They do not have you in their grip. You are not their slave!

Free Your Mind

By using the various methods and solutions outlined in *Debt Cures,* you not only get the amazing feeling that comes with eliminating or reducing debt, but you will also be amazed at how the other areas of your life fall into place. It is a recurring benefit you give yourself. This time, the compounding effect is a domino effect in a positive way. That's why I wrote the book.

Ridding yourself of your debt immediately improves your mood. That will improve your health, your relationships, and your job stress. In fact, you will not feel tied to a job like you used to. Ever hear someone mutter, "I hate my job, but I can't quit"? If you get out of debt and into creating wealth, you can pursue a profession that you love. You can work by choice, not because you have to pay off the credit card bills.

Peace of Mind

Most Americans worry about the same things you do: saving for retirement, saving up a nest egg for that emergency that hopefully will never happen, and saving for their children's education. By curing your debt, you can cure these worries too. You can create wealth and have money for savings, money for investing, money for vacations, money to pay for your mother in the nursing home, money for whatever it is that you used to worry about. You will have more free time to pursue your passions, instead of paying off piles of debt.

> You can achieve peace of mind again!

Debt Cures shows you the path to freedom and peace of mind. You will be able to break free, completely and forever. And that is taking control.

CHAPTER 10

Knowing the Score

*I once kept score on an agency man I entertained from
6 p.m. until 1 in the morning. During that period he
consumed 16 scotch and sodas.*

~ Joseph Barbera

No, the process of getting your credit report and correcting any errors should not be driving you to drink. And no, there is no reason to invite your banker out to wine and dine him. He should be doing that for you.

In this whole process of curing your debt, it is important to remember to focus on the days ahead and smile. And now if you ever go on *Jeopardy!*, and the Daily Double lists TransUnion, Equifax, and Experian, you will answer without hesitating, "What are the three national credit reporting agencies, Alex?!"

Never forget that we will have the last laugh in dealing with the greedy lending institutions and banks and credit card companies. They think that they have us in their pockets for life because we carry their cards in our wallets. It does not have to be so. I know their secrets, and it is time that the entire American public knows them as well.

If a person knows there is a scam, they won't be taken. It's as simple as that.

The Score

You are now up to speed on credit reports. The next item on the agenda: the credit score, the most important piece of information on your financial resume! The higher the score, the better. The credit score is something that the banks can hang their hat on when determining how to pass out interest rates.

You are nothing but a number.

The credit score is calculated using an "algorithm." That is an intimidating word, meaning *complex mathematical formula*. The various data and bits of information from your credit report are thrown into the top-secret computer and cranked and yanked. The resulting score is between 300 and 850. Why they didn't go with 1 – 10 is beyond me. I like to keep things simple; they like to keep us confused.

That number, the powerful credit score, determines what kind of interest rate the banks, the credit card companies, and the mortgage companies will give you.

A few years ago, if you got a credit score in the upper 700s, you were the top choice of lenders. Take a bow. Today you are still considered an "excellent" credit risk, and you should be able to get the best interest rates and the best terms on your credit cards and your home mortgage loans. You, however, are not the ideal customer for the fee-addicted lenders. They want someone who will miss a payment or be late occasionally. Ch-ching, ch-ching.

If you score in the middle, or lower, you are the one they want. The banks and creditors may label you a "questionable" credit risk. It does not mean that they will deny your credit application; it means that they will gladly welcome you into their web of high interest rates and penalties and fees.

It's Nothing Personal

Your credit score is based upon your financial information, nothing else. Because the computer is cranking out numbers and formulas, there is supposedly no room for human bias in the scoring system. The decision-making process regarding your credit is supposed to be made based upon your facts and figures, not your personal information.

Your sex, your race, and your nationality do not matter. How much you have in your bank account does not matter. The credit score is supposed to be an objective tool for the lending industry to be able to compare apples to apples: how this guy pays his bills versus how that guy pays his bills.

Let's take the fictional story of Joe. He is male, single, Muslim, gay, Arab, born in Iran, and wants a personal loan to take his Korean Buddhist boyfriend on vacation. The white, Irish Catholic, married female loan officer has to make her decision based solely on his credit score. She cannot discriminate against Joe, based on his gender, race, religion, nationality, marital status, or sexual orientation. Or the fact that he wore plaid pants and a garish yellow raincoat, and had greasy hair. The credit industry devised the credit report and credit score method in order to make their decisions objectively, and that is all they can use.

Decision Making

The credit score is more important than we sometimes realize. Even if you are one of the rare individuals who does not carry a credit card, have a home mortgage loan, a car loan, a student loan, or a personal loan, the credit report and credit score still have an impact on you. I have never met anybody who falls into that category, but I am sure that there are some of you out there. Be advised. Your insurance company looks at your credit score to determine what kind of policy to give you. Your employer can even look at your credit report and credit score when trying to decide whether to hire or promote you. The credit score permeates into many corners of our lives.

Let's look at Jane, who is divorced with three kids. She applied for a cashier job at the local ice cream shop. She's half Jewish, half Christian, half white, half black. She is overweight, over forty, and has a limp. On the 4th of July, she marched in a parade with a banner that stated "Down With America." Okay, maybe my tale is a little extreme, but she is just an example I created to make my point.

> Credit
>
> scores affect
>
> apartment
>
> leases,
>
> insurance
>
> policies, and
>
> job promotions!

Jane does not get the job and wants to scream that she was discriminated against. The employer simply says, "Oh yeah? Just look at this credit report." The potential employer saw that Jane bounced from job to job, made late payments on the vast majority of her bills, and had several accounts turned over to collections. That very easily can deny a job or a promotion. The employer didn't see Jane as a good employee, a trustworthy asset for the company, and her credit report was proof of that. Jane cannot file discrimination because the potential employer can legitimately use the credit report in his decision making process.

One Score? Three Scores?

Each credit reporting agency has a credit report on you, and each tallies their own score. Not all creditors report in to all three credit reporting agencies. They only have to talk about you to one.

Maybe your MasterCard account reports to Experian; your Macy's credit card reports to Equifax; and your American Express card reports to TransUnion. They each calculate your credit score based upon what information they have on your credit report, so each credit score may be slightly different. It is normal and no big deal.

Secret Formulas

The baked beans guy does not want you to know his family's secret recipe, the formula for Coca-Cola is locked in a vault somewhere, and the complex mathematical algorithm for computing credit scores is not out there, floating around on the internet. If Grandma Elsie would have wanted you to know the secret ingredient in her mashed potatoes, she would have told you. If the consumer lending industry wanted us to know the intricacies of the credit score calculation, it would be in every debt book and discussed in every financial seminar. It would even have its own webisode on YouTube.

The software was created by Fair Isaac Corporation – FICO – so you see the words "credit score" or "FICO score" used. Fair Isaac, a Minneapolis-based financial services company, does not house a database with all kinds of information about you. All three credit reporting agencies use the FICO software. No estimator or calculator or feeble human brain can replicate the processes that the software goes through. The credit score is computed using a proprietary mathematical formula. I like that word "proprietary." It means: I know the secret, and I don't have to tell you.

The credit bureaus and the financial lending institutions think keeping the formula a secret will keep you in the palm of their hand. Not so. We don't need to understand electricity to know how to turn on the lights, and we don't need to understand any algorithms to fix our credit scores. The credit score is comprised of five basic elements. According to About.com: Home buying, the breakdown is as follows:

✔ **35% – Payment History**

Number of accounts paid; Collections or negative public records; Delinquent accounts: total number of past due items; how long past due; how long since you made a late payment.

✔ **30% – Amounts You Owe**

How much you owe on accounts and the types of accounts with balances; How much of your credit lines you've used; Amounts you owe vs. their original balances; Number of zero balance accounts.

✔ **15% – Length of Your Credit History**

Total length of time tracked by your credit report; Length of time since accounts were opened; Time that's passed since the last activity; The longer you show good credit history, the better your score.

✔ **10% – Types of Credit Used**

Total number of accounts and types of accounts (credit cards, mortgage, car, etc.). A mixture of accounts usually generates better scores than only numerous credit cards; they practically throw credit cards at us, yet the credit score goes down with too many credit cards.

✔ **10% – New Credit**

Number of accounts recently opened; Proportion of new accounts to total accounts; Number of recent credit inquiries; The time that has passed since recent inquiries or newly-opened accounts; If you've re-established a positive credit history after encountering payment problems.

What It Means

In a nutshell, your FICO score is primarily concerned (65%) with your payment history and what you owe. It seems like it should be so easy. Pay your bills. Pay on time. Don't owe too much. It could be that easy if the myriad of financial industry-created fees was not allowed to run rampant and trample our credit histories and our pocketbooks. Another element that adds to the fact that the deck is stacked against the American citizen is how the FICO software manipulates the numbers. We know it is complicated, but it is also surprising and disturbing.

What They Do with It

A FICO credit expert, Hazel Valera, in a workshop for the Millionaire Real Estate Club of Las Vegas, stated that the FICO software analyzes your habits over the last two years. Of all the gyrations that the computer cranks through, six rating factors are positive and eighty-eight are negative. That's right. That's a landslide, and the odds are not in the favor of the working citizen. The software code is looking for eighty-eight things that can be used against you. The software is designed to find things to make your score drop.

The free credit reports sometimes include a free credit score that the credit reporting agency calculates, but that is not the actual FICO score. Some credit card companies are satisfied with those scores, but mortgage lenders will only use the official FICO score. Make sure that is the one you get. There is a small fee for the FICO score, but you want to know what they know, so get your FICO score.

Approval Process

When you apply for a credit card or a department store card, they usually check your credit history with one credit report, especially if their card is a fast approval offer. They quickly approve or deny you, based on that one score.

For a mortgage, the mortgage broker or the lending bank usually gets your credit reports from all three credit reporting agencies. They do not take your best score, and they don't take an average. They grab the middle score. The lender can look at only two reports if they want, and you guessed it, they take the lower score. The lower your score, the better for them, and the better odds that they will be able to play Fee Bingo on your account.

Remember that your credit report is always changing. Your credit card companies turn in your payment information each month. Therefore, the credit report is a living document that needs your ongoing attention. Verifying it for accuracy needs to happen at least annually. More often than that is even better. I suggest a credit monitoring service.

One More Score

We will learn how to raise the credit score in the next chapter. There are several easy techniques! Before we tackle that topic, I need to explain that there is one more credit score that entered the marketplace, just in case you hear the name VantageScore.

The big three credit reporting agencies united together to use the same formula for a consistent score that they named the VantageScore. (Rumor has it they also didn't want to pay Fair Isaacs for every FICO score.) The FICO scores range from 300 to 850. The VantageScore system ranges from 501 to 990. Does that make any sense? No. In both systems, the higher your score, the better risk you are, and the better rate will come your way. VantageScore was made available in March 2006, but for the most part, mortgage lenders, credit card companies, and banks are still primarily using the FICO score. It may seem a bit confusing (because it is). If you are swimming in different scores, just make sure the one you pay attention to is the FICO score; that's still the one that carries the weight.

Good, Better, Best

The following table is a general rule of thumb regarding how FICO credit scores are judged by creditors:

Less than 619	High risk
620 – 660	Uncertain
661 – 720	Average (acceptable)
721 and higher	Very good
Over 750	Excellent

How We Rank

Recent credit scores among the U.S. population approximately rank out:

Up to 499: 1%
500 – 599: 12%
600 – 699: 27%
700 – 749: 20%
750 – 799: 29%
Over 800: 11%

40% of us fall in the "Over 750" ranking. Excellent. 13% of us fall under 600, which is very high risk. With a score of 600 to a score of 749, those 47% are the bread and butter of the industry.

Fair Credit Reporting Act

Until the Fair Credit Reporting Act came along, we, the consumers, had to pay for our credit reports. They, the credit reporting agencies, who keep tabs on our every move, made us pay to find out what they were saying about us. Ridiculous. This Act required that the credit reporting agencies supply us, me and you, the good people of America, with free copies of our credit reports, upon request, once every twelve months. However, the credit score is not technically part of the credit report, so they did not have to provide that for free. If you are supplied with a free score, verify that it is indeed the FICO score. Usually there is a fee for the FICO. You can always go to the website at www.myfico. com anytime to purchase your actual FICO score.

Ed and Sue were a lot like the rest of us. They knew their ATM codes, the phone number to the pizza joint, and their kids' shoe sizes. They knew a lot of numbers, but last year, if you would have asked them about their credit score, they would have given you a blank stare. Now, they have their credit reports in hand and they see that they are indeed Average Americans. Their FICO score lands in the zone that creditors love, right in the mid-600s. Fixing their credit score has become priority number one for Ed and Sue.

A Long Road

The road that led you to where you are today, holding *Debt Cures* in your hands, may have been a long and winding road. Maybe you have fallen upon hard times and your debt has grown like a weed. Now you know that the banks, the credit card companies, and the lending institutions have been the ones watering the weed and helping it to grow faster. The federal government is holding the water can and watching the weeds grow and choke out the good grass. Instead of coming to the aid of the American citizen, the feds sit back and admire the weeds.

> What is your FICO score?

America is the land of the free and the home of the brave. Slavery was supposed to have ended with the Civil War, but some folks are still enslaved to the banks and the creditors. All I can say is, "Not any more!" We have already covered a lot of information in these first few chapters. Mainly, you now know that obtaining and fixing any inaccuracies on your credit score is crucial, and increasing your FICO score is essential, for your current and long term situation. Doing so puts dollars back in your pockets and helps you pull the weeds out of your garden.

The Right Path

"By persisting in your path, though you forfeit the little, you gain the great." Ralph Waldo Emerson was a very wise man. Maybe you have been on the path of mounting debt and as a result, mounting pressure. It is time to relieve that burden. If you persist in your path toward curing your debt, the only thing you forfeit is worry. The gain is great. You get your life back.

Let's get you moving on down the right path.

CHAPTER 11

Show Me the Money

"No one saves us but ourselves."
~ Gautama Siddhartha (Buddha)

Ed and Sue requested their credit reports online. They received their credit reports and their credit score from all three credit bureaus, along with their FICO score. As they meticulously reviewed their credit reports, line by line, they found some errors, along with one erroneous credit item to dispute. They immediately filed the dispute and corrections online, and kept copies of all the paperwork. Ed and Sue deserve a shiny gold star for their efforts. They now want to do everything possible to increase their FICO score. They are smart, responsible citizens, just like you.

They want to do everything possible to boost their credit score and, of course, they want fast results. Here are a few more simple techniques to help Ed and Sue, and you, make credit score improvements.

IMPROVE YOUR CREDIT SCORE OVERNIGHT!

Even if you have the worst credit in the world,
you can get almost perfect credit in 30 days!

Get It

Get your credit reports! We spent pages and pages discussing credit reports and credit scores because that is where it all begins. There are entire books devoted to the subject of credit reports, and expensive financial seminars for which you could pay big bucks to learn what I just said: Get your credit reports! Why? Because that is what the financial world uses to judge you, and they are indeed passing judgment.

The credit score is your passport to a better tomorrow. If you follow the concepts discussed in these chapters, you could see a huge improvement in your credit score! A better score gets you better rates, which means lower payments. Paying less money and paying over a shorter amount of time means you keep the money, not the banks. Improving your credit score opens the door! You could improve your financial health and it can be miraculous!

Now you see that the process does not have to be complicated. Requesting a piece of paper (okay, several pieces of paper), looking over those papers, and acting on what you see there. It is as easy as one, two, three! You have heard commercials that say change your hair color or change your wardrobe and you can change your life. Change your credit score and you really can change your life!

Fix It

Get each of the three credit reports. You now know that it is quick and easy, and it is the first step on the road to debt free living! Review your report. Correct any errors! If there are any items that you need to dispute, start the dispute immediately! The credit reporting agency has thirty days to resolve the matter. If they can't within the thirty days, they have to remove that questionable item from your credit report. Make sure that they do!

If you can tackle one credit report at a time, go after the one showing the middle score. That is the score that the banks look at. It is your priority right now. Once you get that credit report free of errors, take the one with the next lowest score, and then the next. Keep all three in good shape!

Many times, they cannot prove the accuracy of the item you are questioning within the 30 days. That means they MUST remove it from your credit report. Instant credit pump up! One short month can bring huge improvement!

Monitor It

Review your credit reports regularly! Be sure they are accurate and free of errors. It is also a good idea to monitor your credit reports for any unusual items that pop up because identity theft is very common these days, and you do not want to be the next victim. A credit monitoring service can do this for you.

Most people balance their checkbooks once a month. You should get in the habit of looking at your credit reports too!

Delete It

Do you have any collection activity happening? This item on your credit report is one of those negative pests. But there is a cure! Call the collection agency and simply ask if they will delete it from your record if you pay. Instead of showing the collection as "paid," they can delete it from your record! Delete! Gone!

About half of all collection agencies will do this. Amazing, I know. They will completely remove it from your credit report if you pay off the debt, or at least pay a large chunk of it.

If you are working with a collection agency who will delete it, do it! Find the money (any way you can!) and get this item taken off your record! This is an unbelievable opportunity to make your debt problem disappear virtually overnight! Getting a negative item like this wiped off your credit report has a huge and immediate impact on your credit score! If you

> Negative items could be 100% removed from your credit report!

can take advantage of this, use the methods talked about later on to get the money to pay it off. It is worth it, now and for your financial future!

Increase It

Increase your credit score with a quick call to the credit card companies! For every card you have, call each one and ask that they increase your credit limit. This request is usually much easier for them to agree to than any other request you might have; they assume you will charge more on your account and that means more bucks for them.

You know how to make phone calls. What a great method that anyone can try!

You do want the increase in your credit limit – not to make more purchases, but to boost your credit score more. Your credit score improves dramatically if you do not use all of your available credit. The fastest and easiest way to accomplish this is to get more available credit. All you have to do is ask! By not using all of your available credit, your credit score can go up as much as 50 points!

Spread It

Play the spread! If the credit card companies won't increase your limit (but most should), spread out your debt among all your credit cards. You want every credit card to show the highest possible available credit. The FICO score system only wants you to use 30%–35% of your available credit on each card, so attempt for that amount. The credit card may give you a credit limit of $1000, but you should only charge $300.

It may seem silly, but play their game. Spread out what you owe, so no one card has a high balance. Do not max out your cards. Use this simple technique and your credit score can greatly improve!

Pay It

To get your cards down to that 30% or 35%, can you pay off some of the balances? Instead of spreading the balances around, maybe you can pay some down. If at all possible, pay off your cards, or get them down to a low balance. Get each credit card to the magic 30% level. I'll help you find the money to pay them!

Find It

Do you have money sitting in the bank or buried in the backyard for that "rainy day"? Well, it's raining. If you have a debt that is in collection, or if you have a high balance to pay down, go ahead and use the money now to get out of this mess. Unless you are earning huge interest on it, you are better off to pay some of these problem areas and make them go away!

Some people are afraid to dip into that "emergency" fund, but it is only paying 4% or some low interest! Your credit cards are costing you way more than that. And if you can clean up your credit report quickly, you will be on your way to wealth creation. You won't need to dig a hole in the backyard because you won't have the money fear and debt worries hanging over you any more! Take care of this problem and the future can take care of itself.

Maybe you don't have any savings that you can use. It is still critical for you to pay off these problem credit items. You need to get the money. Borrow it! I see your eyes fly wide open. We're talking about paying off debt, and I tell you to borrow more debt? Yes! Borrow money from friends and family to pay down the problem items on the credit report. What goes on with you and your family and friends is private – it won't show up on a credit report. Most people you know would probably charge you lower interest than a bank, or if you are really lucky, no interest at all!

Check It

When you do these methods to pump up your credit score, make sure that the credit report does indeed reflect your hard work. If there was an item that was not yours, or you pay off a debt that was in collection, or you pay down your debts, be sure that the report indicates what you have accomplished. The whole point of doing the work is to get the credit score improved!

If your fixes do not show up, then contact the credit reporting agencies. They may let you just send in your proof of payment instead of having to go through the dispute route with them. Do what you have to do to make sure what you have fixed shows up as fixed!

Why Bother?

> You can improve your credit score virtually overnight!

Your credit score is the heavy hitter in the credit world, and you want to be able to hit it out of the park. If you don't pay attention to your credit score, it can end up hitting you over the head month after month after month. The number you receive as your credit score is the determining factor for your ability to obtain credit and the way credit is given to you. A low credit score can potentially prevent you from receiving loans, or worse, you will get credit but your interest rate will be significantly higher than someone who has excellent credit.

The number matters. A low credit score can cost you big bucks over the life of your loans. If you have a mortgage, a student loan, and a car loan, a low credit score means you will pays thousands of dollars more in interest fees.

My Point

For example, let's take three regular guys with three regular credit scores. Doug applies for a home mortgage loan in the amount of $275,000. His credit score was 700, so he is considered a pretty good risk. For a 30-year fixed rate mortgage, he qualifies for an interest rate of 5.6%. His monthly payment will be $1,579.

Tom has a credit score of 675. He qualifies for an interest rate of 6.1% for the same mortgage loan. His monthly payment is $1,666.

Enter Regular Guy #3. Dave also wants a 30-year fixed rate mortgage in the amount of $275,000. His credit score is 620. He is approved for an interest rate of 7.3%. His monthly mortgage payment is $1,885.

All three gentlemen are approved for a 30-year fixed rate mortgage for $275,000. It is the credit score that makes all the difference. Because his credit score was lower than Doug's, at the end of the 30-year life of the mortgage loan, Tom will have paid a whopping $31,596 more in interest dollars. When Dave can finally burn his mortgage papers at the end of thirty years, he will have paid $110,377 more in interest dollars than Doug, who had the better credit score.

Keeping the Score

If it did not make much sense to you before, now it becomes crystal clear why we should care about raising our credit score. $110,000 is a lot of money. To a rich man, to a poor man, to every man, that is a lot of money. It does not have to leave your pockets and enter the coffers of the financial bloodhounds. For very little effort, you can boost your credit score and see big results.

If you do have a good credit score, it is imperative that you keep it that way. It is all too easy to skip a credit card payment or pay the mortgage late "just this once," but doing so can impact your credit score. Although it does not seem fair, one late payment on your mortgage gets reported on your credit report. That could mean a higher interest rate for you in the event you decide to refinance your current mortgage or if you apply for a home equity loan or if you move and need a new mortgage. It is akin to the grade point average; one bad grade makes it plummet, and it is so hard to raise it back up again. So when your credit score is at a good level, make the effort to keep it there.

MORE EASY STRATEGIES FROM BAD CREDIT TO GOOD CREDIT!

Some of these techniques are plain old common sense, but some strategies for improving and maintaining your credit score are unexpected. Just follow the steps outlined here and you will see an improved credit score!

1. **Pay on time.**

   We all know we should make timely payments, but we probably didn't realize that every late payment shows as a negative factor on the credit report. Now that we know the credit score is purposely looking for negatives to ding us on, we don't need to give them easy marks to use against us.

2. **Pay more.**

Do whatever you have to do to at least make the minimum monthly payments on time each and every month. That is the bare necessity. If at all possible, make more than the minimum payment. The required minimum payment used to be just 2% of your balance. As of January 2006, that has been raised to 4%. Even so, only paying 4% each month means the meter keeps running on finance charges and stretches out the amount you continue to owe, and the date for paying it off entirely appears to be nowhere on the horizon.

3. **Don't skip.**

Your ultimate concern is to keep paying. Do not, I repeat, do not skip payments. If your account gets turned over to a collection agency, it hurts your credit score, and it hurts it for a long time, for up to seven years. If you are having trouble making your payments, contact the creditor and try to work out a different payment arrangement. Ignoring the problem won't make it go away; it only makes it worse. Pay whatever you can and work responsibly with your creditors. Keep your accounts out of collection. Your actions today affect your future. Paying your bills today means no stress tomorrow!

4. **Don't close.**

This strategy sounds unusual to many people, but if you have a good track record with old accounts, it makes perfect sense to keep them around, reflecting your good credit history on your credit report. Don't close old accounts. One of the rating factors of the credit score is how long you have had credit with each creditor.

Even if you no longer use an account, if you have made the payments timely over a long period of time, keep it open. You don't have to use the card. Just reap the rewards of good credit history. According to credit expert Hazel Valera of Clear Credit Exchange, in her remarks to the Millionaire Real Estate Club of Las Vegas, the best boosts for your credit score are accounts that are five years old with a credit limit of at least $5000, and no more than 30% of that being utilized. Accounts like these with a good payment history can get your score into the 800 range.

5. **Stay low.**

This point ties in with what was said above. Creditors and lenders do not want to see that you are maxed out on all your accounts. Regardless of whether or not you are making all the minimum payments every month, your score will suffer if you are carrying a balance that is 35% or more of the available credit limit on the account. They give you credit; they just don't want you to use it.

For example, if you have a credit card with a $2500 limit, you will want to keep the balance due on that card under $875. In order to play this numbers game, you may have to spread your balances out over several credit cards. Instead of having a high balance on one card, having low balances on several cards is actually better in terms of how the credit score is calculated. You and I may agree that it should not matter if you carry $3000 of debt on one card or $600 on five cards. In fact, in my logic, it should not be that way, but that is how it works. The important thing is that you understand how they rank you. Knowing the rules means we know how to play their game.

Maintaining low balances, and having them distributed among all your cards, so you use just 30–35% of each credit limit, will be good for your credit score. Before you spread one high credit card balance over several cards, though, take a minute and look at the interest rates. If your other cards have high interest rates and you can't pay them off quickly, you could end up with more in interest fees. It might be best to keep the balance on the one low-interest credit card. Don't shoot yourself in the foot by blindly following this tip.

6. **Don't go crazy.**

Everywhere you turn, there are offers for credit cards. For the purpose of your credit scores, and having it be the best reflection of you, you need to limit how many cards you apply for. Every new account actually hurts your score! Don't just open an account for a free gift or a special savings discount that day. Do you really need another t-shirt anyway?

Most department store cards have high interest rates, and most of your department store purchases can simply be made with the credit card you have. So why bother?

7. **Avoid inquiries.**

Don't apply for so many loans and credit cards within a short period of time. Doing this will call for a creditor or lender to look at your credit report and score. This is called an inquiry. You don't want too many of these! Every inquiry is listed on your credit report and stays there for two years. Keep in mind, inquiries are a negative rating factor for your credit score, especially if they're made in quick succession. Remember: there are eighty-eight negative factors! The score system is not "user friendly"!

If you open a new account, lay low for many months before you open another account or try to get a loan.

Let's Review

The concepts outlined in these chapters are easy and can be applicable to anyone. You don't have to be a member of any club, and you don't have to do a song and dance. By simply following the methods prescribed, you and your credit score can achieve a true "financial makeover!"

> **Knowledge is power and it can be yours!**

If you flip back through the pages of this chapter, you can see that getting your credit score up and keeping it there is not an insurmountable challenge. The number one piece of advice is an age-old characteristic of any good, decent, hard working citizen. Pay your bills. In the days of our grandparents, that was all they needed to heed. There were no credit reports and FICO scores and complicated top-secret formulas computing what kind of customer we would be. There was, "Sure, I know Fred. He owns a farm outside of town. Great guy. My bank loaned him some money and he always made his payments. I trust him." Those days have gone the way of using horses to pull the plow, and now you arc only a number, but we can follow the example of our proud heritage and pay our bills on time.

Keeping old accounts open and keeping balances low is part of the modern day world that we live in. Now that we know it, we can do it. Getting too many cards can be a problem as Big Brother is watching and monitoring every account and every inquiry.

Now that we know, we know what to show. The key is knowing. Knowledge is power and they can't wield it over us anymore.

I have one more story that can help fix credit reports in a snap. All it takes is two magic words.

CHAPTER 12

Two Magic Words
x 3

"Shazam! Abracadabra!"
~ Old Magicians

No, those are not the two magic words. They are fun words to say, but are not the ones that have any impact on your financial resume. Feel free to go ahead and try though. Maybe if you fold up your credit report into a tiny square, cover it with the palm of your hand and say "Abracadabra!", a high score will magically appear when you open it again. If that works, let me know.

Chances are, it won't; and you'll be right back to where you started – staring at your credit report with bleary eyes and wondering if there's any kind of "quick fix." *Well, there is.* And it doesn't involve canaries or silk scarves or any other kind of hocus pocus. In fact, it is much simpler than that.

Bad Information = Bad Credit

As I have said, repeatedly, in one way or another, credit reports make the credit world go round. Credit problems bring your credit world crashing to your feet. The frustrating part is that most bad credit is just bad information.

How to fix it? Two magic words. (And no, although some people would like to mock me and say "Kevin Trudeau," those are not the magic words.) There are actually three sets of "two magic words." Each set is very effective in simply eliminating or significantly reducing your debt.

It's Been Forgiven!

Bankruptcy is a fact of life for many people today. The American Bankruptcy Institute reported that in 2007, bankruptcy filings rose 40 percent. In numbers, that means that the filing total by consumers went from 597,965 in 2006 to a whopping 801,840 the very next year!

However, this doesn't tell the whole story, because almost a third of the filings in a year involve couples, husband *and* wife. A 2001 study found that the total should be multiplied by 31.9% to get a more accurate total in terms of the real number of people actually affected. That makes the 2006 total closer to 789,000, and the 2007 total 1,057,627!

Think about that! Over one million people last year were affected by bankruptcy in our country. That means one out of every 300 people in the US filed for bankruptcy last year! Add to that the high amount of corporate bankruptcies, and that's *millions* of people being affected by this every single year. That is a lot of us, folks. I'm sure all of us know someone whose life has been severely altered by this issue.

People filing bankruptcy believe that under the law they will have a fresh start, a clean slate, that their debts will be discharged. As it turns out, some creditors and collection agencies think they are above the law. Many people that have filed bankruptcy are still facing financial hardships on old debt because collectors are coming after them.

If you are part of this growing group, I have the first set of two magic words for you: *discharged debt.*

The story of a North Carolina factory worker named Dan will show you how this works. Dan completed a bankruptcy in 2002. A year later, he tried to buy a new house. His mortgage process was held up, not because of the bankruptcy, but because his credit report showed that he owed $9500 to his credit card company. This outstanding debt was giving him a poor credit rating and the mortgage lenders could not give him a mortgage because of it. Dan was told that he would first have to pay off a $9500 credit card debt in order to clean up his credit report and be approved for the mortgage loan.

Dan showed proof that this debt had been discharged by the bankruptcy court. The bank said he had to take it up with the credit card company. His credit card company – let's call it *GreedyBank* – had failed to update his records and cancel the debt. They did not report it to the credit reporting agencies, so his credit report still showed the debt sitting there, no record of discharge. Dan offered repeated proof of the discharge, but GreedyBank, of course, did nothing.

The bank's hands were tied because their mortgage approval is based upon the credit report. The credit reporting agency said that GreedyBank had to give them the information. Dan fought with GreedyBank to correct his credit report, but they still did nothing. Dan, at his wit's end, finally gave up and paid the debt to clean up his credit report so that he could buy his house!

Imagine! Poor Dan had to pay almost $10,000 to clear his credit and his name, for a bill that had been legally eliminated. Do you find this outrageous? I do!

It has come to light that credit card companies often fail to cancel bankruptcy discharged debts. It is not an oversight. It is deliberate. They hang on to these debts as a means to pressure consumers like Dan to pay amounts that are no longer required to be paid. It makes my head spin just thinking about it.

Sometimes creditors sell these loans to little-known firms who then try to collect the funds. These companies are a fast growing and big money industry. A few of these companies are even traded on NASDAQ.

Never heard of such a thing? You are not alone. Even seasoned bankruptcy judges are shocked by the revelation of what is being called "the secondary market in bankruptcy paper." Because the stakes are high – bulk sales of these debts have been reported in the billions of dollars – the field is growing, as is the debt total involved. Growing competition by hundreds of companies (I counted 250 on one partial list) is increasing the price of the debts as well. This just adds to the value for the creditor; why cancel a discharged debt when they can make good money off it? It's maddening.

An article in *BusinessWeek* as recent as November 2007 uses the headline, "Prisoners of Debt: Big lenders keep squeezing money out of consumers whose debts were canceled by the courts." The problem exists, but to date, nothing is being done about the abuse. Our bankruptcy laws are supposed to protect citizens, but this is a great big loophole and lots of money grubbers are crawling right on through.

The FCC has issued formal opinion letters stating that credit bureaus are supposed to report when debts have been discharged, but there is no law requiring this. The Fair Credit Reporting Act requires the bureaus to assure accuracy in their reports, but they rely on the creditors to let them know. Accountability measures are vague, if they exist at all. Is it up to the creditor or the credit reporting agency? Neither one seems to care.

In Dan's case, the credit reporting agency didn't realize his debt had been canceled because GreedyBank never forwarded that information. GreedyBank didn't bother discharging the debt since they knew there was a possibility to still make money off it. It's a case of grade school mentality; "I don't have to, so you can't make me." Basically, no one is watching the store, and creditors are robbing unwary consumers of millions of dollars. Dollars that were from debts that had been legally discharged, wiped off the books!

What's wrong with our country's lawmakers?! A person goes through the ordeal of bankruptcy, has debts discharged, but then nobody really wipes them out and the debt still lingers on. Bankruptcy law prohibits the collection of discharged debt, but obviously no one is enforcing that law, and it has turned into big business.

Luckily for Dan, he filed a motion in bankruptcy court charging that GreedyBank never updated his credit report. GreedyBank did not respond to this charge, so the judge ordered the company to re-pay Dan the $9500, plus an additional $14,000 in fines and attorney fees.

Although Dan did pay the debt in order to get his mortgage, he was able to get his money back. Just one more golden reason to monitor that credit report. Make sure debts that have been canceled are removed.

It's your right and sometimes you have to fight for your right. But it's worth it. Remember these two magic words: "**discharged debt.**"

Just so you know, these debt-buying scum use other strategies besides intimidating consumers and exploiting the credit bureau system. Junk debt scammers try to wear down the victim by repeated nuisance phone calls. They send letters that look like they're from responsible collection agencies or law firms. The scammers rely on the fact that creditors often fail to update the bureau when debts have been discharged. They've found a glitch in the system and they are taking advantage.

Another thing the junk debt company does is change the old account number and assign a new one. This is actually good and makes it easy for you. If a new credit or collection company calls you, ask for the account number. If neither the company name nor the account number match anything in your records, and you previously filed bankruptcy, you need to use the magic words "*discharged debt.*" This is a magical way to absolutely eliminate that debt. Poof. Be gone.

Not My Debt!

Sometimes you can hit a different kind of wall trying to solve a problem on your credit report. Let me tell you a story.

A good friend of mine, Kurt, applied for a credit card and was rejected. He was surprised to be rejected because he had an excellent credit history. Kurt went round and round with the credit card company until he was blue in the face. He was informed that his application was being declined because the credit report showed a $15,000 balance on an American Express account that had never been paid.

Kurt had never, ever, had an American Express account. He made repeated phone calls to tell the credit card company that the debt was not his and never was. He sent letters explaining that he did not owe the $15,000 to American Express or any other creditor! In reply, he only received standard form letters. Kurt spent months trying to resolve this, and then he had a lawyer friend draft letters as well.

Most of us know that sometimes our letters may go unnoticed, but an attorney's letterhead usually gets someone's attention. Not in this case. Kurt only received more form letters. He truly felt like he was beating his head against a brick wall. How many different ways could he tell them, "It's not mine"?

It's Not Mine!

He was on the phone for the tenth time, or the hundredth, with customer service – tired, frustrated, exasperated:

> Kurt: I have done everything I could to correct this error. I have never had an American Express card, ever, in my life. I do not owe $15,000 to American Express. I do not owe $15,000 to anyone. This debt is not mine! I don't know what else to do. I must be the victim of *"identity theft."*
>
> Customer Service: Oh my goodness, let me transfer you.
>
> Manager: Hello, sir, we are so sorry for your inconvenience. I will delete that from your record right now. I will issue you a new platinum card today, and for your trouble, I will express mail it, so you should get it immediately.

It's Not Yours!

The two magic words here are *"identity theft."* A few years ago, it was a rarity, but now it is a daily occurrence, and the people doing it are getting better and better every day. The FTC estimates that each year, nearly **ten million** American consumers have their identities stolen. This means that today, as you read this, about 27,400 people will have their identity stolen in some way! The commission also states that 15,000 to 20,000 of these consumers contact them each week. Ten million people each year! That's in one year; in five years, we are talking about fifty million people!

Two magic words can improve your credit score!

A 2006 survey estimated total losses to victims from ID theft at $15.6 billion! Losses to businesses from ID theft amount to $50 billion every year, for totally unnecessary costs. And those costs are passed on to all of us.

It is terribly frustrating when it happens to you. Consumers spent from four to 130 hours of their time fixing ID theft problems. Problems usually involve the misuse of a credit card account, misuse of accounts other than credit cards, and the opening of new accounts in another person's name. Many victims suffer multiple types of identity theft. The best advice to get the issue taken care of immediately is to say these two magic words to your bank or your credit card company. The banks will pay attention to you then. They hate identity theft as much as you do.

While I was writing this book, a friend called to lament that someone was using her debit card information and racking up charges all over Chicago! Meredith still had her card in her purse – someone had somehow gotten the information from the magnetic strip and made a fake card. There are sophisticated card readers that will steal your info, and there are shifty cashiers in the best of establishments. You never know when it could happen to you. Jolted from the complacency of thinking it would never happen to her, Meredith now gladly pays the small fee for credit report monitoring.

Remember the two magic words "*identity theft.*" It is highly possible that there is an item on your credit report that may not be yours at all! And the bad credit score that you get as a result actually does not belong to you. You could be denied credit because of something that some crook did, and you pay the cost, literally. If you are not getting a good credit score, you need to be alert to the fact that there could be an unexplained item on your report, and you could be the victim of identity theft.

If there is something on your credit report that is a total mystery, you need to tell the credit card company or the bank that it is just not yours! Two magic words = identity theft. You should be able to get immediate improvement!

Identity Theft Facts

It is a sad fact that in this world we live in, people will steal anything, especially your financial well-being. Not that anything good can come of identity theft, but Kurt was finally able to resolve this issue with the mysterious $15,000 that had appeared on his credit report.

Don't take it lightly. Identity theft is a real threat. I hear stories every day from people like Kurt and Meredith. It is more common with every year that goes by. Sometimes people are too careless with their private financial information, but usually identity theft happens because the bad guys are very good at what they do.

The easiest way to be alert to possible identity theft is to monitor your credit report. If Kurt had been using a monitoring service or if he had pulled his own free credit report, he would have noticed this whopper of a debt on his own.

Stay on top of your affairs and you can head off problems a lot quicker.

Basic Security

Be smart online!

Besides the obvious tips, like not to give out your credit card number or social security number over the phone, you should invest in an inexpensive home shredder. Any receipt or statement with your personal information should be shredded. I have a friend who throws her receipts in the garbage and then pours spaghetti sauce over them. A shredder is probably a little neater.

A lot of the identity theft occurs online, so be smart when you are on your computer. Some basic safety tips to remember include:

- ✔ Always log off when you have finished your online banking or credit card transaction.
- ✔ Only use your own computer to do your personal financial business. Do not use the computer at the public library; do not use your laptop on the free wireless network at the coffee shop or the bookstore.
- ✔ Don't click on pop-ups.
- ✔ Don't download anything unless you are certain that it is safe.
- ✔ Make up an extremely creative password.
- ✔ Run antivirus and/or security software.

"Silence Is Golden"

Maybe your credit or debt problems don't come from identity theft or debt discharge from bankruptcy. You still could be haunted by a past debt that was supposed to be written off as uncollectible. For whatever reason, you could not pay and your debt was deemed uncollectible. In this case, your old lender collected a tax write-off and you went about your life. But maybe that lender also sold your debt to a scavenger debt collector.

A story about a friend's daughter will show you what I mean. Jennifer recently graduated from college, with a big smile, big dreams, and a small pile of debt. She quickly found a job and started paying off her college debt. Other problems soon hit her. She incurred major dental expenses. Her roommate stole from her. Jennifer was smart and kicked her out, but now she was stuck paying twice the amount of rent she had planned on in her budget.

Jennifer did what any of us would do – she started using credit cards to help with her living expenses and the dental bills. Before long, her credit card debt was over $3000. She slowly made payments, but found it hard to keep up with the high interest rate.

She decided that she needed to go to grad school to further her career goals, but she was not able to pay off the credit card debt. So Jennifer did what many of us do – nothing. She simply could not pay that credit card bill. The creditor stopped contacting her and time passed.

A few years down the road, Jennifer received a letter from what appeared to be a law firm that said they represented an acquisition company and that she owed them nearly $2000. The letter also stated that unless she contacted their office within 30 days, they would consider that the debt was valid. It was further implied that there would be a lawsuit, and she would be responsible for the debt, plus interest and legal fees.

Don't be intimidated by "official" looking paperwork or serious language. They are just trying to scare you. Don't let them. The creditor and account number referenced in the letter were not familiar to Jennifer, nor did they match any of her records. She sent back an immediate reply stating that she was disputing their claim and wanted verification of the alleged creditor and debt. Not surprisingly, she never heard from the firm again, nor another word about the debt.

Jennifer is not alone. This tactic affects a lot of people, and not everyone stays calm like Jennifer. I want you to remember this last set of magic words: "*The SOL*" (or, if you prefer, **Limitations Statute**). These simple words are your bulletproof shield.

Remember what I told you in Chapter Four? You DO NOT have to pay a debt that is too old! If a creditor or a bogus law firm is hounding you, remember to keep calm, be smart, and say little, except for the two magic words, "*The SOL.*"

If he's not aware what **SOL** stands for, go ahead and spell it out for the debt predator; be sure to remind him that you are aware of the statute of limitations. His time is up. Goodbye. Tell the caller that the debt is not collectible and hang up. Under no circumstances do you admit to the debt. (And as you're hanging up, if you want to tell the collector that he is "SOL, buddy," you go right ahead.)

As I've said before, a word to remember is "alleged." You should call the debt that they say you owe exactly what it is: alleged. You may request details on this so-called debt, such as the account number, what it was for, when it was incurred. Go back to Chapter Four for the list of SOL's for each state. Know your rights and the law, and you can reduce or eliminate your debt completely. And all you have to do is remember the last set of magic words, "*The SOL*" (or **Limitations Statute**).

The Real Magic

There are no guarantees against identity theft, junk debt buyers, or discharged debt scams, but with common sense, awareness of the dangers, and careful attention to your financial records and credit report, you can diminish your chances of being the next victim.

Victim is not what we are. We are no longer allowing the banks and credit card companies to treat us as their victims. They have taken advantage for much too long and it is time that they get put in their place.

You do not need supernatural powers to vanquish the consumer lending industry or to get your debt back in control. There are basic steps to take, everyday common sense stuff. And then there are these secrets that I am exposing in this book. The creditors and lenders want to keep their devious tactics to themselves for one reason only: money. If you know how they operate, you know how to beat the system.

These "magic word" sets will work for a great number of consumers. If, however, they don't apply to *your* particular situation, there is still the legal route out of debt – bankruptcy. Bankruptcy is a totally legitimate, legal option, so do not feel ashamed if you have already filed for bankruptcy or are facing it right now.

When all else fails, you should consult with legal and financial advisors. If they decide that bankruptcy is viable for your situation, consider their advice. There are hundreds of thousands of folks each year who take this route out of debt. And maybe there are even more "magic words" out there. Readers are sharing their success stories. Maybe you have one of your own, with your own set of magic words.

Take Control

I know that many of us find ourselves getting frustrated with the system. We get angry, and the two words that we want to say cannot be printed in this book. Swearing at your banker or creditors may release some tension, but it does not have any real effect on improving your finances.

The way to take charge is to take control.

CHAPTER 13

Class Is Now in Session

*"Education is not the filling of a pail,
but the lighting of a fire."*
~ William Butler Yeats

In Chapter 3, Hanky Panky, I told you a little bit about the student loan scandal. Anyone who is now facing the prospect of obtaining a student loan is probably not feeling very optimistic about the trust factor. You are very wise.

A Matter of Trust

My first advice to you is exactly what your gut is telling you: Don't trust the financial department at the college or university. Recent events have shown us that the people in charge of guiding folks to the best student loans were only guiding kickbacks right into their own pockets. Students and parents are naturally overwhelmed with the costs and the decisions of college, so they look to the college for help. They listen to the school's advisor only to later learn that the advisor couldn't care less which agency had the best deal for the students, only who had the best under the table deal for him.

As of April 2007, six major universities (St. John's, Syracuse, Fordham, New York University, University of Pennsylvania, and Long Island University) agreed to over $3 million in reimbursements to students because of the revenue sharing agreements they had with the private student loan agencies. Obviously these students were not getting the best deal.

Keeping with my motto that knowledge is power, let me give you a little back-to-school primer on the student loan industry. This is one of those areas where you want to look before you leap, and bring your reading glasses. Read the fine print before you sign anything. The money director at the school will shove a bunch of papers in front of you and say, "Okay, here's your 'financial assistance' package. Sign here." Who knows what you could be signing? They don't tell you that you can shop around for the best rates and that everything is negotiable.

Federally Guaranteed Loans

You can get federally backed student loans (which is what you want; we'll discuss why in a minute) through the Department of Education or companies like Sallie Mae. These federal loans usually do not cover the entire amount needed, so many people need to get additional funds by taking out a private student loan. When you look at the cost of tuition and the number of students enrolling in college, it is no surprise that the largest growth area in the debt market is private student loans. It is big business, with a capital B.

Federally guaranteed loans are the most desirable. They offer the best interest rate and the best terms. You get the loan at cost, and no private company is making extra bucks off you or passing a secret buck to a double-dealing pal. Over 6 million federal student aid applications are processed online each year to get a piece of the $67 billion that the Department of Education gives out in loans, grants, and student aid. For information, call 1-800-4-FED-AID (1-800-433-3243) or go to www.ed.gov.

Let me give you a quick overview of federal student loans. The basic student loan is the Stafford loan. There are two types that fall under this umbrella. The Federal Direct Student Loan Program (FDSLP) are government direct loans to students. The Federal Family Education

Loan Program (FFELP) are loans given by private lenders but arc guaranteed by the federal government.

Both types are Stafford loans and carry a fixed interest rate (currently 6.8%). All lenders give the same rate, but you may be able to get a discount for making your payments electronically. These loans also have a set 4% loan fee, which comes right out of the money you receive. The usual term for repayment is ten years, and you have to start repaying six months after graduation.

The beauty of student loans is that you make no payments at all while in school. Some Stafford loans are subsidized by the government, which means if you have financial need, the government pays the interest while you are a student. If you do not have financial need, you still can get a Stafford loan. It will not be subsidized and you pay the interest along with your payment after you graduate. Most students that receive the interest subsidized loans come from families who have an income of less than $50,000. Only about a quarter of students getting this type of loan have family income of $50,000 to $100,000.

> ...you make no payments at all while in school.

There is another federal loan called the Perkins Loan. The schools have a fund provided by the government for these loans. They decide and disburse the Perkins Loan to students with serious financial need. This loan has only a 5% interest rate so it is the best loan out there, but you have to have real need to get it.

If the loans you are able to get through the federal government are not enough to cover college costs, then a private student loan is needed as well. For federal loans, the credit score is not an issue. However, these private loans fall under the category of regular consumer loans and the rate you get is based upon your credit score. If your FICO credit score is less than 650, you may not qualify for a private student loan. That's yet another reason to stay on top of that credit score. A bump of 30 to 50 points is sometimes all it takes to get a better rate on your loan. As we have talked about, the best interest rate is so important. You'll pay less and have it paid off in less time.

Graduation Day

You tossed your cap and are a college graduate. Depending upon your loan, in six months or nine months, you have to start paying back your student loans. You will get a letter with the date and the amount of your repayment. As you probably know, student loans are with you until you pay them off or death do you part. There is no escape clause. Bankruptcy does not wash away the student loan debt.

> When it comes to student loans, they will chase you until you die.

But what if you fall on tough times and can't repay the student loan? For starters, if you don't pay your student loans, the IRS can withhold your tax refunds. Your wages can get garnished. And if you are thinking about becoming a homeowner down the road, you won't be able to apply for a federal home loan through VA or FHA.

Rehabilitation Programs

When it comes to student loans, they will chase you until you die. However, it is a little known fact that your loan can be discharged in the event of a permanent disability. That is not how we want to get out of paying our loans.

Suppose for whatever reason, you defaulted on your student loan and now the collection hounds are after you. They will say, "Give us the money now. We want the entire balance. Pay it off in full to me." The guy works on commission and he wants to make a big profit on you.

You say, "I can't." There is a federal rehabilitation program available that you should use instead of paying it off in a lump sum. The terms are quite simple. If you have a federally backed loan, this is the route to take.

You make payments for the agreed amount, say $100, each month for twelve months. You can never be late or short during this rehab time. You have to actually make the payments too, not have them garnished from your salary. Once you have fulfilled this trial period, your loan will be returned to the regular student loan servicing center, and the fact that it was in default status will be DELETED from your credit report. You go back to just like it never happened.

If you had paid it off, like the collection agent wanted you to, your credit report would show a defaulted item paid up, but it would still be hanging around on your credit report for seven years. This way, it disappears. By doing it the rehabilitation way, poof, it is gone!

This method is available for all federally guaranteed loans. The collection agency guys are not going to tell you about this. They want you to cough it all up to them. Hopefully you won't find yourself in default status. But if you do, come up with a way to make the monthly payments through the rehabilitation program and get back in good standing. Once you get back on track of making the payments on time every month, you get your IRS refunds again as well. For more information, visit online at http://www.ed.gov/offices/OSFAP/DCS/rehabilitation.html.

Consolidation

You also need to be aware that student loan consolidation is only allowed once. Over the course of your education, it is likely that you will have several student loans. Loans are usually given each semester, so over the four or five years of college, you could have 8 to 10 loans of various amounts with different interest rates. Upon graduation, you are allowed to lump them all together in one loan with one payment. The average weighted value of all the interest rates determines the interest rate, and the total amount of loan value will push out the time period for payments. For example, if the total loan is now $10,000, you may get ten years to repay. If the total loan adds up to $100,000 you may get a 30 year term to repay. See http://loanconsolidation.ed.gov/ for more details, or call the US Department of Education at 1-800-557-7392. It makes sense to consolidate. You don't want to make eight payments when you can make just one.

A word to the wise: you can prepay your student loans. Assume your monthly payment is $100 and you are able to double it. The extra $100 goes right against principal and that dramatically reduces the amount of time and the amount of interest you pay. If you can at all afford it, pay it down!

Repayment and Forgiveness Programs

Bankruptcy does not discharge student loans, but there are little known programs that exist that can indeed eliminate your student loans. The federal government itself is one way. The Office of Personnel Management (OPM) authorized government agencies to set up student loan repayment programs to recruit highly qualified candidates for government service. It is not a bad deal at all. The employee only has to agree to work for the feds for at least 3 years and the federally backed student loans can be repaid up to $10,000 per year for a maximum of $60,000. It is not considered forgiveness of the loan, but actual repayment. That is a nice deal. For more info on the student loan repayment program, see http://www.opm.gov/oca/pay/StudentLoan/.

There are also several loan forgiveness programs that most people don't know about. You can have your student loan debt forgiven (which means they cancel it out, adios, bye-bye, it's gone) by doing volunteer work, teaching, serving in the military, or pursuing legal or medical studies. See http://www.finaid.org/loans/forgiveness.phtml and let me give you some highlights:

Volunteering:

AmeriCorps. You must serve at least 12 months to receive $4725 for your student loan repayment. (800-942-2677)

Peace Corps. You serve for at least two years and can defer your student loans. (800-424-8580)

Volunteers in Service to America (VISTA). You must serve 1700 hours. You receive $4725. (800-942-2677)

Teaching:

Those willing to teach in low-income areas will receive partial loan forgiveness each year for up to five years. Some states also have programs that offer loan forgiveness or repayment for teachers willing to teach in a shortage area. A list of programs is available at the American Federation of Teachers at http://www.aft.org/teachers/jft/loanforgiveness.htm.

Military:

The Army National Guard has a student loan repayment program, which can be as much as $10,000. Veterans, their dependents, and those interested in careers in the military should check out http://www.finaid.org/military/.

Legal and Medical Studies:

For those who are willing to serve the public, some law schools will forgive their student loans. See http://www.equaljusticeworks.org/. Doctors and nurses who work for a certain length of time in needy areas can get loan forgiveness through programs offered by the US Department of Health and Human Services. See http://nhsc.bhpr.hrsa.gov/ and for nurses, visit the site at http://bhpr.hrsa.gov/nursing/loanrepay.htm.

Occupational and physical therapists are in demand, and loan forgiveness is a recruitment tool. See http://www.apta.org//AM/Template.cfm?Section=Home and http://www.aota.org/. Any medical students interested in possible loan repayment programs should check out http://services.aamc.org/fed_loan_pub/index.cfm?fuseaction=public.welcome&CFID=7086849&CFTOKEN=264504b-ee8d996b-6b94-4aac-8449-0362f3450d85.

Something New

Something new that has just come along is the College Cost Reduction and Access Act of 2007. It is a new loan forgiveness program to encourage public service, geared for people who will make a low income but who have decided on a career in public service. Their salary and their student loan debt can be polar opposites, so to keep people in these low-paying but very necessary jobs, the government has devised this program.

Ten years of full-time employment in public service is required, and during this time, the person must make the monthly payment on their student loan. The beginning date of the program is October 1, 2007. After 120 payments and ten years of service, any remaining student loan debt is discharged. Obviously, this program is only beneficial to those who have loan terms longer than ten years.

Public service jobs that qualify under the College Cost Reduction and Access Act include teachers, librarians, child care workers, social workers, government workers, military service, police and fire workers, public interest legal services, and public health workers. For more info, see http://www.finaid.org/loans/publicservice.phtml.

Class Dismissed

Before we tackle the other topics at hand, I have another *Debt Cures* piece of advice for you. College is expensive. Outrageously expensive and I see no end in sight. There is a great and smart way to get an education from a top school and not pay top dollar.

Let's assume you were accepted to UCLA or some other big name national university. You can defer your acceptance for two years, and make sure you get it in writing. For the first two years, go to your local city college and take all the basic required classes. Most of the time, the core classes are the same and sometimes the textbooks are even the same. You'll pay $100 a semester as opposed to $10,000 a semester. Living at home can save you a bundle as well, plus there are meals and laundry facilities right there.

You have the deal in writing and after two years, you transfer all your credits to UCLA. You complete the second half of your education in your major and get your degree from a top notch school. The prestige of the UCLA degree is yours. You got the same education as if you would have attended all four years there, and you paid half the price.

Now that is smart.

CHAPTER 14

Home Is Where the Start Is

"Home Sweet Home"

One of the most common ways that the banks use to try to forge a life-long relationship with you is in the form of a home mortgage. It is an easy catch for them as many of us want to own a home. You certainly can, but there is no reason that the bank has to stay hanging around you for the next thirty years.

There is an old song called, "Breaking Up Is Hard to Do."

Breaking up is not really all that hard after all.

This is one relationship that you want out of – and it is a lot simpler than you ever could have imagined!

One of the most common desires of all Americans is to become a homeowner. Most people aspire to having their own place, a sense of security, a sense of stability, a place to put down roots. A home is a place to raise a family or a place to grow old. We all have our varied reasons for wanting to have a home of our own, and financially, it is smart to want to be a homeowner.

In nearly all cases, your home is a very good investment. There is not much financial sense in throwing your money away in rent for years and years. So now you have done it; you bought the house, planted some flowers, and got a puppy for the backyard; or you got the river front condo in the heart of downtown that you have always dreamed about. Congratulations. Now what?

That is when the second most common desire of all Americans kicks in. We all want to pay off our mortgage sooner than 30 years! You can!

Big Bucks

Of course you want to pay off that mortgage quicker; we all do. The house payment is often your largest monthly expense, and most people take out a thirty-year mortgage. That is an awful lot of years to pay. If you take out a shorter-term loan, the interest rate might be better, but the payments are higher. Maybe you can't afford that high of a payment or maybe you just want to play it safe with the 30-year mortgage. Maybe all your lender will offer you is a 30-year mortgage.

> Pay off the 30-year mortgage!

Using these methods from *Debt Cures,* you do not have to pay on that loan for thirty long years! There are several options to pay off the mortgage sooner, and save THOUSANDS and THOUSANDS in interest. Never is the expense of interest more obvious than in the house payment. And thirty years is a very long time to keep paying it. Curing the house payment conundrum cures a lot of debt headaches!

With a traditional thirty-year mortgage, a homeowner ends up paying about double the purchase price of the home. That's a lot of money going to interest, or the bank's pocket, instead of yours. It is possible to pay off that 30-year mortgage in much less time! The *Debt Cures* strategy of quick pay-offs provides you with all the knowledge necessary to create a huge and immediate impact on paying off your mortgage debt.

Shave Years Off Your Mortgage

Pay off the mortgage faster and cut out all the interest that is going out of your wallet and into someone else's. How? Obviously, you can pay more on the principal each month. Any extra towards the principal balance reduces the amount that the interest is calculated on. Some people pay double payments every month. Some folks throw an extra hundred in with their payment each month.

Most of us, however, can only afford to make our current payment. That mortgage payment amount is the max that we are able to pay, so we think we are stuck paying that same amount, year after year, for the next thirty years. Wrong. By paying the same amount, but using the *Debt Cures* strategy, you can, in fact, dramatically decrease the life of your loan and the interest you pay!

Split Your Mortgage Payment

The best things in life are often simple, free and easy. Take a walk on the beach. Gaze up at the sky on a star-filled night. Take your existing mortgage payment and split it up into weekly payments!

What could be easier than that! Paying bills by the week is often the best thing for people on a tight budget to do anyway. Having to make one big lump sum payment at the first of the month can be a hardship, and it can be a little depressing to watch that large chunk of change leave the checkbook.

Let's take the example of Jake. His mortgage payment is due the first of every month, like it is for most of us. His monthly payment is $4000. Jake used to pay his mortgage with one check on or around the first of each month. I would assume that is what most of us do, because we never knew there was a different way.

Most mortgage loans allow for prepayment, so what Jake learned to do was split the $4000 into weekly installments of $1000 each. He is allowed to prepay, and he does not want to pay late and get charged a late fee. For his payment due August 1, Jake makes weekly payments of $1000 on July 7, July 14, and July 21, and then the final payment on August 1. He has made his entire payment by August 1, so there is no late fee.

This incredibly simple and little known technique is one of the great *Debt Cures* solutions!

Simple, Yet Amazing

It does not seem like it should make any difference at all, paying your mortgage this way, but it makes a tremendous difference. The amount of interest that you pay is greatly reduced each month because the bank or mortgage firm is getting a good portion of their payment early. You are not paying nearly as much interest, and more is going toward paying your principal. It really works!

You can shave years and years off the life of your mortgage! That is THOUSANDS OF DOLLARS SAVED! Why pay all that interest when you don't have to? Your monthly household expenses will not change and it may even make it easier to budget. Knowing that you will pay one-fourth of the whole house payment each week may be easier than making one big whopper of a payment.

> Reduce your mortgage without paying a single dollar more!

Tom and Tammi get paid twice a month, so they wondered if they could apply this same technique, but instead of paying weekly, they would pay bi-monthly, with each paycheck.

For the August 1 mortgage payment, Tom and Tammi pay $2000 on July 15 and $2000 on August 1. Same idea as above. Their monthly payment has not changed in amount or due date. They are paying the whole amount by the first of the month. They are not paying anything more out of their pockets, but Tom and Tammi have knocked SEVEN years off their mortgage. Just like that! That is THOUSANDS and THOUSANDS of dollars in interest.

Another quick and easy method is to make *just one* extra mortgage payment each year toward your principal. Don't think this will amount to much? Think again. By making this extra payment, you could shave as much as *three years* off of a 20-year fixed rate mortgage. That adds up to a lot of extra money in your pocket – money that the lenders don't get. That is thousands of dollars that you are saving by simply making an extra payment toward principal every twelve months! This is a simple method that will keep you *years* ahead of the game!

A guy I know always applies "extra" money to his mortgage whenever it happens to come his way. If he receives a tax refund, he puts it toward his mortgage. A bonus at his job, a cash gift from his dear old Aunt Edna, a good day at the casino; whatever the source, it's money he wasn't planning on, so he uses it to knock down the principal balance on his house.

There's More Than One Way to Skin a Cat – and a Mortgage

I don't know the origin of that saying, but my point is that there are many ways to accomplish the goal of paying off that mortgage sooner.

- ✔ Get a loan from a family member to pay down the principal. The interest savings will allow you to repay your generous kin.

- ✔ If you pay points on your loan, pay them up front; don't roll them into the loan. If you're not paying them up front, you'll be stuck with a higher balance that you'll be paying interest on each month.

- ✔ Consider a loan from your 401(k) plan to pay down your mortgage. If you can get a lower rate than your mortgage, it's a good tactic. And you are paying yourself back.

- ✔ Use your home as a forced savings account. Make a higher payment each month; for example, put $500 more directly toward the principal. You build up your equity faster and decrease the interest. If you need money, instead of having it sit in a savings account, you use a home equity loan or a home equity line of credit. Again, usually there is a good interest rate and this interest is also tax deductible as home mortgage interest.

- ✔ If you are at all able, consider pre-paying the entire year of your mortgage, each year at a time. You will save thousands in interest and you won't have the burden of a house payment each month.

Prepay Is the Way

Most banks will allow for the prepayment of your loan. If they don't, then this method is not for you, so just be sure to find out. That is the only thing to be aware of. If you cannot find the sentence on your home mortgage contract about prepayment, simply call and ask your lender. If, for some reason, your current loan does not have the prepayment option, ask for it. We have learned a lot about the power of asking! Very often, a simple question proves to be a great debt cure!

If you are taking out a new home loan or refinancing your current mortgage, check and be sure that you have this ability to prepay before signing on the dotted line. If, for some reason, the mortgage company says "no" to the prepayment option, find a new lender. There are a lot of banks and lending institutions out there. Don't get stuck with a 30-year mortgage and not have this exciting option!

No matter how great your interest rate is, this method can save you an unbelievable amount of money!

Use any of the techniques stated above and that 30-year mortgage can be gone in half that, or even less. That is worth having a "let's burn the mortgage" party! Owning a home is the American dream. Having your home paid off in half the time is better than a dream!

Ever heard of a mortgage accelerator loan? These loans use special accounts to encourage borrowers to apply all extra money toward their mortgages. The savings can be huge!

If you'd like to pay off that mortgage, but you lack the discipline to do so, a mortgage accelerator loan may be a great idea for you! All you have to do is refinance your home and set up an equity line of credit. Once this is in place, you're halfway there. The final step is to arrange it so that your paychecks from work are directly deposited into your new credit account. It is much like your regular checking account, with one distinct advantage: the money in the account reduces the balance of the mortgage, and any money not paid for bills is applied against the principal balance.

With this special loan, your principal balance is decreased, and you end up saving bundles of interest! So, in essence, the paycheck goes toward paying off the house.

Any money not spent on the usual bills would not earn much in a savings account, but in this scenario, the overall life of the mortgage is reduced. Translation? You are ahead of the game. It is sort of like an automated way of paying off the mortgage – you may have good intentions, but extra money in the checkbook is often spent on coffee or other miscellaneous items. With the accelerator account, the extra money is applied to your mortgage before you have a chance to spend it.

If you do need that extra money, it is yours. The account is a line of credit or home equity loan so you don't have to do anything; you have ready access. This accelerator loan is a terrific product. There are currently two companies that offer this loan in the US. For more information, you can check it out at: http://articles.moneycentral.msn. com/Banking/HomeFinancing/ANewWayToPayOffYourHouse.aspx.

A similar product is the Money Merge Account. Combining your checking and savings accounts with an advanced line of credit, this system exists to aid you in paying off your mortgage in one-third to one-half the regular time. There is no refinancing involved, no change in the amount of your monthly payments.

Check out this example, which is explained in more detail on www.unitedfirstfinancial.com: You have a 30-year, $136,000 mortgage at 5.25%. If you paid each month for 30 years, you would pay $270,784 – nearly twice the cost of the home. Standard operation for many folks, and the banks are quite happy with that status quo. The Money Merge Account program, simply by applying money to the principal all the time, can help repay the same mortgage in just over 11 years. Total repayment of $181,217 – an incredible savings of $89,566! Same mortgage, same interest rate, little or no changes in your monthly expense, but wow, what a nice sum.

It is amazing what putting money against the principal balance can do. Even as little as $15 every two weeks applied to your mortgage can cut one and a half years off! Now that is a great incentive! Every little bit matters.

Score Matters

Getting the best interest rate on your house is also a very important reason why you want the best credit score possible. The credit score is here to stay, so make it work your way. The mortgage lender is looking at your FICO score, hoping he can hit you with a high interest rate. You want a high score so you can get a lower rate. The difference on what a person with good credit pays over the life of a mortgage versus what a person with the lower FICO score pays over thirty years could practically buy another house.

Take a look at these two people, and see the difference a score makes. What goes up makes the interest and payments go down.

Sam followed the *Debt Cures* methods prescribed here in these pages and raised his credit score to 720. That qualified him for the best interest rate of 5.5%, making Sam very pleased. Diane hadn't yet learned of the *Debt Cures* solutions to her debt troubles. She has some work to do to clean up her credit report; her FICO score was in the low 500s. That is considered poor, and she gets hit with an interest rate of 9.3%.

Diane also doesn't realize what a huge difference her rate is compared to Sam's. She even asked, "So what is the big deal about a few percentage points?"

It is a very big deal.

FICO Score	Interest Rate	Payment	30 Years of Interest
500	9.3%	$1,651	$394,362
560	8.5	$1,542	$355,200
620	7.3	$1,373	$294,247
675	6.1	$1,220	$239,250
700	5.6	$1,151	$214,518
720	5.5	$1,136	$208,853

Lesson Learned

Diane takes a quick look at the chart, not paying attention to the last column showing the total interest accumulation. She sees that her monthly payment will be about $1,650, while Sam pays only $1,100 for a mortgage of $200,000, the same amount that Diane is borrowing from her bank.

> Diane: You are telling me that simply because I have a lower score on my credit report, I have to pay $500 more every month than you?

> Sam: Yep.

> Diane: So every year, I have to pay about $6000 more for my house than you do for your house, right next door to me?

> Sam: Yep.

> Diane: That doesn't seem fair! That's a lot of money!

> Sam: Yep.

> Diane: Is that all you can say?

> Sam: Nope. I can say plenty. If you compound the interest over thirty years, it equates to even more than $6000 a year more than what I will pay. At the end of thirty years, I will have paid almost $209,000 in interest. That's a lot of money. You, on the other hand, will end up paying almost $395,000! Just in interest!

> THUD!

That was Diane hitting the floor.

When Diane was revived, she knew that she had to do something. It was time to take control over her financial matters. Sam turned her on to the techniques of *Debt Cures*.

Bye-Bye PMI

Often overlooked by people when buying a house is the issue of PMI, Private Mortgage Insurance. Don't have a 20% down payment for that mortgage? You'll get hit with an additional fee, called PMI. The theory behind it is that since you don't have a substantial down payment, you don't have a lot "invested" in that property, so you are more of a risk to just walk away from the debt. That's what they say, anyway. For every person out there who bought their first house and didn't have 20% for a down payment, I bet you wanted to sock them and scream, "If I had 20% to put down, I would! I don't want to pay this stupid PMI! This is all we can afford, you idiots!"

PMI is just another scam to get money out of you. It is money out the window for you, and another luxury vacation for them. And there is nothing you can do about it.

Or is there?

Avoid It Like the Plague

If at all possible, do not pay PMI. When you are shopping for a house, try to find one in a price range where you will be able to put down at least 20%! The more you have for a down payment, the better interest rate you get, the lower principal balance you have, the lower your payment will be, and the less you pay over the life of the loan.

And who wants to pay this extra thing they dreamed up called PMI?

Are you paying PMI?

If, for whatever reason, you cannot come up with 20% down, or you have already bought a house and are currently paying PMI, listen up. Do whatever you can to raise the money to bring up your equity to 20%. Borrow from your parents, borrow from your kids, have a bake sale in the driveway. Get the money.

In the event you can't come up with the full 20%, don't get depressed. Eventually, your regular monthly payments will bring up your equity to 20%. When that happens, call your lending bank or mortgage company to have PMI removed. You have to monitor it and notify them when you have reached 20%. If you do not, they can keep taking it every month for the whole 30 years.

Another option to rid yourself of PMI is to get your home reappraised if the value increases or you paid a price that was under market value. The increase in the true value of your home over what you paid for it is known as appreciation. Appreciation reflects when an asset you own, your home, in this case, rises in value. This is money you didn't need to work for and you can put it to good use. Simply call your mortgage company and request that your home be reappraised as it is undervalued. If your lender will not cooperate, another lender will! Take control.

For mortgages after August 1, 1999, the lender is supposed to automatically stop taking PMI when you have reached 22% equity in your house. It does not mean that they will. They can continue to rip you off for the monthly PMI charge if you have a history of late payments or missing payments.

Get Rid of It

PMI may not seem like much each month, but it is a useless fee. You get absolutely nothing from paying it. It is essentially a penalty every month. For a mortgage balance of $200,000, you could pay over $1000 a year in PMI! That is $1000 of your money up in smoke!

A great technique to get the mortgage paid down faster and to have a lower payment every month is to get rid of PMI. Borrow from your family to get the 20% or simply call and ask that they remove it. That $1000 is your money!

Bye-Bye Interest

A way for folks to cut their mortgage from 30 years to 10 years can seem a little more complicated when you hear people throwing around sentences with "banker speak" like: Many homeowners have negative amortization loans with a variable rate.

This means that even though the homeowner makes their payment, their principal balance actually increases. Variable rates are a tricky thing. As market interest rates go up, the interest rate on the mortgage gets raised. As the loan's interest rate increases, the payment significantly increases. These folks are victims of the banks and lending institutions because they trap them in the beginning with a great teaser interest rate and then the rates go to the moon. The lenders don't tell these people, "Hey, you are getting screwed here. You should go and refinance your loan."

But I will tell you! Hey, you are getting screwed here. You should refinance your old mortgage loan.

Re-Fi

Let's illustrate with an example. Ed and Sue bought their home five years ago for $300,000, with a variable rate mortgage. Their original monthly mortgage payment was $2500. Now that five years have rolled by, interest rates have gone up as well as their principal. They are now paying $3100 per month, and the balance is $315,000.

> Refinancing your mortgage could save you thousands!

So what is the solution to this mess? Ed and Sue should keep paying the $3100, the amount of the monthly payment they are currently paying now. They should shop around and refinance the mortgage to a fixed rate. The rate they have now is astronomical. The lower rate at the beginning of the mortgage is long gone and they are now paying as high as 12%. Ed and Sue can find a fixed rate mortgage for 6% or 7%. As we have seen, that will make a remarkable reduction in the amount of interest being paid. That one simple solution saves a boatload of bucks. Enough to go buy a new boat. Or a new business.

By losing the old variable rate loan and switching to a new fixed rate loan, their principal will not go up, their balance will not go up, and their monthly payments will not go up. Their peace of mind will go up. They will continue to make the same monthly payment as always and now they will pay off their home much, much faster.

If you have a variable rate mortgage, what is your rate? What should you do? Refinance!

Another benefit of refinancing is that required piece of the puzzle – the appraisal. After a few years have gone by, most people's homes have appreciated in value. The new appraisal can help you by showing that you now have a home with a higher market value, and you have greater equity in it. This can lead to a better interest rate for you. Always try for the lowest interest rate available. It never hurts to ask!

Another way to bring the payment down, for a first-time mortgage or a refinance, is to put as much as possible in for the down payment. I understand that is a hard thing to do, so this is a prime opportunity to ask your family for help. Any money that they can loan you will save you a ton of interest! The larger your down payment, obviously the less you have to borrow, plus you qualify for a better interest rate. Saving on interest is like saving money over and over again; better in your wallet than theirs.

Numbers Talk

Let me paint a picture. A borrower, Buddy, has a loan that equals 100% of the appraised value of his property, and has a FICO score of 620. With the current market trends, we are assuming that the value of the home has not increased or decreased since the property was purchased. After an initial five years of making Interest Only payments, the rate has adjusted to 9.5%, and the payments have become principal and interest, amortized over the remaining 25 years of the loan. We are also assuming that the adjusted rate of 9.5% will remain consistent for the remaining life of the loan.

Since Buddy has been making interest-only payments for five years, the principal loan balance has not decreased during this time. Buddy will have to continue paying Private Mortgage Insurance (PMI) because the loan balance has not dropped below 80% of the value of the property. A friend, who is not named Buddy, ran these figures for me and has the spreadsheet showing the dollars and cents.

Scenario A:

Buddy's monthly payment is $3901.45, principal and interest of $3494.79 and PMI payment of $406.67. By paying this amount monthly, the PMI would not be removed until 137 months of payments have been made.

Once the PMI is removed, Buddy makes the minimum principal and interest payment of $3494.79 monthly, and the loan would not be entirely paid off until the end of the 25th year.

If Buddy chooses to continue paying $3901.45 each month – with that $406.67 PMI amount now going toward paying down the principal loan balance – the loan would be entirely paid off in 22 years and 6 months. By continuing to make the $3901.45 payment each month, after the PMI has been removed, Buddy would save approximately $53,750 in interest.

Scenario B:

If Buddy pays every two weeks instead of making one monthly payment, he would make a bi-weekly payment of $1950.73, principal and interest payment of $1747.39 and PMI of $203.33. By paying this amount every 2 weeks, the PMI would not be removed until 89 months of payments have been made.

Once the PMI is removed, Buddy's payment of $1747.39 every 2 weeks would entirely pay off the loan in 19 years and 3 months, saving him approximately $181,730 in interest.

If Buddy chooses to continue paying $1950.73 every two weeks – with the PMI amount of $203.33 going toward principal – the loan would be entirely paid off in 17 years and 1 month. With a $1950.73 payment every 2 weeks, even after the PMI has been removed, Buddy would save approximately $221,750 in interest.

Scenario C:

If Buddy decides to make weekly payments of $975.36, principal and interest of $873.70 and PMI of $101.67, PMI would not be removed until 89 months of payments have been made.

Once the PMI is removed, Buddy's payment of $873.70 weekly means the loan would be entirely paid off in 19 years and 1 month, saving him approximately $181,730 in interest.

If Buddy chooses to continue paying $975.36 weekly – with the $101.67 going toward paying down the principal loan balance – the loan would be entirely paid off in 17 years, and would save approximately $222,600 in interest.

Whew.

Debt Cures Method

If Buddy uses the *Debt Cures* methods and increases his FICO score to 750, he can refinance to a loan with a 5.5% rate that is fixed for 25 years. He would still have PMI, but it would be at a reduced rate, since his FICO score is significantly higher.

In the following scenarios, let's assume Buddy has the improved credit score and loan terms outlined above, but that he is still making a total monthly payment of $3901.45. Under these new circumstances, let's see how quickly he will pay off the home loan.

Scenario A1:

Monthly payment is $3901.45, principal and interest of $3578.12 and PMI of $323.33. PMI would not be removed until 42 months of payments have been made.

Once the PMI is removed, with minimum principal and interest payment of $3578.12 monthly, the loan would be entirely paid off in 13 years and 3 months, saving him $483,093.03 in interest.

If Buddy pays $3904.45 each month – with the $323.33 PMI now going toward paying down the principal loan balance – the loan would be entirely paid off in 12 years and 1 month, saving approximately $497,060.

Scenario B1:

Payment every two weeks instead of making one monthly payment – $1950.73 in principal, interest of $1789.06 and PMI of $161.67. PMI would not be removed until 37 months of payments have been made.

Once the PMI is removed, with payment of $1789.06 every 2 weeks, the loan would be entirely paid off in 11 years and 9 months, saving approximately $502,770 in interest.

Paying $1950.73 every two weeks, the loan would be entirely paid off in 10 years and 10 months, saving approximately $515,255.

Scenario C1:

A payment each week instead of making one monthly payment – $975.36 in principal, and interest of $894.53 and PMI of $80.83. PMI would not be removed until 36 months of payments have been made.

Once the PMI is removed, principal payment can go down to $873.70 weekly; the loan would then be entirely paid off in 11 years and 7 months, saving approximately $506,350 in interest.

If Buddy chooses to continue paying $975.36 weekly, the loan would be entirely paid off in 10 years and 9 months – about $515,530 in interest saved.

Some of you numbers people eat that stuff up. Others like a condensed version: You can see the progression. Paying every two weeks saves interest over paying once a month, and paying weekly reduces the interest paid versus paying every two weeks. Reducing the principal balance directly affects the interest paid out.

In fact, Buddy could pay off that mortgage even quicker if he wanted to! He could pay earlier in the month, as opposed to weekly. In addition, with great credit, Buddy could find a mortgage with a lower interest rate (depending on what's available at the time). There are tons of people out there with rates even above 9.5%, and that should not be the case. Don't allow yourself to settle. Use the *Debt Cures* methods and refinance and pay off your mortgage in even less than ten years!

By doing what Buddy did, you could get a better FICO score (which leads to a better rate). That means less money to the bank and *more money* to you. Looking at C and C1, Buddy's interest savings at best, with the 9.5% rate, is $222,600; with the 5.5% rate, he saves $515,500. Both are great, but that better interest rate nets Buddy an extra $292,900.

Buddy loves *Debt Cures*. The banks don't.

More on the Story

Besides refinancing, and all the prepay options discussed earlier in the chapter, there are more techniques. In this era of subprime mortgages, I know that some of you want a solution that can work for you.

The record number of foreclosures is mind-boggling. In 2008, $500 billion dollars of mortgages will adjust (the ARM is called the Adjustable Rate Mortgage for a reason) and the adjustment will be a killer for a lot of people. Over $300 billion of those mortgage dollars are subprime mortgages. Many people won't be able to afford the payment with the new interest rate and home prices dropping all across the country. That means that people will owe more on their home than it is now worth. Not a pretty situation.

My down and dirty explanation: Subprime mortgages are handed out to people who don't possess the best of credit. This is a practice that many lenders are involved in, and I don't agree with it at all. They anticipate that folks with bad credit eventually won't be able to make their mortgage payments on time. What happens next? The bank slips in to repossess the home, only to turn around and sell it once again.

With the housing industry suffering at present, these greedy lenders are seeing their plans backfire. When they repossess these homes, they are now unable to make back what they originally loaned it out for. The "Subprime Lending Crisis" keeps making news as many of these sub-prime lenders are going bankrupt. They should not have been making the loans in the first place, but I digress. If you are in this situation, keep the faith. You may not lose your house to foreclosure after all.

There is an option called a short sale. What happens: You, the home owner, need to sell but can't get what you still owe out of the house; the bank agrees to accept an offer for less than the total amount owed to pay off the home, hence they will come up "short." Normally when you sell your house, you pay off the bank and have a little equity left over. In this case, you have no equity and still owe the bank a little (or a lot!), but they allow the sale. It prevents a foreclosure and saves everyone headaches in the long run. In many situations, someone who knows you will buy the house at a discounted price and then resell it back to you when conditions improve.

For example, take Hilton. His aunt buys his house in a short sale for cheap, only to later resell it to him when he has his credit back under control. He now no longer needs to take an ARM. He can take a fixed mortgage with a good rate because he has used *Debt Cures* to clean up his credit. His loan is less, his interest is lower. His story has a happy ending. Yours can too. For more info on short sales, visit http://www.mortgagenewsdaily.com/wiki/Short_Sale_Defined.asp.

In this way, you can take out a low-interest loan and the cost of the house (and the amount of the loan) is less than the original purchase price and loan amount. But you can still pay the amount you were originally paying the first time you owned the house, in order to pay off that mortgage even quicker. That's right – stick to the *Debt Cures* strategy, and you can get that mortgage paid off in even less than ten years!

Another method to prevent foreclosure is loan modification. It is similar to refinancing because it is a permanent change to your loan. You can negotiate a different rate or a longer term in order to get a payment you can afford and not lose your house. You are able to change your terms and save thousands of dollars. It is different from refinancing because there are no closing costs, taxes, or fees. Normally, the banks would not be inclined to do this because it means less money for them. However, these are not normal times. They realize that something is better than nothing, and keeping you in your house is best for them. If they foreclose, they have to sell it and hope to get enough to pay off what you owe.

A bird in the hand is worth something. If the bank agrees to your loan modification request, they may ask you to pay for an appraisal. That is reasonable and worth the small expense to keep you in your home and with a payment you can afford. To quote Winston Churchill, *never give up*. Keeping your house is worth it.

The banks and the lenders do not want us to know that we can reduce our payments, reduce our interest, and reduce the life of the loan. The banks want to keep all these strategies a secret so they can continue to sit back and count our money for the next thirty years.

No thanks. I like to count my money myself, thank you very much. I think I'll stop paying all that interest and start using my money for my own purposes. Like creating a little bit of wealth.

CHAPTER 15

No Bankruptcy

"There is a bankruptcy attorney in your area
ready to contact you!"
~ tag line on bankruptcy lawyer website

There are infrequent occasions when bankruptcy may be the right choice for you. Most of the time, it is not. You would never know it though. Bankruptcy is advertised nearly as often as credit cards!

It is no wonder that so many people turn to bankruptcy. Debt is out of control and when the pressure is mounting, it can be hard to think straight. The ads are on the radio as you drive to work, the commercials are on television while you watch your favorite show in the evening, and the phone book and the internet are full of ads for lawyers who specialize in bankruptcy. Finding a lawyer to handle bankruptcy is easier than finding a hairdresser.

They make it sound like a bed of roses. If you have not filed bankruptcy, it is a good bet that you know someone who has. Talk to that someone. Did bankruptcy magically make all their problems disappear?

POP QUIZ
True or False?

1. Credit card fees have risen 160% over the last five years.

2. Credit cards are swiped 2.2 million times every hour.

3. Consumer Debt exceeds the National Debt.

4. A CEO of Providian said, "The goal is to squeeze out revenue and get the customers to sit still for the squeeze."

5. In 2004, thirty states sued banks regarding predatory practices.

6. The Federal Trade Commission used to have two lawyers to handle the collection agency suits. Presently, more than 100 attorneys are processing these suits.

7. 83% of all divorces are attributed to money problems.

8. The number one cause of bankruptcy is health care bills.

9. Between 1994 and 2004, over 10 million Americans filed for bankruptcy.

10. Being in debt now does not mean that you will be in debt forever.

If you answered "true" to all of the above, you are correct. If you answered "sad, but true" to all but the last statement, you are also correct.

Sad, Sad World

Those statistics above are astonishing. We are a credit card society. The convenience is wonderful. The fees are not. The industry has made it too easy to get too many cards and too much credit. Many people mistakenly believe the credit card company or the bank would not give them a card unless they could afford it. "I must be doing okay. The bank just gave me another credit card."

You *are* doing okay, in their eyes. The old joke about corrupt voting practices in Chicago was "vote early, vote often." The credit card industry may have a similar motto – pay little, pay late, pay forever.

The outlandish fees that they are raking in are unbelievable. The biggest increase in revenue is fees! And the big wig of the big bank wrote in an email how he wants us all to sit still for "the squeeze." Outrageous. But then again, this is the company who paid $400 million to settle allegations of fraud and other egregious acts against its own customers. How much more preposterous can it get?

How about the fact that thirty states filed suit against the big bucks credit card banks for their ludicrous ways, and the federal government of these states stood by the credit card banks! Debt collection agencies have also become an empire. They think they are above the law. It takes 100 attorneys to handle all the complaints filed against these guys and yet the government does not step in and tighten the laws!

> You do not have to sit still for the squeeze!

It really is a sad, sad world.

Last Option

Instead of thinking bankruptcy is the only option, consider it a last option. I understand the temptation. You had a string of bad luck and now you are saddled with debt. Your marriage is crumbling, your health is shaky, and those medical bills are already overwhelming; you don't want more! It can seem that bankruptcy is the only way out.

You are not alone in your thinking. Millions of people file for bankruptcy. America is supposed to be a nation of wealth, and look how many of our citizens are throwing their hands up in the air and filing for bankruptcy.

As far as the banks and credit card companies were concerned, too many people were filing for bankruptcy. Why did they care? They weren't getting paid their fees! So the bankers went to their buddies in the government, and in 2005, the federal government made it more difficult for people to file for bankruptcy. That's what friends are for.

No Relief

Talk to those who have filed bankruptcy; they will tell you life is not "easy street." They have a black mark on the credit report now, and the predators sweep in like vultures to pick their bones. These folks are targeted now as a "poor credit risk;" the banks can't wait to charge them high interest rates for the "favor" of working with them.

These were the same "helpful" bankers who forced them into bankruptcy. In the film *Maxed Out*, a bankruptcy judge was asked about all the cases he had reviewed, regarding how much of the credit card debt was principal versus the amount that was interest and fees. He stated that on average the amount due was triple the principal.

Jim and Juanita both lost their jobs and they had no emergency fund set aside to pay basic living expenses. They used their credit cards to pay the bills, and ended up borrowing from cards to pay on the others. "We started robbing Peter to pay Paul…" Juanita told the reporter in the documentary film that aired on PBS, *Secret History of Credit Cards*. The penalties and fees accumulated very quickly.

They had been good customers for years, but when they fell behind, they were not given the courtesy of kindness for all those years of good payments. They were hit with late fees and over the limit fees. The interest rate soared from 9% to 25%. As Jim said, "Forget the fact that you had the credit card for a number of years and were paying on it regularly, were never late. And as soon as you miss one payment, it's like all deals are off."

It did not take long, and they had $80,000 of debt on ten credit cards. It became impossible to pay, and they filed bankruptcy. And Jim and Juanita still get credit card offers in the mail.

There Is Relief

There are literally millions of people like Jim and Juanita. They are looking for a way out. The sad part is that it did not have to come to this. If the banks would pull back their aggressive fees, perhaps they would not have to be worried about bankruptcies.

The good news is that there is hope for everyone, whether you have filed bankruptcy or not. With *Debt Cures,* you will see that you can eliminate your debt, or negotiate it away, and cut your rates to wipe out up to half or more of what you owe. Using these techniques could stave off the vultures and the need for bankruptcy.

CHAPTER 16

Big Business

*"A business that makes nothing but money
is a poor kind of business."*

~ Henry Ford

As I stated in the first chapter, credit card companies are stealing from the American citizen; the federal government, instead of standing up for the rights of its citizens, is in bed with the bankers and the lenders and the fat cats, counting their money together and allowing it all to happen.

One giant credit card company improperly assessed late fees – because they had their employees hold or shred customers' checks. Another, Providian, allegedly charged customers for things that they never ordered, like credit insurance. They wound up paying a large settlement amount, but no one went to jail and the scandal blew away with little media attention. Providian paid their settlements – $400 million – but stayed in business. Some credit card issuers referred to it as "king of the bad boys."

What does that tell us? Obviously, there are more bad boys.

I don't know if there is a secret handshake or if they exchange high-fives, but according to www.bcsalliance.com and attorney Robert Hinsley of www.consumersdefense.com, the consumer lending industry is overrun with bad boys.

"Bad Boys"

One credit card company (we'll call it Big Bank) took the liberty of doing a truly dastardly deed. They changed the due dates on customer's monthly credit statements. They did not notify anyone of the change; they just slipped it in, and it slipped by most people. Now that is a sneaky tactic.

> The Big Banks think they can get away with anything!

We hard-working bill-paying citizens get used to what bills are due on what day. My credit card bill is always due on the 17th of every month. Well, if I had been a Big Bank customer, they could have changed my payment due date on my statement, and I would not have noticed. I would have paid by the 17th. If they moved my due date to the 13th, I would have been late, because I would not have realized the date switch. Most customers did not notice, and that was the whole point.

The honest citizens were not aware that the due date had been moved, so they sent in their payments like always, which now meant they were late. Big Bank slapped them all with a late fee at twenty-nine bucks a pop. If they were late two months in a row, the bank jacked their interest rate up a whopping ten percent. Ouch!

Big Bank must want to be king of the hill because they pulled another fast one. They let a month go by without sending monthly statements to their customers. Because they did not receive a statement as their reminder, many customers paid late, or missed paying that month. Big Bank dinged them all with the $29 late fee.

When customers realized what happened, they called to complain. They had never received a statement! Blaming it on a computer mistake, Big Bank refused to remove the late fees! They stated that they are not required to mail a monthly statement, and it is the customer's responsibility to know when to pay their bill.

These folks need a refresher course on responsibility to customer service!

The Contenders

I wish I could tell you that Big Bank is alone in their wicked ways, but many of the credit card companies are throwing their hat in the ring for the "bad boy" competition. According to Houston attorney Robert Hinsley of consumersdefense.com, there are a lot of serious contenders for the title:

- ✔ $45 million settlement; Citibank; alleged to have improperly assessed late fees.

- ✔ $36 million settlement; Sears; allegedly raised interest rates after they stated that they would not raise rates.

- ✔ $8 million settlement; MBNA; alleged to have improperly assessed late fees.

- ✔ $7.2 million settlement; Advanta; allegedly charged higher interest rates to customers who were promised a low rate.

Notice the key word in all the sentences above – they all settled. They stayed out of court and stayed on their course. What's $45 million in fines to Citibank, after all? They can pay a settlement like that and still stay one of the top players in the most profitable industry in America.

One suspects that it is like the NASCAR teams, making illegal modifications to their racecars, hoping that no one will notice, and if they do notice, it's a slap on the wrist, a fine to pay, and life goes on just the same way. When the consumer lenders do get challenged, they pay their settlements with a wink and a shrug, and the next week, the aggressive practices continue. The unscrupulous practices appear to go on, and the government is winking right back at them.

And More Bad Boys

Another apparent rival to the throne is industry giant Capital One, who was sued over its alleged marketing ploys. MSNBC.com's Bob Sullivan reported that the Minnesota state attorney's office claimed Capital One misled consumers with promises of fixed interest rates, and then raised those rates – by 400% in some cases!

The lawsuit was initiated when a Minnesota resident signed up for a Capital One card after seeing a commercial on television. She specifically asked if they would let her keep the 4.9% rate for as long as she had the card. She allegedly was assured they would. She got a card. Less than a year later, and after paying her monthly bills on time, her rate was increased – more than doubled, in fact, nearly tripled – to 14%.

Capital One is claimed to have sent out mail offers that point blank spelled out that the card was a fixed rate. The ads supposedly stated repeatedly that the rate was 4.99%. The attorneys counted the word "fixed" seventeen times! Capital One allegedly went heavy on the adjective and the advertising, and then silently switched to a higher rate and hoped that their customers wouldn't notice. If that is true, can I say "cheater" seventeen times?

If a customer phoned in to Capital One and wanted to accept the mail offer, the customer service representatives supposedly had a cheat sheet of what to say to avoid customer's direct questions. Apparently, even if you advertise a card with a fixed rate, and say it seventeen times, you don't have to come through with a credit card for your customer that has a fixed rate. Or a "low" one. Not if you are a big bad boy bank anyway. Capital One allegedly doled out interest rates of 20%; some even as high as 26%. Their ads never used the word "high" or "bait and switch" or "look out, we're out to get you."

Another separate Capital One dispute did get some coverage in the media. A man who had to undergo emergency open heart surgery mailed in his Capital One payment late that month. Capital One allegedly received it just one day late. According to Texas attorney Robert Hinsley, when this citizen called to explain why he was late, "they coldly told him 'too bad' and they jacked up his interest rate from about 7% to 21%." Who needs heart surgery here?

On September 30, 2004, Capital One had credit card loans amounting to $46.1 billion. Their *quarterly* earnings were $414.4 million! And that was 50% more than the year before! With earnings like that for three months, for one bank, it is obvious that there is a lot of money revolving through the banking industry of revolving credit. Do you hear the voice in the back of your head now whispering, "Obscene"? If not obscene, it is an awful lot of money.

And they spend an awful lot of money. Capital One spent $827 million in marketing its credit cards in the first nine months alone of

2004. They were spending $827 million in ads, and the year wasn't even over yet. Think about that same amount of money being put to a good cause! It is obscene; and shameless.

No End in Sight

The banks and credit card companies continue their shameless ways with outrageous rates and fees galore. They feel not shame, but pride, as they continue to break profit records with fee income as a primary source of those profits. The executives shrug their shoulders at the criticism and say that they are in full compliance with existing government regulations. And instead of putting the breaks on the banks, the feds have become advocates for the consumer lending industry. The fact that the banks are key campaign contributors to many a politician would not have any influence, would it? What do you think?

In a 2007 article for reuters.com, Harvard Law School professor and bankruptcy expert Elizabeth Warren states that, "One would expect the government to come down on the side of the consumer. Instead, it regulates on the side of the banks.... The lobbying dollars are all on the side of the industry. That's why they get to make all the rules."

The attitude and aggressive ways of the credit card industry are like being on a runaway train. Americans are saving less because they need to spend up to 90% of their disposable income paying down their credit card debt. Bankruptcy filings and foreclosures are at an all-time high. The debt crisis in America is like a financial cancer that grows and spreads silently while we sleep.

According to Gabriel Stein, an economist at Lombard Research, "Households, in their quest for sources of financing, have now been moved from mortgage borrowing to credit cards. This is extremely bad news for the U.S. economy over the course of 2007 and suggests that households are at their last gasp to find some form of credit." Who is responsible for putting the stranglehold on the person gasping for their last financial breath? My answer: the banks, the credit card companies, and the entire consumer lending industry. That is one area in which I can use the word "responsible" and "consumer lending industry" in the same sentence.

File a Complaint

The credit card companies rely very heavily on the hope that the average citizen is not aware of what is going on, and if they are aware, the banks rely on the fact that most people do not do anything about it. That is because most think they can't. Now we know better.

You can fight back by reporting your credit card issuers to the proper authorities, and I will give you that information below. If our elected officials get enough complaints, maybe, just maybe, some legislation will be enacted to curb the craziness, and the greed, of the credit card industry.

Who to Contact

1. **Your state's Attorney General's office.** Most people would probably never think of contacting their state attorney general. The office seems too official or intimidating, not something that an ordinary citizen could have contact with, but they are in essence the top dog lawyer for your state. They work for you. These attorneys know their stuff and are aggressive.

   This is exactly the place where you want to start. The attorney general will listen to your complaint, and more importantly, will act on your complaint. They keep track of all complaints filed. Even if you are the first one, when the next guy makes a complaint, and then the next guy, they all add up. The attorney general will not know of the corrupt goings-on unless you notify them of your complaint.

   Most of the lawsuits that have been filed against the credit card companies came from attorney generals. The Providian case was set in motion by the California Attorney General. It all started with one complaint.

   You should be able to find your state attorney general's office listed at www.naag.org.

2. **Elected Representatives**. Yes, I know I have been telling you that the Washington officials and the banking officials are joined at the hip pocket. They are. Campaign contributions make the world go round. They have their good old boys (and girls) network, and that is a fact. It is also a fact that these people are

your elected officials, and if they think their job is in jeopardy, they may listen to you.

As your elected representative, they have a duty to you, and you have a duty to them. If you do not voice your complaint, then nothing will ever happen. Make your complaint heard. Speak up. Write. A staffer will read your letter and it may just get thrown into a pile, but if that pile gets big enough, then something will get done. If the suits in Washington start getting enough complaints, they will have to do something about it. If we don't complain, they can sit back, light another stogie, and keep on doing what they have been doing – nothing.

Email and snail mail addresses are available at: www.house.gov and www.senate.gov.

3. **Banking Regulators**. Their mailing address is: Division of Credit Practices, Bureau of Consumer Protection, Federal Trade Commission, Washington, D.C. 20580; or file a complaint online at: www.ftc.gov.

4. **Better Business Bureau**. Contact them online at: www.bbb. org.

5. **Comptroller of the Currency**. Their phone number is: 202-874-4700.

It is the right thing to do to complain, complain, complain. Credit card companies get away with their outrageous behavior because too few of us hard-working consumers complain. If your senator received hundreds of letters from consumers threatening to vote him out of office, he will sit up and listen. The squeaky wheel sometimes gets rewarded, so start squeaking.

> Your voice,
>
> and
>
> your vote,
>
> matters.

What to Say

Contact your elected officials and inform them of what the credit card company did to you specifically. Don't give a general rant against corporate America. Give your story of how their greedy practices are hurting your everyday life. "My credit card company raised my interest rate to 22%.

I have been a long-standing good customer and I always pay my bills. Now the monthly payment is so high, I can't pay my utilities and my car insurance." Whatever your exact beef is, spell it out. Give dates, rates, dollars; present your complaint professionally and cordially.

You can be bold. The person in Washington was elected by you to represent you. Let him or her know that you are fully aware of the lobbyists and the campaign contributions. You can point blank ask what they have received from the lobbyists and credit card companies.

Don't be intimidated. Tell them you want regulation of the credit card industry, and that you want to see how they vote on banking and credit card issues. Express your opinion that the terms of the credit card companies need to fully disclosed. They should not be able to sneak in a rate hike. They should not be able to keep raising fees either.

Lastly, make sure you mention that you will be voting in the next election and your vote goes to the person who will take a stand against the banks and the credit card industry.

Just Do It!

Your actions matter. Bringing this issue to their attention is worth your time and effort. If we want things to change, we have to do something about it. By not complaining, we are letting the credit card industry, and the federal government, get away with it.

Contact your elected officials in Washington! Spread the word to everyone you know and have them do the same. Most everyone has an issue where they have been wronged by their credit card company. Send a quick email to your senator and representative, telling them about it. If you have a specific serious complaint, tell your attorney general!

Universal Default...

The scam of universal default is extensive throughout much of the consumer lending industry, and an area that many people are shocked about when it happens to them. Beware: if you are in default with one credit card or lender, you could then be zapped by your others.

Congress has let the banks and credit card companies go unchecked for too long. They devise whatever methods they can to get more fees.

...Is a Universal Scam

If the credit card company nabs you for universal default, they lower the boom and give you their worst rate. The *average* default rate is around 24%, so that means that some cards charge even higher. The credit card companies have no problem with the concept. If the bank across the street gets to raise the customer's rate because the customer had a bad day, we all get to raise our rates. Any hint of price control structures elsewhere makes people crazy. We scream about that in other industries. The credit card industry seems to exist in a protected bubble that we humble citizens just can't seem to pierce.

The whole deal of universal default makes me want to scream. If a person in a tough financial position makes a late payment or misses a payment with one bank or credit card company just once, for whatever reason, and however minimally, all the rest of his credit cards and creditors could sock him with a higher interest rate now. He gets blindsided! He is being punished by all the lenders, and it can be severe. The dreaded downward spiral happens and he starts defaulting with all his creditors. The vicious cycle really is vicious and vindictive. How in the world is that helpful to anyone?

Even more unbelievable is that an error on the credit report can trigger universal default! And nothing can un-trigger it!

It is highly possible that the item on the credit report that caused them to sing "universal default" is actually erroneous information. It doesn't matter. Even if you get the error corrected on your credit report (after reading this book, you, of course, will do that), that is not an instant fix. The error correction can be posted to your credit report, but the credit card companies can still keep your rate jacked up! You have no legal right to force them to return your rate back to what it was before the universal default kicked in. What is wrong with this picture?!

That Is 100% Stupid!

Let's use the analogy of a teacher making an error in his grade book for your final exam. You earned an A, but the teacher inadvertently drops down a line while recording grades and gives you an F. This means you fail the course and have to repeat it next year. You show the graded exam to your professor and he fixes his grade book, but does nothing to correct the overall situation. You still fail the class and have to repeat it. That would not happen. There would be a course of action to take to say the failing grade was due to an error and now the error has been fixed. Let me pass. Right now, the government looks the other way at universal default errors and lets you fail.

According to a 2005 survey, the latest data available, 44% of credit card banks surveyed take part in universal default. This survey was of forty-five different banks. These forty-five banks issued 144 different credit cards. That's a lot of universal default going on. Check your card member agreement, the fine print, to see if your bank has this policy. If it says that it may use "default pricing based on information in your credit report," then indeed, be prepared for universal default.

Maxed Out

In the 2006 documentary film *Maxed Out,* director James Scurlock turned the cameras on the consumer lending industry. The people he interviewed, average everyday American citizens, were "just being preyed on [by lenders] and manipulated and squeezed so hard that they can't ever hope to recover. And that's not right." I agree that it is not right, but people need to know that there is hope and that they can recover. Scurlock stated that he made the movie about the debt epidemic in America because "debt is the one issue that affects all of us – rich or poor, black or white, gay or straight, liberal or conservative."

Scurlock and his crew made a lot of interesting discoveries. In the film, he talked with a consumer attorney who spends the bulk of his time taking on the credit reporting agencies over errors. In the depositions of credit bureau attorneys, he has been told, on record, that over 90% of all credit reports have errors on them. Again, this seems like an area where the federal government should step up and require a more diligent and accurate reporting, an overhaul, a clean up to the system. Alas, they don't. It is up to us to be the watchdog of our credit reports, as we have learned how they impact every dollar we spend.

Also shocking to the makers of the movie was that the consumer lending industry is exploiting the extremely poor, the naïve college students, and the people who have declared bankruptcy. We'll take them, the financial industry, to task for that in the next chapter.

A Debtor Nation

Credit card mentality is deeply embedded in our American culture. Information gathered by the U.S. Census Bureau claims that the average American has at least nine credit cards. Consumer debt now exceeds the national debt. The American people owe approximately $6.7 trillion in household debt. Of the more than one billion credit cards in circulation today in the United States, 600 million are retail cards, 320 million are bank cards, 140 million are oil company cards, and 30 million are travel and entertainment cards. We have a card for everything.

"What's in your wallet?"

In 1980, credit card debt was $50 billion. At the end of 2000, unsecured credit card debt was $654 billion. Welcome to the new millennium. Three out of five households now have an average credit card balance of more than $11,000. If Average Annie carries that average balance of $11,000, and if she only makes the monthly minimum payment, with an interest rate of 24%, it would take Average Annie twenty-two years to pay off that $11,000. Twenty-two years. Why? There is over $47,000 in interest piling up on that $11,000 balance. Average Annie does not want to spend the next twenty-two years of her life paying off an $11,000 credit card balance, along with four times that much in interest fees. Average Annie is ready for *Debt Cures*.

Americans Are Not Saving

Most Americans are not able to save nearly enough for their retirement. No surprise as to why, or to where, their money is going. If they are like Average Annie, they are chipping away at a credit card debt that continues to grow and grow and grow, without them even making any more credit card purchases. It is an incredibly unfair system. Saving for the future, for retirement, for an emergency fund, can seem like an impossible dream when faced with the daily nightmare of mushrooming credit card balances.

In an April 2007 Market Watch article posted on Yahoo Finance, it is stated that the Commerce Department released its personal saving figures for 2006, and drum roll please, Americans are not saving. The sad fact of the matter is that the Commerce Department statistics show that people are actually spending one percent more than they earned. People really are falling into a financial hole. That figure is the worst since the Depression era, but hey, ask the feds and the lenders, and they'll say that everything is peachy keen. Maybe for them, but for the average American citizen, times are tough.

> Americans' savings: "...the worst since the Depression era."

According to the CNNMoney website, consumer spending accounts for seventy percent of the U.S. gross domestic product. Their website states, "The world economy is leveraged to the U.S. consumer. And the U.S. consumer is leveraged to the hilt." David Wyss, a chief economist at Standard & Poor's, made the statement: "We've never had so many who owed so much."

Revolution

No one is more pleased than the credit card industry. Bankrate.com states that 40% of credit card issuers' profits come from fee income. They pat themselves on the back for another great year and light up fat cigars. Meanwhile, the most common New Year's resolution for many Americans has become "to get out of debt." Resolutions used to be typical things like, "lose ten pounds," "find my true love," or "keep the house clean." Now, most Americans are buried with debt that has escaped their control, simply because the lending industry is out of control; and the number one concern for today's hard working bill-paying citizen is to get out of debt.

Meanwhile, the credit card companies drop millions each year in congressional campaign contributions. It is no surprise that any legislation that comes out of Washington basically rolls out the red carpet for the credit card companies to steal the American public blind.

George Orwell once said, "In a time of universal deceit, telling the truth becomes a revolutionary act." Call me a revolutionary.

Debt Cures was written specifically for you, to get you out of their control. Now the only thing for you to be concerned about is thinking up a new New Year's resolution.

CHAPTER 17

Stealing Candy from Babies

"Monsters are real."

~ Stephen King

The American consumer is in deeper debt than ever before in the history of the United States. The amount of debt grows by $2 billion each day. I cannot even fathom that. Are we a nation of wealth, or have we become a nation of citizens who are oppressed by the banks, the mortgage companies, the credit card corporations, the department stores – the entire consumer lending industry?

The competition for the consumer pocketbook is at an all-time high. Because the lending industry is drunk with power and thirsty for fees, they have broadened their markets to be able to reach into even more pocketbooks. And under mattresses. And into piggy banks.

The Age of Reason Is History

Long ago, in a galaxy far, far away, a customer had to be deemed a good credit risk in order to get a credit card or a loan. If a person had a bad credit history, then the reasonable thing to do was not give him money until he could improve his credit and learn how to manage his money. Decisions were made based on sound business practices, not get-rich-quick schemes of the lenders. The old banker's rationale was, "I will loan you some money and charge you a little bit of interest for the right to have this money now. You will pay me back in installments. You will be able to make your purchase, and have affordable payments. I will have helped you; you are able to repay me, and I will have made a profit on the money you pay me back. It is a win-win, and we are both happy."

The rosy glow of mutual respect has faded. The consumer lending industry rationale of this century goes a little more like this: "I will loan you some money. I will charge you as much interest as I possibly can. I will create fees so I can get more money out of you. I will set your monthly payments low, so you think I am doing you a favor, but I do so in order that you will keep paying me every month while I keep layering on the finance charges. Hmm, what other name can I think up for another fee? You used your credit once to get you through a rough patch, and I have you in my lasso for life. I like you. I like making money off of you. You make me very happy. I don't care what you think of me. The federal government is my friend and they let me do things my way. You should not complain. You should be grateful to me. I helped you out of the rough patch, remember?"

I envision a large, ugly Jabba the Hutt-type character delivering that soliloquy.

The New Math

It is not unrealistic for a person like me or you to expect that by paying our monthly payment, we should in effect be reducing the balance. It ought to be simple mathematics. *A* minus *B* equals *C*. *C* is my new balance. I do it again the next month, and now this is what I owe, something less than last month. Every month, what I owe should get smaller and smaller and smaller.

The credit lenders have their own math. This is what you owe, and this is what you need to pay, just 2% to 4 % of the entire balance. Throw in some fees every month and now what you owe is more than where you started. The equation looks like: A – B + FEE + FEE + FEE = C, and C is now greater than A. In my algebraic mind, C = an unreasonable balance, and FEEs are equal to underhanded tactics. The industry calls fees their way of making money. I call it criminal.

The New Targets

The gazillions of dollars of profits that the consumer lending industry is currently making is not enough for them. They are now tapping into markets that, only a few years ago, the industry leaders would have thought pointless, lacking potential, and a total waste of their time. The new attitude is predatory, and the credit card companies are stalking new prey: college students, the impoverished with poor or no credit history, and illegal aliens.

Exploiting Illegal Aliens

The *Wall Street Journal* front page story on February 13, 2007, revealed that Bank of America has a new credit card, especially and exclusively for immigrants – aliens who are here illegally and/or have no credit record or Social Security number. Bank executives insist that they are doing nothing wrong, and technically, they have not broken any laws – they're just working the legal loopholes. Behind closed doors, I imagine they feel smug that they are the first to get their fingers in the wallets of the eleven million undocumented immigrants. Someone probably got a raise for thinking of it. They maintain that they are in compliance with all U.S. banking and antiterrorism laws. Illegal immigrants can go to the Mexican consulate and get a *matrícula consular,* an identification card that allows aliens to open bank accounts. An article on BusinessWeek.com quotes a bank branch manager stating that *matrícula* holders are "bringing us all the money that has been under the mattress."

> The credit card industry has spun out of control.

But I doubt that Bank of America has considered the ramifications of their new program, or that they really care. They have opened Pandora's box, and all they care about is that they have a new group of people to lay their fees on. When dollar signs are in their eyes, it is hard to see anything else.

Credit card companies are purveyors of the American Dream, to whomever they can sell it to. Not only is there irony in the fact that the bank launching this program is named the *Bank of America*, but another interesting tidbit of information is that President Bush's first Director of U.S. Citizenship and Immigration Services from 2003–2005 was a man named Eduardo Aguirre. His job before that? He was president of international private banking for Bank of America. You connect the dots.

Nothing is sacred, and everyone is fair game. The credit card issuers are like junkies who will do anything for their next fix. They'll now take aim at target populations that, in years past, they would have been laughed out of the boardroom for even mentioning. Now, anything goes. If an executive, twenty years ago, would have said, "Let's go to the poor neighborhoods and the very poorest parts of the country, and let's get them to sign up for our cards," that employee would have been shown the door. Now he gets a bonus.

Exploiting the Impoverished

James Scurlock, the maker of the documentary feature-length film *Maxed Out,* states that the most shocking discovery for him was learning how the financial industry is exploiting the impoverished people of our nation. It is incredulous and sad. Scurlock maintains that the increase in these credit offers is actually causing poverty.

Instead of eating their Wheaties for breakfast, the big bucks lenders must eat something like "Greedies" to get them stoked for the day. Scurlock and his crew traveled with a journalist to New York, Pennsylvania, and Mississippi. In an MSNBC.com article by Jessica Bennett, Scurlock says, "If you had told me that Citigroup, one of the largest financial groups in the world, was trolling the backwoods of Mississippi for customers, I would have questioned your veracity. But they are; and they're finding people. They're going around very poor neighborhoods, in very poor parts of the country, finding people who have some home equity, finding people who have been responsible, who've saved, who have something left; and they're taking it from them."

Remember the mother and her son, who could not even sign his own name? Remember how they were faced with the prospect of losing their house? They were just one of the many families who got caught in the net when the big banks went fishing for small fry.

Exploiting College Students

If any group were to be given the title of the most sought-after by credit card companies, it would have to be the college kids. They want them while they're still young and not schooled in the ways of debt. Nineteen-year-olds are not nearly as sophisticated and wise to the ways of the world as they think they are, and they like to spend. They have little money of their own, so they barely make their payments and they're immediately caught in the web. It is worse than stealing candy from babies. It is setting them up to fail before they are even out in the working world.

Daniel was caught up in the hoopla of campus life as a freshman, and of course, he opened up a new credit card account the first weekend. The credit card company had the university name on the card, and they were right there on school grounds with their tables set up, tossing out Frisbees and free t-shirts. Daniel assumed it was all legit. And technically, it was. Daniel thought he was a responsible guy. And technically, he was. He pulled good grades and was planning to major in Finance, of all things. He made his minimum payments, and more offers came his way, with lots of nice perks. By the end of freshman year, Daniel had five cards and was five thousand dollars in debt. Daniel, and thousands of college students like him all across the country, learned their lesson the hard way. Their purchases ended up costing more than they ever imagined. They could have bought several Frisbees and t-shirts for what the credit cards ended up charging them. What little money they had in their piggy banks before they left for college has been raided by the big, bad wolf.

Credit card issuers love the campus bunch, because they turn out to be one of the most profitable groups of customers for the credit card industry. College students are not screened the same way that all other applicants are. They don't even have credit reports yet, so a credit score does not come into the picture. All they may need to qualify for a credit card is the simple fact that they are a student at a college or university. The credit card companies know they can get them hooked. Some college students now graduate with huge student loans and heavy credit card debt. It is not a coincidence that 25% of all bankruptcies these days are filed by young people under the age of 25. That, to me, seems like a crime, but no one is being held accountable. The credit card issuers and the federal government just look the other way.

Take, for example, twin brothers, age eighteen. Alex goes to college and is handed a credit card at his university. He is allowed a card just because he is a student. Zach decides to wait a year before going to college. He works full-time and when he applies for a credit card, he is denied because he has no credit history. Zach could pay his bill, so the credit card companies do not want him. In the nonsense upside-down world of credit cards, that is how it works with giving credit to young people these days.

Firing Back

It is often said that debt is the one issue in this country that touches everyone. Debt doesn't discriminate. Maybe that is because the credit card companies are going out of their way to get their paws on everyone. College kids never used to be targeted for credit cards. That was ludicrous. And poor people? Come on, get serious. And bending over backward to give cards to illegal aliens? What are you thinking? A decade or two ago, these groups of "consumers" were not aimed at by the financial lending industry and they, the consumers, were better off because of it. Now, everyone is fair game; except the game itself isn't fair.

Promising futures... tragic endings.

Most parents have no idea that their kids are getting these credit cards and are shocked when they learn how much debt has piled up. Usually, it is the parents who come to their aid, helping their children pay off the balances. The credit card issuers know this, and literally bank on it. Sadly, it is not always the case. In the movie *Maxed Out*, two mothers told their stories. These two mothers did not know each other previously. One had a son; one had a daughter. The two students went to different colleges, and are a sobering example of what is happening on campuses throughout the United States.

These two co-eds were just like Daniel, good kids, smart kids. Because they were good kids, they were ashamed of how the credit card debt had mounted, too ashamed to tell their parents. Their separate stories ended the same tragic way. Suicide. All they left were apologies, along with the stack of credit card bills. The mothers were devastated to lose their children and devastated to learn what had brought on the despair. Imagine the grief and sheer agony for one of the mothers when, a few months later, the mailbox held a credit card offer in the name of her dead child, stating, "We want you back. 0% APR for six months."

Nothing should make a person take such a drastic measure, ever. No mother should ever have to endure that kind of heartrending loss.

It's a Mad, Mad World

Do not let your debts poison your life. Creditors do not own you. You may owe them some money, but you do not owe them your life. There is always a way out. These kids were too young to realize that. The two mothers went to Capitol Hill to testify that credit card companies should be banned from college campuses. As they waited their turn to speak, they were surrounded by credit card industry lobbyists and power brokers, discussing their golf scores and their campaign contributions. As these moms listened to the guys in the expensive suits, they became well aware that they were not operating on a level playing field. These moms had lost their children, due to the evils of the lending industry's methods, and yet their words fell on deaf ears.

Good, decent parents with good, decent kids get trampled in the high stakes world of politics. Lawmakers' deaf ears perk up only when the money starts talking. Elizabeth Warren, the Harvard Law professor and credit expert, is infuriated at how the financial industry can run amuck and ruin people's lives. Laws won't change because, she says in the PBS documentary *Secret History of Credit Cards*, "It is credit card companies who make big political contributions; it's credit card companies who have been the number one givers in Washington. Not big oil, not big pharmaceutical – big consumer financial services. They're giving money in Congress; they're giving money in presidential campaigns. Why would they be giving so much money? What they want to be sure to protect is their ability to go out and sell credit cards when they don't have to tell what the terms are, and they can change the terms after someone has taken out the debt."

> Credit card companies make big political contributions.

No other industry has that ability. The words that come to my mind are "crooks" and "shysters." The Consumer Credit Hearings of 2005 were a sham. The practices of the consumer lending industry were supposed to be reviewed by a Congressional committee, but the members of Congress had a more important vote to get to, or a doughnut waiting, or something like that. In the feature film documentary *Maxed Out*, some of the credit card industry representatives from various major banks are shown making their pretty statements into their microphones to the effect of, "Gosh, we're really great. We give credit cards to people and we are wonderful." No questions were posed to them, and that was the end of the hearing. Nothing happened. No debates. No discussions. No proposals of legislation or guidance. Nothing at all happened. What is the point of a hearing if you do not ask any questions? I'm still scratching my head over that one.

The Facts in Black and White

Think of how we buy on credit. Most of us cannot plunk down a full cash payment for our houses or our cars. We have to pay them off over time, and we have to pay a little interest for doing so. That is a no-brainer. It is also accepted as a no-brainer that we know what we are going to pay.

For every contract, except for credit cards, the terms are stated up front and do not change. When Ed and Sue bought their house, there was a statement that they were given called "truth in lending." They were shown the amount that they were borrowing, the interest rate, and how much total interest they would pay over the life of the loan.

Most of us cringe when we see that total figure, but it is put before our eyes, so we are aware of what we are paying over the life of the loan.

The interest rate is right there in black and white, what it will be for each year of the loan. The terms are stated clearly, and you sign your name, agreeing to those terms. A month later, the mortgage broker can't call up Ed and say, "Oh, I see you were thirty seconds late on your car payment so I am going to increase your interest rate on your home mortgage payment. More money for me! Too bad for you! It's always a pleasure doing business with you, bye-bye!"

The same standard contract rules apply for car loans too. When they bought a second car for Sue a few years ago, Ed and Sue again signed a contract that stated the terms clearly. The amount borrowed, the interest rate, and the total amount that will be paid over the duration of the loan were plain to see. That is how contract law is supposed to work. In *Secret History of Credit Cards*, Warren said, "I've read my credit card agreement, and I can't figure out the terms. I teach contract law, and the underlying premise of contract law is that the two parties to the contract understand what the terms are."

Credit card companies do not have to play by these rules. Ed and Sue bought a new television a few years ago for $1200. Unexpected medical bills came up when their son broke his leg and they were not able to pay off the balance in full. They were hit with a higher interest rate and a late fee for paying one day late. The balance had to roll over for a few months until they could pay it off, and that $1200 television ended up costing them nearly $2000 in a very short time.

The credit card issuers can raise interest rates, and lower credit limits, and tack on various fees, seemingly at whim. "It's Tuesday, let's raise the rates." Why do they do this? Because they can.

Turning on the Lights

How many times have you heard the phrase, "Let's shed a little light on this"? When we put something under the light, we see it for what it really is. When a child is afraid, the first thing we do is turn on the light and show them that there is nothing to be afraid of.

When it comes to *Debt Cures,* you get the benefit of the light shining and exposing the credit card industry for what it really is. Now you can see that there is nothing to be afraid of. The monster under the bed isn't real, and the monster behind the credit card fees can be defused. They might try to pick on the unwitting college student or poor person, but the bully never wins. In the end, he gets his comeuppance. No more stealing candy from babies. The candy is yours, and you get to decide who to share with.

CHAPTER 18

Three Ring Circus

"A few clowns short of a circus."

"Ladies and gentlemen, children of all ages, step right up and you will be amazed. Right before your very eyes, we will try to make your money disappear." That may be the favorite line of circus ringmasters and the credit card industry, but we're on to the tricks of the trade. Their dog and pony show is being told to take down their tents and hit the road.

(No offense intended to the trapeze artists and acrobats and all the great talents of the circus. Personally, I enjoy the lion tamers.)

Yingling and Friends' Circus

In the documentary *Secret History of Credit Cards,* the president of the American Bankers Association, Edward Yingling, was interviewed. He is the guy that hangs out with the politicians and fights for the banking and credit card industry to be able to keep on doing what they are doing. That's right – appalling interest rates, exorbitant fees, and a penalty mentality. An excerpt of the interview follows:

> INTERVIEWER: Have you ever read the contract that's sent to you with your credit card?

> EDWARD YINGLING: Yes. But I'm a lawyer. *[laughs]*

INTERVIEWER: Do you understand it?

EDWARD YINGLING: I do understand it. I think it'd be very hard for a lot of people to understand. And I think it's a constant battle to try to figure out how you make disclosures and those types of things in plain English so that somebody will read them.

The mortgage lenders and the folks who give us our car loans have figured out a way to make a contract that we can understand. We usually don't like the gargantuan figure that represents the total interest that we will have paid at the end of the contract, but at least there are no surprises. Paying interest is hard enough when you know what you are paying. Paying surprise fees and interest rates that magically grow overnight like Pinocchio's nose or Jack's magic beanstalk gets a little absurd.

Master Illusionists

They want to keep you blindfolded!

Credit card contracts are designed by credit card company lawyers to keep the credit card issuers and banks in business. If they keep us, the consumer, the everyday citizen, guessing in the dark, they really don't care. When Yingling talked about credit cards and the confusion that most people have regarding their terms, he was not at all apologetic. He stated that, "The product is not a promise to somebody that we will lend you that amount of money forever at that interest rate." The credit card companies just don't want us to know when things change. What we don't know will hurt us.

Professor Elizabeth Warren argues that credit card companies should put a one-line sentence on the monthly billing statement, directly under the amount of the minimum payment, that simply states, "The balance of xx dollars at the current interest rate of xx percent will take xx months to pay off." Full disclosure should be so easy, but Yingling said that would be impossible. He claims that there are too many variables to run such a calculation for every statement, and the customer would make more purchases, causing the calculation to be moot. That is not the point that Ms. Warren was making. Down and dirty: show how long this balance at this interest rate would take to pay off in full. If we can put a man on the moon, and the credit card companies can, at the drop of a hat, pull thousands of FICO scores, computed by a complicated algorithm, the calculation of a pay off timeframe should not be a problem.

But they do not want you to know. And they keep changing the interest rates.

Send in the Clowns

Their pals in Washington aren't going to do anything about the industry and all the complaints either. I hear the saying, "Power corrupts and absolute power corrupts absolutely." It seems to fit.

Let's return to the interview.

INTERVIEWER: How profitable is the credit card industry?

EDWARD YINGLING: The credit card business is profitable.

(Let me interrupt for one brief second. That is the weakest response to an interview question that I have ever heard.)

INTERVIEWER: I thought it was the most profitable sector in the banking industry.

EDWARD YINGLING: I think it depends on how you define sectors....

(Another interruption. When we start saying things like, "It depends on how you define...," it usually means we are avoiding the subject.)

INTERVIEWER: MBNA's profits last year, one and a half times that of McDonald's.

EDWARD YINGLING: Well, McDonald's didn't do too well last year.

(Sorry, I have to interject again. This interview took place in September 2004. I didn't look up profit numbers for McDonald's, but doesn't McDonald's do well every year? The credit card banks do better than McDonald's. Admit it.)

INTERVIEWER: I know that there are different ways to gauge profitability, but it seems they're [credit card banks] doing quite well.

EDWARD YINGLING: They're doing quite well; I would agree with that.

INTERVIEWER: Citibank is more profitable than Microsoft, Wal-Mart, and the executives are highly paid.

EDWARD YINGLING: Right, right.

In the beginning of the interview, Yingling was asked to describe the benefits of credit cards. He talked for a couple of paragraphs about how much his industry has done for the consumer. His conclusion – "When you think about it, it's really an incredible system...."

If you are interested in reading the complete interview, you can go to: http://www.pbs.org/wgbh/pages/frontline/shows/credit/interviews/yingling.html.

Trained Animal Acts

It is not just the credit card companies who like to play games with your money. Lending a helping hand is no longer the motto of the money lending industry. Car dealers, bankers, and anyone who is in the position of making some money off a person by giving them a finance deal, all have been known to take advantage of their trusting consumers. The temptation to pocket a little more if they can is too strong and the unwitting customer makes it too easy. Bankers, automobile finance departments, almost any kind of lender – they all try to present the image that they are your friends, the ones that you can turn to when you need financial help. All too often, their so-called "help" gets the trusting customer into deeper debt and deeper trouble.

Anthony had a mortgage on his current house for $200,000. He had a buyer and a contract for the sale of this house. Anthony found another house to buy in the country, with a little land and room for horses. Before the first sale was complete, the banker gave Anthony a new mortgage, another $200,000, on the new property. The pending sales contracts for both properties were being handled "for sale by owner," with no realtor involved.

The sale of his current house fell through when the buyer's employer was bought out by a foreign company. The buyer lost his job. The bank would not give him a mortgage with no job. That meant, "no contract." Anthony no longer had a buyer for his house. Anthony's purchase contract on the country property was not contingent on the sale of his current house, because he thought it was a sure thing. Anthony was now stuck with two mortgages that he could not afford.

His banker had known that this was a possibility, but gladly gave him two full mortgages, no offer of a bridge loan, and no friendly advice that the payments of two mortgage loans might be too steep for Anthony's income. The lender had all his financial information and ignored basic customer service. He only saw a jackpot for himself. With a smile, the banker said, "Glad that I could help you out."

> We use our credit cards 52 million times a day.

Who helped who in this scenario? The banker is now collecting interest on two mortgages. Anthony is saddled with two house payments. By not defaulting on the mortgage payments, his other expenses are being paid by credit card. The situation is a freight train ready to derail. Maybe it could have been avoided if the helpful, friendly banker had given financial advice, or had simply looked carefully at Anthony's income, and said, "I'm sorry, but you don't qualify for two mortgages." Instead, he just looked at the dollars that would be coming to him and his bank.

There are more stories than you would ever care to read about people who get caught up in debt. It happens so quickly. Something puts us in a bind, and we turn to our credit cards to make it through. I imagine that since you are flipping the pages of *Debt Cures*, you or someone close to you needs the solutions and the methods to get out of debt and on to the real task at hand, creating wealth. Everything in this book applies to each of us. Get out of debt. Get on your way to wealth. The credit card industry may delight in our pain, but our pain is no more.

Fire Eating Sword Swallowers

What irks me is that the financial lending industry does not have to be so greedy. They are doing just fine, and the credit card banks needn't worry about ever going out of business. Here in America, we use our credit cards 52 million times a day. That's 36,242 times a minute that cards are being swiped. Shopping malls, grocery stores, restaurants, gas stations, fast food joints. Our credit cards see a lot of action. The credit card issuers get a percentage on every purchase. Over 36,000 purchases a minute should be bringing down a hefty income.

Also, for the record, I have no quarrel with credit card-issuing banks, charging a reasonable interest rate. That is part of the deal with credit cards. Charge some interest. Make a healthy profit. The banks and card issuers would make cushy incomes with that factor alone, but they are not satisfied with that, and they want more. They are out for – you know what I am going to say – *obscene profits.* I have but one word to say to them. Tough.

We can fire back. And you already know how. Pick up the phone.

Human Cannonballs

1. **Call all your credit card companies and ask that they lower your interest rate.**

   The problem is not that you use your credit cards. The problem is that the banks and credit card companies are also using your credit cards! They did not steal them out of your wallet to make false purchases, but they sure are using them to their full advantage, to get you for every possible dollar in interest. How do you fire back? Negotiate a better interest rate!

   Kathleen had a large balance on her credit card and an alarming 22% interest rate. With one quick and simple phone call, Kathleen got her rate lowered. The customer service representative was very pleasant and Kathleen said very politely: "Hello, I am looking at my credit card statement and I noticed that my interest rate is higher than it used to be. I know that when I got the card it had an introductory interest rate. Is there any way I can have that rate back?"

   All you have to do is ask!

   Repeat these words: "Can you lower my rate?" Those are the golden words to know. The credit card company lowered

Kathleen's rate. You are a very pleasant and polite person, and I bet they'll probably do the same for you!

Let's use some rough estimates to calculate the savings for Kathleen. There are interest and loan calculators on the internet that you can use. I am just trying to illustrate the point, so my figures are approximate. Kathleen's interest rate got knocked down from 22% to 9%. She had a balance of close to $8000. Even making just the minimum payment would allow her to pay off the credit card in half the time and save over $13,000 in interest! That really is astounding!

You can make your calls and work out your own figures. Then tell all your friends, so that they too can wield the same power.

Your telephone is a great weapon, so use it. Ready, aim, fire!

2. **Call all your credit card companies and ask that they remove annual fees.**

Many cards today do not charge annual fees because of the competition between credit card issuers. Once one company stopped assessing the annual fee, most followed suit in order to keep customers. Annual fees used to be standard though, and some credit cards that offer perks and rewards, like airline flyer miles, often charge an annual fee; sometimes it may not show up on your statement until after the first year or after an introductory period of six months. Review your statements each month.

Ed and Sue still had an old card that carried an annual fee, along with a couple rewards cards that charged annual fees too. There are simply too many credit card options out there today to pay an annual fee. Don't do it. If you see an annual fee show up on your statement, call and ask that it be removed. Most of the time, they should remove it. Two minutes of your time is certainly worth fifty bucks per card. "Hi, this is Ed Jones. I see on my statement that I was charged an annual fee, and I was hoping that you could waive that fee."

If at first you don't succeed, try, try again. Talk to a manager. Odds are in your favor that the fee will be removed. If not, stop using that card. It can be that simple. Remember, the ball is in your court. If you tell them that you are going to transfer your balance elsewhere, they usually will drop the annual fee.

In the big picture of life and money, you might think at first that getting rid of an annual fee is no measurable savings. If you had a card with a $50 annual fee and mindlessly paid it every year for thirty years, you would be wasting $1500. That $1500 could be used for other purposes, or invested, and over time would be worth several thousands more. We would never hold a fifty dollar bill in our fist and light it with a match and watch it burn away to ash. Yet that is exactly what we are doing if we are paying any annual fees to our credit card companies.

3. **Call all your credit card companies and ask for a higher credit limit.**

If you are a good customer, a balance-carrying-paying-the-minimum-each-month kind of good customer, the credit card issuer will raise your credit limit before you can say "thank you very much." If they have you where they want you, they certainly want to keep you there. You don't have to give a reason as to why you want a higher credit limit, but if they ask, you can say the words they love to hear – balance transfer. Tell them that you are planning to do a balance transfer from another card and want to be able to put the whole amount on their card, but that would require a higher credit line than you currently have. They would be delighted to help you out.

The real reason that you want a higher credit line on your card is for your credit score and your goal of improving it in any way you can. As I stated before, credit scores are lowered if your balances are too close to the credit limits. If you have a $1000 credit limit on your credit card, and your balance is $800, the FICO calculation counts that as a negative rating factor. Although I think that is stupid, we can work with it. Keeping your balances low, ideally at about 30%-35% of the total available credit, is good for your credit score. So make the calls and get your limits raised. The same $800 balance on your card with a new $2000 or $2500 credit limit will boost your credit score.

Ed called his credit card companies and asked each one to raise his credit limit. Some asked him why and some didn't bother to ask. Each one agreed to raise it. Doing this may not show a dollar savings at the time of the phone call, but improving the credit score helps all future dealings. And what is your plan for the future? To create wealth! Good credit can take you there. In fact, it can get you all the way to Millionaire Acres.

4. **Call all your credit card companies and ask that they remove late fees.**

This one is not a slam dunk. If it is your first late fee, you have a good chance that they will waive it. "Hello, this is Sue Jones. I see on my credit card statement that I was charged a late fee this month, and I have never been late, and I am hoping that it could be waived." If you have a good payment history with that card issuer, it is highly likely that they will waive the fee as a "courtesy." It was not so "courteous" of them to charge the fee in the first place, especially since you are such a good customer, but they do it. They do it all the time and they hope that you don't bother to ever look at your statement.

If you are perpetually late, all bets are off. But it never hurts to call. You never know for sure until you try, so explain that you mailed your payment on time and you have no idea how it could be late. For the first time that you make a late payment, it is definitely worth one phone call to save $29 or $39. In most cases, they should waive it. The odds go down with every late payment you make. Your pocket or theirs? You make the call.

Prior to reading this book, you probably assumed, as most people do, that one late payment is not a big deal. Now we know how the credit card companies pounce on that one late payment and try to use it to spin a web of fees. Now that we know, we won't give them the opportunity anymore. As unfair as it is, that one late payment can mean a late fee, an end to a good interest rate, and a trigger of universal default. So call and try to remove every late payment, and then stop making late payments. Pay on time. It really is in your best interest.

The Strongman (and Woman)

There are hundreds of examples of ecstatic people who have used the *Debt Cures* methods, and real results happened immediately! Not only do these phone calls save you money today, they save you money for the life of that balance. Simply calling the credit card-issuing bank produces awesome results. Lowering your interest rate can cut your debt in half! Sometimes even more. That is instant gratification, and that is power.

> You can join thousands of success stories!

Dennis had a credit card balance of about $15,000, with an interest rate of 14.99%. One phone call, which kept him on the line for ten minutes, netted a new interest rate of 9.9%. Making only the minimum monthly payment, Dennis can pay off his balance about two years sooner and save close to $5000! That is a great way to use ten minutes of your time. Sometimes the savings are not as substantial as Dennis', but any dollar in your pocket will serve you better than paying it to the lending institutions.

You can join the success stories!

Bettie: With one quick phone call, my rate was lowered from 12% to 6.9%! That will save me close to $2500!

Ty: I called my credit card companies and all three raised my credit limits and dropped my interest rates! I now carry interest rates of 12%, 14.9%, and 15.3%. Not the greatest, but a real improvement. I will call back in a couple months and ask again!

James: I was on the phone with the customer service representative for about five minutes. She was very polite, and it was easy! My rate is now 12.99% – down from 17.99%! This can save me about $1200! What a relief!

Jay: I had great credit, always paid my bills. I was shocked when I saw my interest rate went up for no reason. When I called, I was told that I had been late on a payment to another credit card – so they could raise my rate! I was angry, but the customer service person gave me back my old interest rate. I will pay attention to my statement every month from now on.

Joanne: I can't believe it! My interest rate is now 8.9%! It was an outrageous 22%, and I was not even aware that it was so high! This lower interest rate will save me thousands! Maybe even $10,000!

Max: My balance was not going down every month, it was going up! Fees, fees, fees! I had no idea. There was an annual fee, plus I was over my limit, and I didn't know it. They were charging me an overlimit fee of $35 each month.

They waived the annual fee and the overlimit fee as a "courtesy." Now I know to pay attention to my monthly statement and check for fees! I will pay down my balance and call back to ask for a better interest rate!

Wallace: I was skeptical, but with one phone call, my late payment fee and my overlimit fee were removed. I am amazed.

Sherri: I had a promotional deal that ended. I called my credit card company and asked for the same rate, since I still had a balance. They could not give me the special 4.99% anymore, but instead of my rate going to 13.9%, they gave me a rate of 9.9%! This will save me close to $1000!

Michael: I called up my credit card company and asked what my rate was – she said 12%. I asked what kind of rate specials they had, and I now am at 9.9%! They really do have specials. She told me to call back every month to see if they are offering anything better!

Denise: I have a very high balance on my credit card right now – over $12,000. I know the interest alone was killing me. I was afraid to find out what the interest rate was, but I asked. I had a 13% interest rate, but the customer service person knocked it down to below 10% – anything under 10% is good for me right now.

Tori: I have an automatic payment set up each month from my checking account to pay on my credit card. My minimum payment went up, and I didn't know it, so what I paid was less than the minimum. The credit card company said I was late and they raised my interest rate! It really made me mad!

I make timely payments every month – it comes right out of my checking account to be sure that I do! And they still screw me! My interest rate nearly doubled! I was so angry. I calmed down and then I made my call. They put my interest rate back to where it was, but it is so unfair that they can mess with my interest rate like that. I have always been a good-paying customer. I am just grateful that I knew to check my statement and that I knew to make the call.

I could go on and on, but I hope you get the idea. These kinds of methods have helped people just like you. The stories of success are as varied as the population across America, and each one is a nudge to you to pick up the telephone. Go ahead! What are you waiting for? The simple things in life are indeed often the best, and this simple technique works! Why pay off those ridiculous fees?! You do not have to! Make the calls! And send in your success story!

You Are the Ringmaster Now

Obviously, the banks, the credit card companies, and the entire consumer lending industry do not want you to know that you can save hundreds and thousands of dollars by calling them and making these simple requests. They want you to think that they are the mighty ones, and we, the common people, are weak. It's not true. Even the great and powerful Oz was exposed to be a mere mortal. You have absolutely nothing to lose, so pick up the phone and get started. Rehearse what you plan to say before making the call if you need a confidence boost. The most important thing that you need to remember: Knowledge is power. You have the power!

CHAPTER 19

Slaying the Dragons

"Perhaps I am stronger than I think."
~ Thomas Merton

The banks and the credit card companies want to keep you under their thumb, making you think that they hold the control and that you must bow to their every command. Hogwash and poppycock. Truth be told, you are not at the mercy of the banks, but they don't want you to know it!

The credit card companies need us, the average worker bees, the honest citizens of America. The competition among banks and credit card companies is fierce, and they need to maintain and attract new customers. If lowering your interest rate keeps you as a customer, they probably will do it. You may have to talk to a supervisor, but when it is your money at stake, talk to ten people if you have to. Threatening to switch to another credit card bank usually works. It is the card issuer who is faced with a choice: Give you a fair rate and still make some money; or don't lower the rate, and not get another dime off this account, because you can, and will, switch banks.

Don't be intimidated and don't give up. Persistence pays off! After the first telephone call you make with a successful result, I guarantee that you will feel invigorated! Ed and Sue did. They tackled each credit card and were rewarded for their efforts with reduced rates, removed fees, and raised credit limits. It took a couple hours on the telephone, and it was worth every minute. The increase in dollars saved was equal to the increase in their self-confidence. Instead of feeling victimized, they feel victorious.

What's in a Number?

Many people don't understand what a big deal the interest rate really is until they see the numbers laid out before them. We'll use the figure of $8000, since that is the national average credit card balance in America. If the minimum payment is 4% of the $8000 balance, your monthly payment is $320. Let's say that you borrowed $8000 from your father, and he charged you no interest at all. Even dads are allowed to charge a little bit of interest, but for this example, your father did not. If you paid him back $320 each month, you would have repaid him in full in 25 months. Two years and one month. No interest. You are now debt-free and have a fantastic father.

Now, let's show what happens when you pay interest to your credit card company. Same balance of $8000 and the minimum monthly payment is $320. Every point you can lower your interest rate will save you money!

Interest Rate	# of Months Until Paid Off in Full	Total Interest Paid
6%	125 months	$1,125
8%	130 months	$1,575
10%	136 months	$2,071
12%	143 months	$2,622
16%	159 months	$3,131
20%	180 months	$5,612

Donna has $8000 in debt and only can make the minimum monthly payment. With a few phone calls, she got her rate down to 8%. At the end of her payments, she will have paid $1,575 in interest fees. Cheryl has no idea that she can call her creditors and reduce her rate. She has a card with an outrageous 20% interest rate. It will take her 180 months to pay off her $8000 balance. That is fifteen years! She will end up paying $5,612 in interest. That is nearly four times higher than what Donna will have paid for the same amount of credit. Somebody needs to tell Cheryl to pick up the phone and make a call.

Your Life Won't Always Be This Way

If you carried the average $8000 balance and did not have the fees and penalties and interest tacked on by the credit card companies, you would be able to pay off your debt and live your life without the relentless pressure of bills and creditors and collectors. It is a numbers game, and they want to keep you oblivious, somehow thinking that you are at fault for what they have created. You have nothing to be ashamed of. The debt that they are burdening you with is an illusion, manufactured by the credit card industry!

Is there a "Not tonight, I have a headache" fee?

We live in a country that allows the creditors to create fees, one for every day of the week, and twice on Saturdays and Sundays: stop payment fee, annual fee, over-the-limit fee, late payment fee, finance fee, cash advance fee, declined check fee, research fee....

Did I miss any? You get the point. Those are all fees that you can see on your monthly statement. I did not make up any of those. The banks did. Plus, the interest rates have skyrocketed in recent years, and often, the cardholder is not even aware that his or her rate has gone up. Credit card debt is out of control, and debt collectors have whirled and whorled out of control as well.

Debt Avoidance ≠ Debt Riddance

Being in debt over your head is a dreadful situation, but it is just that – a situation; and remember that it is only temporary. The banks and credit card companies want you to be in debt forever, but with the methods of *Debt Cures*, you will get to the end of the tunnel.

The goal is to get rid of your debt, not just simply close your eyes to it. Don't ignore your debt problems. First, you conquer the bad debt, and then you move on to the creation of wealth. Always keep that thought running in your mind, and it will help you through the unpleasant times of debt and debt collectors.

A common reaction to debt problems is avoidance. I hope you have learned by reading these pages so far that avoiding the issue does not make it go away. You will only make things worse in the long run, so don't bury your head in the sand. Don't sit at the bar and tell Joe to pour you another strong one. Taking action is the best thing to cure your debt and to boost your confidence.

Lame Excuses

Don't dream up excuses to tell your creditors. You are not the one to blame, but you are the one who has the power to turn the tables. Lame excuses are what the creditors tell. Try asking a credit card customer service representative what a "membership fee" is and they will recite a paragraph of meaningless babble, instead of just telling you it is a way of charging you an annual fee without you knowing that you are paying an annual fee. Membership has its privileges. Or something like that.

Some of us, of a certain age, remember when the comedian Steve Martin had dark hair and an arrow through his head. He had a comedy bit where he promised to tell you how to be a millionaire and never pay taxes. That's right; how to be a millionaire and never pay taxes. "First, get a million dollars." Big laughs. "Then, when the Internal Revenue Service calls you up and says you have not paid your taxes, you simply say, 'I forgot!'"

The IRS certainly does not work that way and neither do your creditors. You have real reasons as to why you are having trouble paying your debts, but the real truth is that the lending institution really does not care what your reasons are. They want your money; not your excuses, not your stories, and not your jokes.

The Next Battle

Ed and Sue's next-door neighbors, Steve and Maria, had fallen on hard times when they both suddenly lost their jobs. Steve and Maria had believed that it was a smart idea that they both worked at the same place. They only had to have one car, so they saved in commuting costs. Always responsible with their money, they even had their car paid off. Steve and Maria never anticipated that they would both suddenly be without jobs, with no notice to prepare. One day, they showed up for work and there was no company to work for. With both of them out of work, the bills piled up so quickly, it scared them. They let fear overtake them, and they worried about everything. In their panic, they wrongfully assumed that bankruptcy was the only way to get out of the financial mess that they had unexpectedly found themselves in.

The first thing that Ed and Sue told Steve and Maria to do: Lose the worry and the fear. It does nothing to help the situation. Lying awake at night or arguing with your spouse does nothing to cure the debt. The next thing they did was give them a copy of this book.

Ed and Sue were so energized by their success in making the phone calls to the credit card companies that had saved them thousands of dollars, they encouraged Steve and Maria to do the same. They told Steve and Maria to go one step further – call the credit card companies and negotiate a settlement.

Steve and Maria really were at the end of their financial rope. They were shocked to learn that negotiating a settlement directly with the credit card companies was even a possibility. They had made an appointment with a bankruptcy lawyer and were not asked any questions over the phone, just, "We'll see you next week." They were surprised to hear that there might be other options. The credit card companies want to get their money and do not want to resort to collections if they don't have to. Jump the gun and beat them to the punch.

Steve called his credit card company and explained that he had not been making his payments because he and his wife had both lost their jobs, and were, in fact, meeting with a bankruptcy lawyer next week. He explained that they currently had no income and had wiped out their savings paying their house payment. Based on the *Debt Cures* advice, Steve sent in his financial statements showing his net worth, which proved that he had no ability to pay. It took a few phone calls and some letters, and Steve and Maria were able to settle their credit card fees for half of what they owed! Fifty cents on the dollar is not bad!

Take Note

Make notes of your conversations with creditors and bill collectors, and take down full names of everyone you speak to. You can record the telephone conversations, if you want, depending upon what state you live in. In California, Connecticut, Delaware, Florida, Massachusetts, Maryland, Michigan, Montana, Nevada, New Hampshire, Pennsylvania, and Washington, it is illegal to record a phone conversation unless you have the other person's consent. In the rest of the 38 states, I believe it is allowed (but check with your attorney!).

Make sure you have the settlement in writing before you send in money, and make sure you have a source that will loan you the money so you can indeed pay the settlement by the specified date. If you do not pay the credit card company by the specified deadline, they can call the deal off.

Settling with the credit card companies is a little known opportunity that few people are aware of. If you go to bankruptcy court, the credit card company's chances of getting anything almost evaporate, so they usually are willing to negotiate with you.

Another reason to settle directly with the creditors is to avoid the dragons of the financial lending industry, the debt collection agencies. They breathe fire and just may eat babies. And I bet a lot of those guys are covered in scales.

The Dragon Has Been Slayed

The dragon had seemed so big, and scary, and powerful. We cowered in the corner of the dungeon and assumed the worst, that he would scorch us and then have us for dinner. Then the dragon slayer strolled in, calm, cool, and collected. He saw that although the dragon was ugly, he was not as strong as we were led to believe. The dragon slayer didn't carry a sword or a fire extinguisher. Under his arm, he carried a book called *Debt Cures,* and it was a mighty weapon indeed. Fear was banished from the kingdom and the people were restored to prosperity. The fortune teller came to town and predicted, "In your future, I see great wealth."

CHAPTER 20

Stop Debt Collectors Cold

"Mean, gritty, dirty and low"
~ description of a movie called *The Debt Collector*

Debt collection agencies pretty much operate in one of two ways. The credit card company may hire them to be the hit man, the guy who threatens cement shoes unless you pay up. When the debt collection agency is hired as the bounty hunter, the collector gets paid a percentage of what they collect from you. The more money that they can wring out of you, by any tactic, the more money they make in their commission fee. They turn over the collected money to the creditor and they pocket their fee.

Sometimes the credit card company sells the debt to a debt collector. This practice is becoming more and more common. "Debt buying" is turning into a profitable venture for a lot of corrupt schemers. Basically, the credit card company sells the right to collect on the debt, and the agency then gets to keep whatever it collects from you. The creditor gets his money up front and is done with it. So again, the more money that the collector can squeeze from you, the more money that goes into their velvet-lined cash boxes. The agents that work for the debt collection companies are typically paid on commission, so the more they pull out of you, the more they get, and the more the company gets. The agent's name goes right to the top of the scoreboard posted in their office, otherwise known as the den of wolves.

The "Lyin' Den"

There is a line from an old country song that goes something like: Mamas, don't let your babies grow up to be cowboys. Let me add to that: Mamas, don't let your babies grow up to be debt collection agency employees. These men, and women, are the henchmen of the consumer lending industry. There may not be a word in the dictionary for "henchwoman," but they exist out there. These gals and guys are petty and ruthless and will stoop to any level to squeeze a dime out of you. I think they could eat rocks, and it would not upset their stomachs. There is not a colder breed of humans on the planet.

The tales of their duplicity are endless, and yet nothing is done to rein them in. It is no secret that some collection agencies break the law, yet day after day, their cruel tactics continue. If you are not to the point that you are dealing with collection agencies, good. Follow the advice given so far and you will stay out of their clutches. For those of you who are in the den of dragons, there is a way out.

Contrary to popular opinion, money is not the root of all evil; the love of money is. The greed, the ugly desire to grab the grub at all costs, is what ruins people. The resume of a debt collector would probably boast his or her top three qualities as being boldly unethical, taking pride in having questionable morals, and functioning as a specialist in harassment. Many people make the mistake of trying to reason with their debt collector. Many debt collectors are not reasonable people.

Fair Practices

As we've heard from our parents, our teachers, and our mentors, life is not always fair. We know that. The whole way that the credit card industry does business is not fair, but it is legal, so we march on. We citizens of good character don't have to revolt, exactly. Staging a Boston Tea Party type of demonstration where we all cut up our credit cards and toss them into the ocean, or the local cesspool, is not the solution.

Credit itself is not the enemy. We are going to talk about good credit versus bad credit shortly, and how we can use good credit to achieve amazing wealth. Credit is not the evil that needs to be rallied against. The tactics of the entire consumer lending industry are the wicked devices that need improving.

Because credit card debt is at an all-time high, and the fees and penalties and interest rates are at all-time highs, credit card delinquencies are in full bloom. The collection agencies are tickled. Business is booming for them. Debt is big business, and the creditors and collectors are the sharks who are circling, because they smell blood.

Know Your Rights

The debt collectors do have rules that they are supposed to adhere to, but that does not mean that they will. However, if you know your rights, you can understand that the fire-breathing dragon really is nothing but hot air.

Under a law that was passed called the Fair Debt Collection Practices Act, debt collectors MAY NOT:

- ✔ Contact you earlier than 8 a.m. or later than 8 p.m.
- ✔ Contact you by phone after you have requested in writing that they stop.
- ✔ Contact you at work despite their knowledge of your employer's disapproval.
- ✔ Tell people, like your boss or family members, that you owe money.
- ✔ Tell you that they will take your wages.
- ✔ Tell you that they can have you arrested.
- ✔ Tell you that they will sue you. (Only your creditors can sue you.)
- ✔ Send you papers that look like court papers.
- ✔ Talk to anyone but you. (They are not supposed to talk to your kids.)

This act came about because Congressional findings in 1977 stated there was "abundant evidence of the use of abusive, deceptive, and unfair debt collection practices by many debt collectors. Abusive debt collection practices contribute to the number of personal bankruptcies, to marital instability, to the loss of jobs, and to invasions of individual privacy."

Don't talk; they'll use it against you.

True, and the intentions of the act were good, but "deceptive, unfair, or abusive" is in the eye of the beholder. Yelling at you, swearing at you, and telephone harassment have been determined to be "abusive," but there is still a lot of gray area. Debt collectors push. You can push back.

Pardon my course language, but you don't have to take their crap. Now that you know the basic ground rules, you are better equipped to deal with the obnoxious debt collectors who left their hearts, and their manners, somewhere else when they left for work.

The most important lesson for you to remember is that you do not have to talk to a debt collector until you are ready to face them, armed with knowledge. It is as easy as hanging up the phone. You do not have to return their calls. Until you are ready, do not talk to them. They want you to think that they have a crystal ball and know your every move. They don't. Don't give them any information. Remember, and review, the *Debt Cures* methods detailed previously in Chapter 4 where I talked about how you can eliminate your debt!

Unfair Practices

These collectors are trained to be aggressive and are trained to lie. They operate in a boiler room with a competitive tally board posted to show who had the most kills, or collections. They get an adrenaline rush from sticking it to you. One power-charged collector stated in the movie *Maxed Out* that "it feels great." He likened the high he got to "throwing a touchdown pass and getting paid for it." He was making a nice living, paying his bills by preying on people who were having trouble paying theirs. He called the underworld of collections a "fun industry. It's competitive and you get your paycheck." The daily score-board was a great motivator for him to harass people like you.

Some employees of the collection agencies go the opposite direction, or so it may seem. They are taught to operate on your emotions and get you talking. They use the "sympathetic" approach to try to get you to open up. Some will give a fake name, but they want you to "trust" them. They pretend to care about your problems and will listen to you. Be warned. The information you give them will be used against you.

Janice fell for this scheme. The collector oozed kindness and compassion on the phone. He asked questions that appeared innocent, and he seemed to have empathy with her struggles. He even told her how she reminded him of his own mother. Janice told him that she was working part-time as a waitress, trying to make ends meet. Now he knows the name of her employer and how much she makes because she volunteered the information.

Respect Yourself

Information is power. Do not give it to them. Attorney Richard DiMaggio states that, "The collector is not, and never will be, your friend... Tell the collector nothing. They do not care about you, and any question they ask should be ignored. You may owe a bill, but you owe the collector nothing – not even respect."

Also, a word to the wise: Per the Fair Debt Collection Practices Act, collectors *have to* stop calling you on the phone once they're *asked* to do so. After you do that, in accordance with the Act's requirements, type up and mail them a brief letter that restates your "requests": stop calling me at my home, stop calling me where I work.

> Don't let them mess with your self-respect!

Write It Down

Keeping track of all communication is important. The very first time you get a phone call about any alleged debt collection effort, write it down. Keep a simple notebook detailing the date, the time of the call, the name of the collection agent (whatever name they give you anyway), the name of their company, and what he or she said. Having a log is so much easier than trying to remember it later on, and if you do end up filing a complaint, your notebook will have all the information for you.

Simply enter a few lines of information:

January 10, 2007. 8:10 pm. Telephone call from Bob Bulldog from Expert Liars Collection Agency. Bob wanted a payment on a credit card debt to MegaBank. He said the debt was $4000. I said I didn't know about such a debt. He kept talking. I told him that a debt to MegaBank didn't ring a bell, and asked if he could send me all the information he had on this alleged debt. I told him to not call me at home and to not call me at work. I told him to communicate with me only in writing. Bob did not seem happy, but was not rude. Bob said he would put my request in his files.

This notebook is off to a great start. Notice that the collection agent already did one thing that he is not supposed to do. He called after 8:00 pm. Usually, debt collectors don't wilt on the first try. Bob called back.

January 11, 2007. 8:30 pm. Collection Agent Bob called again. I said that I had asked him not to call me, and that I had sent off a letter today, putting the request in writing. He cut me off and said that they didn't have any letter yet. He said this account was seriously delinquent, and he expected payment. He said it was his job to keep calling until the debt was satisfied. He was belligerent and said he would call my boss and garnish my wages to get the debt paid off. I said he had no right to do that under the Fair Practices Act. I told him to stop calling me and that if he didn't, I would file a complaint with the attorney general and the FTC. I hung up.

It is a very easy thing to do, to keep a record like this. Again, the collection agent called after the hours allowed, and this time, he made a bogus threat. When the very first call happens, you do not know how it will progress, so it is wise to keep a record. Try to jot down exact quotes of what the collection agent said, like, "I will call your boss."

Don't let them bully you. With the methods provided in *Debt Cures,* you can free yourself from debt collectors, once and for all.

Modern Day Pirates

Collection agency employees take pride in their tenacious ability to use fear or humiliation on their unsuspecting prey. Good old-fashioned scare tactics work on a vast majority of people. Grace was certain that she would lose her house because the collector told her so. The collector broke the law by saying that, but he figured that Grace was naïve, and he was right. Barry was a proud man who believed if he did not pay off the collection agency, he was somehow less of a man. Martin was humiliated when the collector began calling his boss, his neighbors, and his family members. The collector asked them questions about Martin and his employment. It was a real disgrace to Martin when his mother and his sister called him, asking what was wrong, and why they were getting phone calls about him.

> They lie, threaten, and intimidate. Don't fall for it!

One puffed-up young man boasted about his skills as a collection agent and said that he was a master of his craft. He compared himself to a pirate on a pirate ship, and the debtor gets walked out on the plank. "You want to push them out on that plank as far as possible without making them jump."

Modern Day Monsters

Here's what one other collector said to a lady: "You shouldn't be having children if you can't afford to pay their hospital bills." He has no legal right to make such a comment! There is no reason in the world that any of us should put up with abuse like that. These collection gangsters think they can dish out whatever they want. Their warped sense of power from getting away with too much for too long has them strutting their stuff like they were some kind of villain from an action cartoon. Collectors will make illegal statements. They will bluff and outright lie. They will try to shame and humiliate you. They will threaten to sue you when they have no legal leg to stand on. Guess what? If they do, you can turn the tables and sue *them*!

Most people do not know this, and they take the awful abuse from the collection agency callers. The collectors specialize in making you feel guilty about not paying your debt. They play on your basic human decency, something they wholly lack. They know that you are a good, honest, law-abiding person, and they will use every dirty trick in the book to try to make you feel bad about yourself. Stripping you of your self-confidence is their standard procedure. Don't let them.

Deception Playbook

Every occupation has its tricks of the trade, and every profession has conferences and training seminars. Debt collectors are no different. They want to improve their methods for getting to you. There are Boy Scout camps; and then there are boys and girls, grown-up boys and girls, who go off to a type of boot camp for debt collectors. These are two totally different kinds of environments.

One group learns how to tie knots; the other group learns how to tie people up in knots. The debt collector campers are taught what to say and how to say it. They are highly practiced in when to fake sympathy, when to pretend to be mad, and when to go for the kill. They study methods of getting under your skin. They might even bite the heads off of chickens, but I can't say for sure.

They are well aware that anyone who has reached the collection process has no doubt suffered in some way – a job loss, a health crisis, a divorce, or even a death in the family. These guys and gals have no qualms, kicking a man when he's down.

Do not underestimate the lies and the deception of a debt collector. They will debase themselves like no other profession. A collection agent from San Diego was sent to prison in 2006 because he lied that he was a lawyer and that he could have the alleged debtors tossed in jail, unless they paid him. That is one of the oldest tricks in the Debt Deception Handbook, yet innocent people still fall for it. Don't fall for it!

Common Threats

If the harasser calling you threatens to have you arrested, he is blowing smoke. You cannot go to jail over any alleged debt. Debt collection is a civil matter. Your alleged debt is not a criminal case, and you cannot go to jail. The "I will have you arrested!" threat is a bald-faced lie. I always used to say that the collectors should be thrown in jail for lying like that; it is refreshing to learn that it has happened. Hopefully it will be the start of a new trend.

There is a long laundry list of threats that all the collectors are notorious for bellowing. One of their all-time favorites is: "I'll garnish your wages!" The truth is that, no, the debt collection agency will not garnish your wages. Most of the time, they have zero power to touch your wages. Nil, nada, none. They must have a judgment against you to do so. A judgment means that there was a lawsuit against you that went to court. You would be fully aware if they had gone to court and someone won a judgment against your wages. No lawsuit, no wage garnishment. Don't let them convince you otherwise. And believe me, they will try.

> They can't take your house or throw you in jail.

Another extremely common intimidation tactic is to threaten that he or she can take your house. Too many people think this is a true danger! They worry themselves sick, thinking that they're going to lose their home. The collection agency cannot take your house, unless the debt they are bothering you about is a debt that is secured by your house. That would only be your mortgage or a home equity loan. Most all other loans are not secured by your house. They love this bogus tactic because it gets people to pay. They have no right and no power to come after your house. Don't believe them!

Sad but true, threats of violence are still a part of the collection racket. The modern collection agents still use thinly-veiled threats, like "We know where you live!" as if a big bruiser of a guy is going to show up, grab you from your house, and throw you in the trunk of a big black car. You are not going to get your knee caps broken or end up at the bottom of the river. Some of these collection guys are as bad as thugs, and sometimes do threaten or imply harm may come your way. They just want to scare you. Such threats are illegal and you need to file a complaint with the FTC.

Empty Threats

Don't fall for their empty threats. You have debt trouble at the moment, period. End of story. This too shall pass. The guy calling you and harassing you could very easily be making a six-figure income, and he has no real sympathy for you or what you are going through. Your woes bore him. He is thinking about how he is going to spend his next bonus. That is why people stay in the debt collection profession – the money. They don't believe they are saving the world economy, or doing a noble deed. They like their income, plain and simple.

Debt collection is a multibillion-dollar industry. The debt collectors don't care one iota about you or your situation. Your circumstances do not matter to them. To them, you are just another hard-luck story, and all they care about is the scoreboard hanging over their cubicle. You will get their attention only when you are able to talk money.

So let's talk money.

A Cure

Damian and Martina had fallen on hard times when Damian's business crashed. They were still able to make the house payment, the car payment, and the orthodontics bill for their daughter's braces, but money was very tight. Martina's salary had allowed them to get by, barely, but they were falling behind on the credit card bills. Every day, a new statement came in the mail, the fees were growing, and they were feeling overwhelmed, like most debt-riddled people.

Damian and Martina had a lawyer friend help them draft their balance sheet and income statement. They gathered all their documentation, showing their original bills and all the fees that had compounded since Damian's business went under. Some creditors they contacted directly to work out a settlement on those debts. For the others, they worked with the collection agency. They reduced their overall debts by 50%! They were able to borrow from Martina's father and mother, who will allow them to pay back the debt when they get back on their feet. What had seemed like an insurmountable crisis was handled by calmly implementing the *Debt Cures* solutions.

Net Worth

Once you learn it is a numbers game, you have to play the numbers too. Even if you are getting calls from a collection agency, you can still contact the original creditor. If they have not sold off your debt, they may be willing to work with you. Tell them your story, but show them the numbers. Numbers do the talking in these kinds of conversations. This is where the personal financial statements, your balance sheet and your income statement, come into play. Maybe all you need is a very simple letter from your accountant. Quite often, it works wonderfully. Know what your bottom line is, and do not agree to pay more than that. Agreeing to pay a sum that you cannot possibly pay will not get you out of the sinking sand, so be real.

If the creditor is already out of the picture, they have sold your debt to the collection agency for pennies of what it was worth. Anything you can pay the collection agency is almost pure profit for them. Most people assume that you cannot negotiate. You can, and you should. Show them your original debts; show them all the arbitrary fees that piled up because of the crazy cutthroat credit card industry; and show them your financial condition and what you can pay. It could very well be that you can afford to pay nothing. Show them that in black and white.

The debt collector will see your financial statements and read your letter, which states very plainly: *this is my net worth, consisting of these assets — my house, my cars, and my wedding rings; these liabilities: mortgage loan debt, car loan debt, credit card debt #1, credit card debt #2, student loan debt, etc.* After looking at this, he or she will be more accessible and more realistic in his demands. He or she won't keep insisting that you pay the whole $80,000 that you owe if it is clear that all you could ever pay is $10,000. And maybe all you can pay is nothing. If you have a negative net worth, show it.

I cannot say it enough. Money talks. If you have no money, they will shut up.

Give It a Try

Present a professional case to the debt collectors and watch their superior attitude morph into a practical one of how they best can settle and still make their dime off your debt. They want to cut and run, so help them on their way.

If you have not already done so, draft your financial statements and a simple two-sentence letter. A sample balance sheet, income statement, and letter are provided as a guide for you and are included in the Appendix.

This successful formula works. In just 24 hours, virtually overnight, you can bring your debt down by one-third, one-half, or even two-thirds! Have a friend with accounting or legal experience help you draft your letter and your financial statements.

The collection agency does not have power over you. You do not have to be afraid of them. You can fight back. You can win.

Michelle was very skeptical and didn't know if she believed that the debt collectors could be taken care of, once and for always. She had nearly $100,000 in debt and thought that she had nowhere to go but bankruptcy. A friend convinced her to prepare an income statement and a balance sheet, along with drafting a letter to the collection agency. Michelle's debts were knocked down to the original $30,000 that she had incurred. Now Michelle is telling everyone to break free from their fears and follow the *Debt Cures* methods. Simple steps that anyone can follow to bring about astounding results!

You Have the Right to Remain Silent...or Speak Out

Do not forget that you have the right to sue the collection agency if they abused the Fair Debt Collection Practices Act. If they were "deceptive, unfair, or abusive," and you have documented your case, it may be a wise move. Creditors and debt collection agencies are frankly quite surprised when they get sued, and it is very expensive for them. When they review the dollars they have to spend for legal fees versus the amount of debt that they are trying to collect from you, it is almost always in their best interest to settle with you. If you do sue

Know your rights!

and get a settlement, the most important term to get in your settlement is that they will have the collection proceeding removed from your credit report. They can have this negative information removed, and you can start over with a clean slate. That alone can sometimes be worth any legal fees that it cost you to sue.

The numbers of complaints against debt collection agencies are soaring. You do not have to take their extremely aggressive practices. Know your rights, and what they can and cannot do. Take notes of the name, agency, date, and time of every collector you talk to, if you do talk to them. You will want to have good records of all communications, even if you have the matter promptly taken care of, and they settle amicably. You don't have to be a jerk just because they act that way. You just have to know the steps to take.

Tough Talk

Don't let them take advantage of you. Believe me, they will try. The New York attorney general sued a national debt collection agency for collecting on thousands of debts that could not even be proven to be real or collectible. Not only do they use every trick in the book, they make them up as they go. The Federal Trade Commission has won a $10.2 million judgment against a company in New Jersey for their illegal collection practices. The company overstated the debts that people owed and used the illegal threats that we discussed earlier. So just because some person on the phone is talking tough and telling you that you owe them, don't fall for it. And don't be afraid to file a complaint.

A Fighter

Sometimes, the only thing a person can do is fight back. An article ran in the *New York Times* about a woman who was put on the debt collection hit list for charges that didn't even belong to her. She got the bank to agree that she had never incurred those charges, but the debt had already been turned over to the collection agent who was barreling ahead full-steam. The article states:

> One New York City victim, Judith Guillet, complained and filed a police report in 2003 after receiving a Chase credit card bill for $2,300, including five charges from Amoco gasoline stations in the Bronx. She has never owned a car or had a driver's license.

> The bank agreed that the charges were not valid, but the debt case hung on because the bank turned it over to a collection agency. Last November, that agency obtained a court order, allowing it to freeze Ms. Guillet's bank account, even though it could not demonstrate that the debt was valid.

> "I felt helpless," said Ms. Guillet, a nurse who is retired on full disability. "I couldn't pay my rent, buy food or pay my electricity bills."

It took two years for this poor woman's bank account to get unfrozen. She was confused and fearful, and as she said, she felt helpless. That is why you need to arm yourself with the knowledge in this book so that you won't feel confused or afraid, and you are never, ever, helpless. Monitor your credit report regularly and always review each monthly credit card statement. If something does not make sense, call the credit card company.

Stop the Hound Dogs

Debt collectors may hound you at first, but you can nip them in the bud and stop them dead in their tracks. In 24 hours, you can take a situation that had you feeling despair to a state of repair. The creditors and debt collectors listen when the numbers speak. If the numbers on your balance sheet and income statement are screaming, "I have nothing," the collector will realize it is futile to keep with the scare tactics. They will become much more sensible in their dealings with you.

When you were a kid and wanted to borrow a dollar from your brother, and he said he didn't have it, maybe you didn't believe him at first. You kept asking him and bugging him relentlessly. He insisted that he was broke. Then you checked his piggy bank and his wallet – the one that he didn't know you knew where he hid it – and you saw that they both were indeed empty. You finally understood that he honestly did not have a dollar to give you. So what did you do? You left him alone.

Debt reduction methods are easy. You have every right to take full advantage of these solutions. They know it. That's why the banks and the credit card companies don't want this book in circulation. The consumer lending industry would most certainly prefer that I keep all their tactics to myself. Sorry, fellas, ain't gonna happen.

Enough is enough. If they would be satisfied with healthy profits and return to fair lending practices, I would shut up. If they continue to keep up with the outrageous methods of pinching every last penny out of the American citizen, then I will continue to expose them for what they are.

An obnoxious greedy industry should be shown for what it is. If they decide to change their ways, I'll be the first to applaud.

CHAPTER 21

Achieving Wealth

"Wealth is the ability to fully experience life."
~Henry David Thoreau

I heard a phrase a long time ago that went something like, "Being rich is having money; being wealthy is having time." That is a very telling statement. That is my wish for you, to have the time to enjoy your money, the wealth that you will create, and to relax and realize that the shadow of bad debt will not cloud your life forever. Bad debt can be a thing of the past, and it never needs to show its ugly mug in these parts ever again.

In the Beginning

Ed and Sue started out in the beginning of this book, feeling like an avalanche was washing over them. The bills were coming, and they kept paying, yet they never could get ahead. Any time they needed a little "extra" money, be it doctor bills or a new furnace or brakes for the car, they had to use their credit cards, and they were never able to pay off the balances.

Every month, it seemed like there was something, and the credit card had to be used to bridge the gap. It was like a carnival ride, where it just keeps spinning and going around and around. A person can lose their equilibrium when they never get to stand on solid ground, and that is how Ed and Sue felt. They felt like they were in a downward spiral. They both had their jobs and could make their house payment and buy the basic necessities of life. Their kids didn't go hungry and they had clothes and school supplies. They worked hard and did not spend frivolously, yet they were not able to save for emergencies, for their kids' college funds, or their own retirement. Ed and Sue never could get ahead and it was frustrating.

Their neighbors, Steve and Maria, were beyond frustrated. They were scared. They had both lost their jobs at the same time, and the bills seemed to pile up immediately. They had carried a balance on the credit cards before they lost their jobs, as millions of Americans do. When they started relying on the credit cards to pay for gas and groceries, and had no immediate job prospects in sight, they started to panic. The credit card bills quickly swelled into a giant mess and the interest escalated the problem. They jumped to the assumption that the only escape was bankruptcy.

We've Got Company

Ask anyone you know, and I bet they have a debt story to share. The odds are stacked against the average working citizen. We have mentioned that the average American has $8000 in credit card debt. I've seen some figures show it as high as $11,000. No matter – the fact is that we are carrying large credit card debt. Throw in the car loan, and the approximate debt goes up to $18,700 per U.S. household. Now add in a mortgage payment, and it is no wonder that just taking care of shelter, food, and transportation is a difficult task these days for most families.

Most debt and credit books on the market today talk about how to cure debt by curbing your spending and "cutting out the fat." They make you think that it is something you did that created the wild debt problem. It is plain to see that the real crisis is not the spending habits of the American public, but the aggressive practices of the American consumer lending industry. Most folks are not in debt because they have a gambling problem or a shopping addiction. Those are isolated occurrences, and not the norm.

Everyday People

What about people like Jody and Richard? Richard works construction and Jody works at a daycare center. They get by, and they pay their bills. They have a two-year old, and Jody just gave birth to another baby. Their ten-year-old washing machine died, and Richard does not want Jody to have to take a toddler and a newborn to the Laundromat. Anyone who has ever had a baby knows that one tiny person creates a huge pile of laundry. Richard bought a new washer and had to charge it to his credit card.

There is Helen, a retired music teacher. Her husband handled all the bills and when he died, she was lost. They never had any children, so she does not really have anyone to look out for her, except one nephew who mows her grass and changes her light bulbs. Helen has prescription medicines that insurance and Medicare do not fully cover, and they cost her hundreds of dollars every month. She was taken advantage of by an unscrupulous contractor who charged her double for a new roof. Her car needs a new fuel pump. Helen won't get her Social Security check for a few weeks, so she had to put the car repair on her credit card.

> Using credit cards should not mean never-ending debt.

Or how about Greg? His divorce cost him more than he could have ever anticipated in lawyer fees, plus he has to pay alimony and child support. His ex-wife got the house and has a very low-paying job. The water heater sprung a leak, so she called Greg to take care of it. His children need hot water to take baths, so he bought a new water heater, but he had to put it on his credit card.

These people cannot "cut out the fat."

The trouble is that everyday working people cannot make it without having to use the credit card from time to time, and once they do, the trap snaps shut and they are ensnared in a labyrinth of fees. Getting untangled from it all seems so complicated that people can get overwhelmed or confused or scared.

Your Tax Dollars

Adding to the frustration that we feel is that you and I go to work every day to earn a paycheck that gets eaten up before the next paycheck comes in. Just taking care of the basics is a struggle. The United Sates is a debtor nation. Credit card debt that never goes away is the invisible money sucker in the room. Some people are spending 90% of their disposable income toward paying off the credit cards and other debts. It is not that we are charging like crazy. It is the fact that they are charging *us* like crazy!

The federal government is aware of the consumer lending crisis, but they refuse to do anything about it. The aggressive and predatory practices of the lenders, and the collectors, are common knowledge. Politics is the name of the game. You and I are not big campaign contributors. The consumer lending industry is. The big credit card banks give big dollars to Washington. In return, Washington lets them get away with murder.

Predators on the Loose

In 2004, thirty states sued the big banks for predatory practices in their credit card-issuing methods. Thirty states! That would tell a reasonable person that predatory practices were going on. There must not be reasonable people in Washington. What happened? Nothing. The feds defended the banks! The credit card banks continue to pile on the fees, the penalties, and the crazy interest rates. These credit lenders continue to target the college kids and the people who can barely make payments, so they can trap them with minimum payments that will take twenty years to pay off.

The issue of educating our kids about consumer credit falls on the parents alone. At all levels, the public education system does not teach students about managing money. Students graduate from high school, and college, with little if any knowledge about personal finance. With the literally billions of dollars that are spent on education, the government and the teacher's union do nothing to allocate any resources to addressing the credit cancer in America.

Why is that? D-o-l-l-a-r-s. The politicians accept campaign contributions from the large lending institutions, and in return, they agree to keep future generations in the dark. Why educate the golden goose when you can continue to take the eggs? It's just another example of the American public getting screwed. How ironic that your tax dollars and mine are spent on an education system that not only is failing in the areas of reading, science, and math, but personal finance as well.

They want to screw us. I say, screw them. It's okay to get angry, as long as you then get busy.

Taking Care of Business

We can grumble all we want, but the best way to fight back is to, well, fight back. We know what they are up to, and we can counterattack.

Earlier pages spent a lot of ink explaining credit reports and credit scores. Now you know:

✔ Get your credit report.

✔ Review your credit report very carefully.

✔ Correct errors/remove false information.

Ninety percent of all credit reports have errors, so you better believe it is worth your while to check yours over completely. A lot of credit scores are bad simply because the credit report has misinformation. Dispute. Correct. Monitor. Your credit report continues to evolve, so you need to continue to review it periodically.

Your credit score, a three-digit number, is the only number you need to think about right now. Forgot about your high school batting average, your IQ, or what the bathroom scale showed this morning. Your credit score is your financial report card, and you want high marks. Improve your credit score overnight by doing the steps listed in Chapter 11. Once you have boosted your score, keep it there:

1. Pay on time.

2. Never skip a payment.

3. Make at least the minimum payment, more if possible.

Get the Word Out

One of my favorite solutions of the *Debt Cures* methods, if I can take the liberty of playing favorites, is that you can save yourself thousands of dollars immediately, just by making phone calls! Anybody can do it, and everybody can benefit. Anybody who has credit cards or any debt balances can make these phone calls and slash their debt. It does not matter if you have $5,000, $10,000, or $50,000 in debt; you could reduce it virtually overnight! Some people have cut their debt totally in half! Some even more! It is painless, easy, and saves you thousands. Nothing gets you on the road to success like a small taste of what success feels like.

> The methods described here can be HUGE improvement!

Ultimately, you are learning that you can be self-sufficient. You do not need to pay someone to make these calls for you. You can deal with your creditors and lenders and not have to pay any fees. Fees are what we are trying to get rid of! You can learn to rely on yourself, to trust yourself. That is important in all aspects of your life!

These self-help techniques can help you in all your financial dealings in the future. Reducing or eliminating debt is a great feeling. Knowing that you are the one who handled the pressure and stood up to the giant monster of greed is downright inspiring. Be inspired. You've earned it. Now take the courage you have acquired and get ready to build your wealth!

Can you understand why this solution makes me feel good?

Spread the word. Tell everyone you know to simply call all their credit card banks and ask them to:

1. Lower interest rates.

2. Waive fees and penalties.

3. Increase the credit limit.

Debt Elimination

If I had to choose one favorite *Debt Cures* method, this would be it. The very idea of 100% debt elimination is such a motivator and an emotional shot in the arm. I would predict that before you read this book, 99% of all readers had no idea that this was even possible. I hope that 100% of all readers will now tell everyone they know.

If your best friend has thousands of dollars of debt that they could be rid of completely, entirely, every single penny, FOREVER – they need to know about this method!

Maybe it is you with the old debt and the bad-tempered collection agent, making you irritable. Don't get ornery. Get even. It only takes one sentence: The statute of limitations is gone. Agencies try to collect on bogus debts all the time. But now we know better. This solution gives you a double prize. You have no debt to pay and you get the satisfaction that the malicious debt collector does not make a single dime off of you.

Or, if the alleged debt is not expired, simply tell them to mail all the information on this alleged debt, because you are not sure if it is yours. You do not want to pay a debt that is not yours. Some debt collectors are not always trustworthy, so you need to protect yourself.

Debt Reduction

Okay, I have yet another favorite. *Debt Cures* teaches you to use financial statements as a tool to reduce your debt drastically. *Debt Cures* is not about debt consolidation. That technique rolls everything into one sum, but it is all still there. *Debt Cures* is about debt elimination and debt reduction and self-empowerment! Okay, I will put down my megaphone and pom poms, but this is great information, and it is worth getting excited about.

By simply drafting very basic financial statements, or a simple two-sentence letter from your CPA, you have the most powerful tool to show the real score. And you are the victor. Prepare a simple balance sheet and an income statement that shows your net worth, and your true ability to repay your debt. Follow the outlined formula to success by tactfully showing in concrete professional statements what you have, and what you do not have. If you do not have it, you cannot pay it. Watch your debt disappear, and stop the creditors and collectors from ever bothering you again!

Prepare a:

1. Balance sheet.

2. Income statement.

3. Letter that states your net worth.

Phase Two

Guess what? I have a fourth favorite. It's a four-way tie. A grandmother can have ten grandchildren, and they are all her favorites, right? I'm the same way with *Debt Cures*. I'm excited about curing debt, and there is still more to come! Do you have student loans and/or mortgage loans? Everybody I have ever met wants to know how to pay off that 30-year mortgage in half the time. Sit tight, I'll get to it. What really gets me enthused is not only sharing the steps to curing debt, but sharing the steps to creating wealth.

Debt Cures is a two-part process. First, you can and will get rid of the fear and the debt that currently feels like it is dragging you under. Once you have taken control of your debt, and learned the industry's disgusting tactics that got you mired in that debt in the first place, you don't want to jump right back into the same old rat maze again. You want to move forward. You will.

Your forward path is the creation of wealth. There are hundreds of testimonials from people, just like you, who have overcome their debt and taken the next step, that of creating wealth. Do you want to join them? I thought so.

You've taken care of the difficult business of facing up to your debt. Now you deserve a reward. How about free money programs? Sound interesting? Even more intriguing is that these free money programs are grants that you do not have to repay. It can be as simple as making a phone call and filling out an application. Billions have been given away to people and all they needed to know was who, when, and how to ask. Now you will know too.

We Shall Overcome

The key to overcoming bad credit is to build good credit. Bad debt and good debt may sound confusing, but I will explain, and if you are up to it, I will tell you how to get a new credit line of up to $1 million. Maybe you have been thinking about starting your own business. We will cover how to get you started.

As you have discovered, *Debt Cures* methods are not difficult. They do not require an advanced degree or that you hire an attorney or that you cut up your credit cards. *Debt Cures* are simple solutions for the American citizen who is sick and tired of getting ripped off.

Dana was deep in debt not too long ago. He had student loans, a car loan, a home mortgage loan, and credit card bills. Sound familiar? He went to his job every day and thought that every day would be the same old rut, trying to get by, living paycheck to paycheck. Dana is exactly the type of person who can benefit from the methods of *Debt Cures*. By following the simple steps outlined here, he can reduce his debt significantly! Or eliminate it! Virtually overnight! So many people think it is not possible for them, but it is, and so much easier than they could ever imagine. You don't have to feel tied to your job, and you don't have to be a slave to your creditors. The best part is that you can cure your debt and be on your way to becoming a wealthy person!

Debt Cures methods are the ticket to your future – a future of wealth, of stability, of self-reliance. Tackle the old debt and learn the techniques of wealth creation!

CHAPTER 22

Rebuilding Credit

"I get knocked down, but I get up again.
You're never going to keep me down."
~ Chumbawamba

You may have been down. Your debt probably felt like an enormous burden that would never go away. But you do get up again. The banks and the credit card companies and the government aren't going to keep you down. You can break free from the bondage of debt and you can build lasting wealth.

The *Debt Cures* mentality is that of getting out of debt and building wealth, not some kind of hocus-pocus get-rich-quick scheme. It is not about trying to land your face on some television reality show and hoping that your fifteen minutes of fame will make you a millionaire. Getting out of debt and building wealth is not a fluke, and not terribly difficult. The methods you have read about in *Debt Cures* have helped thousands of people. You can join them.

Much of what has been covered to this point has been on debt. We have discussed many techniques and solutions to get you out of debt. Too many people associate the word "debt" with the word "bad." That is not the case. There is good debt and bad debt.

Two-Stepping

Debt Cures is a two-part process. The first is used to free yourself from the bad debt. A person who knows the system, and what the government and the bankers and the big lenders are up to, is a person who can beat them at their own game. Not only do you break away from the bondage of the interest rates and the scams and the predators, but you get to move forward. Life is not just a rut that we have to dig ourselves out of. It is an adventure to be enjoyed!

Dumping the debt is empowering! You have educated yourself. You have the knowledge now. You understand that the twofold process of freeing yourself from debt and freeing yourself to build wealth is comprised of parts that are woven together. The *Debt Cures'* methods that help you create wealth begin by doing everything we have already covered.

I like to use the analogy of a brick layer. He methodically, step by step, mixes his mortar and lays the bricks. He mixes more mortar, and lays more and more bricks. By keeping to his steady rhythm, he stacks enough bricks that he has created a wall, and it is very strong. He didn't just quickly and restlessly pile up loose bricks, one on top of another, that could easily fall. He didn't just mix a bunch of mortar and stand there and do nothing with it. The brick layer followed his simple techniques, and by doing these steps together, he created something strong. He built something that can last.

Build Your Wall

Not only are you learning how to get out of debt, you are learning to *stay* out of debt. That is like the mortar that holds the bricks together. The bricks are the building blocks of your wealth. Building wealth is a process of several easy tactics. Following the techniques outlined, you can create a brick wall of wealth and the big bad banking wolf will not be able to blow it down.

Part of the techniques inherent to creating wealth is using credit. To a person who has been deep in debt, it may take some time to come around to the idea that credit can be a good thing. Just about every millionaire in America will tell you that they used good credit to leverage their way to the top. In order for you to get there, you have to rebuild your credit. There is no magic wand to wave, just all the steps previously covered in this book. Simple, easy techniques that will bring you to the point where you say, "Okay, let's talk about good credit."

Good Credit

According to credit expert Hazel Valera, credit is the number one reason that people cannot move forward in their lives. I have shown you how to reduce or eliminate your debt so that you can move forward. You can move on with a peace of mind, knowing that you won't end up in that situation again. You know how the lending institutions operate, and you won't be falling into their traps any longer.

Some people believe that they can never have credit trouble if they never use credit. They are anti-establishment, anti-government, and anti-corporate America, so they do not want to give the big bank boys one dime. I understand that. But always paying with just cash is not the answer. It may prevent bad credit issues, but you need good credit. The best way to be anti-big bank is to play their game, and use their money, instead of them using yours. You need to play with their credit.

Ms. Valera also said that it is detrimental to not use credit! Sometimes people fall into the bad credit trap, but it can also be just the opposite. Good credit breeds good credit. Sure, you can pay cash and try to avoid even having a credit score, but that will not propel you forward. You will stay right where you are. You will have mortar, but no bricks. *Debt Cures* is for those who are willing to move ahead.

> Credit itself is not a "bad" thing.

The credit card companies and the big banks think they are the only ones that can play by their rules. We do not have to become greedy money-grubbing sharks, but we can wise up to the ways of the world and not get taken advantage of again. We will use certain tactics to take advantage of what is available to us.

Imagine the Possibilities

So many people become down when they are in debt because they think they will never get out. Not true! You can get rid of your current debt and move on to a life of creating wealth. You can get a whole new start, a new financial profile! You can start from scratch!

With a good credit rating, you will be able to get the best interest rates on all your loans – your home, your car, and your credit cards! Once you get good credit back, you know how to keep it that way as well. I don't deal in magic fairy dust. There are many ways to rebuild your credit and get you in good standing again.

Being a person with a good credit report opens up the door to all kinds of possible ventures for you. Things you thought were out of reach can be available to you now. The phone will ring and you will not be afraid to pick it up. Collection calls are a thing of the past. You can pay for your son to go to baseball camp, and you can afford your daughter's braces. The little things that worried you are no longer a concern. You have the bills paid off, and have a feeling of control.

Maybe you have wanted to buy a house or get a different car. With your old credit score, you were offered the worst rates and terms. You have learned how to clean up your bad credit report, and now you can reap the rewards and keep building good credit.

Piggyback

This section must now be marked with a big asterisk. Things have changed since the first edition of this book went to print, but instead of deleting this section, I want you to know what existed and what has been taken away. It's one more maddening example of how the big shots don't want you to get ahead. Here's what I said about the piggyback method when the book was originally written (and then they changed the rules!):

"One of the easiest ways to improve your credit is again a little known secret that the banks do not want you to know. The more people who learn these tricks, the more people will be improving their credit scores, and we all know that is bad for business – the bank business, anyway.

Improved credit scores mean less interest and fees being sucked in by the banks and the credit card companies. I say, let's do it!

"If you have poor credit and need to improve it in a hurry, ask a parent or a family member or a close trusted friend to give you a piggyback ride. What that means is they let you join in their good credit rating. They let you ride on their back for awhile.

"Obviously, if your best friend does not have good credit, they are not the person to ask. There has to be someone in your life who does have a good credit history and who will let you be added on to their account. That is how it works.

"They do not have to have a card issued to you. You do not have to ever charge a single cent to the account. You just get the benefit of their good credit because your name will be added to the account, which will soon show up on your credit report as an 'account in good standing.' If you are trying to improve your credit or need to establish credit, this is a marvelous way to do it."

Uh, scratch that. All good things in life must come to an end and this is one of them. Since this book originally went to print, this method has been closed, another door slammed in your face. The folks at the FICO scoring think tank have decided that "authorized users," any name added to an account, really isn't an authorized user– who are they to make that determination?! – and they will no longer include these accounts as part of the credit score for that person. Talk about unfair!

All the accounts out there with additional users – it's now sorry pal, only the first name on the account gets the credit rating. So for all those college kids out there whose parents wanted to give them a head start into the world of good credit, you're outta luck. For all those widows whose devoted sons wanted to help them establish credit in their own names, you're outta luck. And for all the spouses, usually women, who were added to their husband's accounts and thought they were also getting the benefit of the good credit, you're outta luck.

Once again, the innocent person, the little guy (or gal), is getting screwed.

The FICO powers-that-be believed that people were taking advantage of this method and some people who had good credit were allowing those with bad credit to become an authorized user on their account – for a fee. The credit gurus wanted to shut them down and in doing so have created a very unfair mess. And actually, why should they care if a consumer paid someone else for the benefit of their good credit? Consumers pay for all kinds of ways to help improve their credit score. BINGO! That's it. The big guys running the show don't want improved credit scores! They want to keep you and your score down, so they can keep their fees and profits up. I bet if they could figure out a way to do it, they'd say you can't read books on how to improve your credit score!

The piggyback method has now been shut down, whether you were hopping onto the credit of a trusted family member or someone you didn't know. (FICO now maintains that paying a fee to piggyback on someone else's good credit amounts to fraud, so if you did pay for such a service, have your name removed from those accounts. And if you had good credit and allowed someone to pay you to piggyback on your credit, now is the time to end that practice.) The FICO people estimate that 30% of everyone in their system has an additional user named on their accounts. That's over 60 million people affected by this new change. Do they honestly think that 60 million people are paying someone for the privilege of their good credit? Get real. They do not want credit scores to go up, plain and simple!

Now with the new rule, the second user name on an account will not get that account included in their credit score, causing their score to drop. Included in that 60 million is a whole generation of women out there who are the added users on their husbands' accounts. Everything was set up together when they got married and everything has hubby's name first. That was the way of our society. That now means that these women have just lost their good credit rating. That is the way of our credit society. If these women become divorced or widowed, all those years of good payment history will not do them one bit of good. The system is rigged against the honest American citizen.

Once again, let me remind you, knowledge is power. This is just one more example of what they don't want you to know about, but now that you do know, the time is now. The time for what? The time to fight back. If you, or someone you know, are the secondary name on an account, the time has come for credit in one's own name. In the eyes of those passing credit judgment, every man (and woman) stands alone.

Have your wife, your mother, or your college student get a credit card in her own name. Make a few small purchases and pay them off right away to establish a good paying history. Opening the account itself is not enough; there has to be activity for it to enter into the scoring system. The next car purchase should be in her name, even if you have to co-sign. Or have her take out a small personal loan at the bank and of course make the payments timely. This will establish a good credit score under her name and not as a piggyback rider.

I agree that this change made by FICO and welcomed by the banks and the credit card companies is not fair. The big guns don't play fair. The system is geared in their favor and to keep the American public under their thumb. It's all part of the great American rip-off. Millions of people, women especially, will feel the brunt when their credit scores take a nose dive, through no fault of their own, simply because the rules were changed.

One credit reporting agency will begin using the adjusted FICO calculation in late 2007, and the other two bureaus will in 2008. Take hold of the reins now and help yourself and those you know establish good credit in their name now.

Get $500 (or More) of Credit Instantly!

Talk about frustration! I've told you "if you have credit card debt, if you can't get a credit card, I can tell you how to instantly get a credit card. You could have a credit card and $500 instant cash money." And I told you how to do it. You could have been added to someone's account and within a week would have a card in hand and the ability to get cash, and of course have the benefit of

You can have cash in hand TODAY!

that good credit which would boost your credit score. It wasn't magic, but it was as good as a miracle: no matter your credit condition, you could get instant credit with the use of the "piggy back" method! I wrote: "Yesterday, your credit report was causing you to worry. Today, you are taking the steps to up that credit score; and TODAY, you can immediately have credit!" I had no idea that I would have to say, "Tomorrow this great method will be taken away!" I know things change fast, but the timing of this FICO scoring change is exasperating and infuriating to say the least. The ink was barely dry on the first printing of the book when the big wigs came up with their big idea.

Co-Sign = Instant Cash and Instant Credit for You!

Co-signing a loan is an excellent retaliation to the demise of the piggyback method. If your spouse was an authorized user on your credit card, put him/her as a joint account holder. Try to do this as well for your mother and your college student or your friend, if the credit card company will allow it. The piggyback method may have been taken away, but co-signing accomplishes the same purpose. This method is just as easy and just as quick, and the sky is the limit when it comes to dollar signs.

Thought you would never be able to get a loan with the state of your credit report at the moment? Think again! If you need $10,000 cash right now, you can get it! Virtually overnight!

You can get a loan, and you can have $500, $1000, $5000, or even $10,000 in your hands in cash! Never forget that your bad credit report is a temporary condition. While you are mending it, you do not have to be stopped dead in your tracks. There are ways to get instant cash, and this is a fabulous way to do it! That trusted friend or family member who would let you piggyback off their credit card can co-sign a loan for you, and help you on your way to creating wealth and a sense of financial freedom. They – the banks – have not put the kibosh on co-signing for loans!

One slight word of caution, which you already know: You only want to co-sign with a person who is responsible and has a good credit history. When you co-sign with someone, you share the debt. If one does not pay, the other is responsible for it. This has more risk than simply being added to a credit card. There is actual money being received, which has to be repaid, where with the credit card you do not have to access the account if you do not want to.

Be advised: Asking someone to co-sign a loan for you is not something one would usually do on a first date.

> Gal: "I had a nice time tonight. Dinner was great. Thanks a lot. Can I see you again sometime?"

> Guy: "Okay, how about meeting me at the bank tomorrow? We can sign some papers, with you as the co-signer of a loan for me. Then we can grab some lunch."

I don't know. Maybe if she said "yes," it was a match that was meant to be.

Be smart. If someone asks you to be their co-signer, you only do so if you know that they can be trusted to pay back the loan. If they default, the creditor or lending bank then comes to you for full payment. Most of the time, you only talk money with close friends and family anyway, people you trust and confide in. Hooking up together on a loan is a great way to help out your college student or your elderly mother who never had credit in her own name or your best friend going through a financial hard time. They need the loan in their name, but with no credit history, the bank does not want to give them a loan. Without getting a loan, a person cannot establish a credit history. It is one big Catch-22.

Have your spouse get a car loan in her name, even if you co-sign and make the payments. Getting credit in each person's name is the game and getting good credit is the goal.

Co-signing is a great way to build credit, and it works both ways. For example, when Ed was just starting out and had no credit, he could not get a loan. His father agreed to be the co-signer on Ed's car loan. The bank knew that if Ed didn't pay, his father would. Ed did pay and in doing so, built up his credit. And that is what Ed did.

Years passed, and the banks and credit card companies had gotten their claws into Ed, as he was now married with a house and kids and all the bills that go along with that. Real life can get in the way and occasionally a bill can get paid late. The credit score then takes a hit. This time, Ed had credit established, but was looking to improve his credit. His father agreed to co-sign on another car loan, and Ed was able to rebuild his credit score with this account in good standing. Every good account counteracts one that needs help.

Frequent Updates

Your credit report and thus your credit score won't get updated unless there is activity happening. You do not want old bad information just sitting there. Get going and generate good information! Let it keep cranking every month.

> Using credit helps you build good credit.

Using credit helps you build good credit. For a credit score to get generated, you need to have some activity to spark that, and you need to have credit for at least six months. There has to be a timeframe to show a history and a pattern of payments. This will build a credit pattern that shows timely, consistent payments. A credit card with no activity happening does not do this. Open a credit card and make one small monthly purchase and pay it off on time each month. You do not want to pay interest! Having regular activity means your credit report gets updated each month.

One of the tricks of the credit report is to always pay on time. It is so easy to let time get away from you, causing you to end up paying an account late. We all do it. The bills get put on the kitchen counter or the hallway table. The "to be paid" pile gets buried under other mail or the kid's science project, and the next thing you know, you are making a late payment. That is how they trap us. One late payment and the credit score goes down the drain. And interest rates go up, up, up.

Installment Loan

Yes, I realize that may sound strange to tell you to get a loan, but credit scores are computed based on various criteria – one being that you have different kinds of loans, not just all credit cards. Once you have established a credit card and have a new credit path underway, a small installment loan may be wise. Borrow a small amount from your bank or credit union, and keep the length of the loan to one or two years. You do not want to be paying much interest; you want to be creating a new pattern of paying.

This may be a case where you need a co-signer in order to get the loan, so choose your co-signer wisely. It will be like having a co-credit report for this particular loan, and our goal here is a stellar credit report.

Secured Credit Card

If you can't get a regular credit card, you may want to consider getting a secured card. This is an option if you have no credit or poor credit. The secured card is secured because you give the bank a deposit, and they, in essence, let you borrow it back. Because only people with poor credit go for this kind of card, there are a lot of crooks out there, hustling these cards to the people they think they can take advantage of; they charge outrageous interest rates and fees. Go to a credit union that you know and trust. Use it wisely and make sure timely payments are made each month.

Get a card that will turn into a regular card if you prove to be creditworthy after one year of using that secured card. The most important item – verify with the credit union that they turn in the information to the credit reporting agencies. If they don't, don't get the card. The only reason you want the card is to build credit. If it is not going to show up on the credit report, it is worthless.

College Students

Earlier in the book, I discussed the abusive and predatory practices that the credit card companies and big banks are using, and that their number one target is our nation's college students.

We can beat them to the punch and help our children become smart consumers. They need to know the real deal; we can't let them be hoodwinked by the folks at the booths set up at their school orientation weekend, offering beach balls and backpacks. College kids are the number one targets for these predators, who will just literally hand cards over to them. Instant credit means instant credit report. Teach your young adult how to use it wisely and what it does for their future financial success.

There are credit cards for college students that are called "student cards." These are not the same ones mentioned above that allow the student to get in over their heads, and to walk out of college already deep in debt. The student card requires that the parent co-sign, and the card usually has a credit limit of no more than $1000. The idea is for the student to get used to having a credit card, learning to be a responsible consumer, and still have a safety net. It is sort of like a practice credit card, and in order to apply, you have to really seek it out. This card can be a good way for a student to establish a credit report and a credit score.

Give the Gift of Good Credit

The regular credit cards that students get at their schools can do the same, if they learn to use it wisely. There are many discussions that parents have with their children as they grow up, and how to use credit is just as important as the birds and the bees, and the "just say no" to drugs speech. Parents need to be educated about the credit card industry, and they need to inform their children.

The Gift That Keeps Giving

There is no better gift to give someone than helping them with their financial health. If you help your kids learn to avoid the traps that the consumer lending industry has waiting for them, they can maintain a debt-free existence and get on to building wealth.

For your friends and your family, and for yourself, there is no better gift. Money does not grow on trees. It grows because we have learned how to make smart choices and how to fight back against the credit card companies, the banks, and the mortgage companies. They are the poison, the weeds that want to choke out prosperity. They want it only for themselves.

The steps and techniques outlined in *Debt Cures* are like weed-killer, or like the antidote to the snake's venom. We are not destined to be held under their power.

We are destined for wealth.

CHAPTER 23

Building More Wealth

"No one is destined to live a life without wealth."
~ S. Ross Ingram

You already have many wealth-building techniques under your belt. Every step you take to reduce or eliminate your debt is a step towards building wealth. Take these ideas and build on them.

You have learned that you can pay the same amount of money toward your home mortgage every month, but if you break up those payments into weekly installments, you will save thousands of dollars and slash many years off paying that debt. Amazing, simple, and a great step to building wealth. Use the same technique to pay off your student loans! Your car loans! Any bank loans! Just be sure that there is no prepayment penalty, and you are on the way to debt-free living!

Use Your Power for Good

The ability to borrow is power, and you have the power; not the banks, not the credit card companies. Make them work for you. We have seen that they are eager to attack, so your credit needs to be handled wisely. They want you to misuse your credit. They want a piece of you every month, month after month after month. The lenders and credit card companies and big banks are in it to take advantage, and they are looking for every opportunity to do so. Don't give it to them.

Many Americans use credit to buy things that do not increase in value. If you use credit to buy items that depreciate, then you are paying, over a period of months, for something that is only getting less valuable over time. That is not how investing is supposed to work.

Unless you are buying a collectible, most of our cars depreciate the minute we drive them off the car lot. My advice is to buy a car that is a year or two old, and if you can't purchase it outright, pay it off as soon as possible.

Wise Investing

Clothes, shoes, furniture, vacations, eating out – these items are commonly bought using credit, and you end up paying today for something that you ate last month. The best use of credit is to use it for things that will increase in value. Real estate, stocks, bonds, art – there is a chance for tremendous gain when you buy items that will appreciate. That is why your home is a wonderful investment. It is your haven on several levels. With it, you are building memories, and you are also building wealth.

The author of *Rich Dad, Poor Dad*, Richard Kiyosaki, says that the best investment you can make is in yourself. By reading, and learning, you are doing just that. How you invest your time is just as important as how you invest your money.

Bright Idea

A little known wealth creation tactic is using a corporation to build wealth. You can free yourself from debt problems and poor credit by starting your own corporation. I see that scowl. I am not off my rocker. You can have a corporation. Yes, you.

Why form a corporate entity? You start with a clean slate! You get a fresh credit history, plus many tax advantages, and protection of your personal assets. And the chance for a $1 million credit line! Do you think that would happen if it were just little old you?

If you have bad credit, you can start fresh, right this minute, and be on your way to wealth. Starting a company is not as scary as some people tend to think. The benefits are worth it. There are many advantages to having your own corporate business, and best of all, you may be able to access a large line of credit. That means you will not need a huge outlay of cash from your pocket.

It's Not Hard

Let's assume that you are currently in the process of improving your personal credit score. An individual and a business have separate credit histories. You can start a company and immediately take off with excellent credit!

> Forming a company gives you a new credit history!

Forming your own business does not have to be a long, labor-intensive process. You, as the sole owner of your business, can become a corporation or an LLC (limited liability corporation) very easily. You do not need partners or investors.

By incorporating, you get the advantage of corporate tax laws. You can form a corporation without an attorney, and the forms and filing fees will often cost less than $500. However, it is smart to have a lawyer or a financial planner assist you.

Ideas

In order to form a corporation and start making money, the first step is obvious – you need to have a business. Maybe you already have a business, a dog walking business or a hair salon. Perhaps you are a handyman or house painter. Maybe you have always dreamed of starting your own business. Now is the perfect time. Ed had been rebuilding old clocks as a hobby for years. He decided to turn this hobby into a legitimate business venture.

The author Joyce Carol Oates, I believe, once said, "Ideas come from the craziest places." Let your ideas flow. When you are just getting started, it may seem overwhelming to think of all the possibilities, because they are countless. With a business, you can branch into many divisions and still enjoy the overall umbrella of protection of being a corporation. Ed may end up launching all kinds of brilliant ideas. If he starts a separate division down the road someday for watch repair, it will not affect his clock-rebuilding department. With a corporation, you can have different business activities under one corporate roof.

Corporate Credit History

Your business gets a corporate tax ID number and does not use your social security number. If your credit history under your social security number is less than great, rebuilding a new credit profile is easier than you think. The corporate credit history uses the business ID number, and the credit score is a totally separate number.

Corporate credit scores operate the same way, but have a different number system. A score of 80 is considered excellent – equivalent to a personal credit score of 800. The same responsible tactics apply – pay on time, do not use all your available credit, etc. There are several corporate credit rating agencies. Dun & Bradstreet is probably the most well known.

Getting Started

A new corporation makes a new credit history by getting credit in its name. Sometimes banks are hesitant to loan money to a brand new corporation. Just like with an individual, the bank wants to see the track record of your paying history. If you are just getting started, there is no track record yet.

There are credit-builder companies available on the internet that will provide you the contact information of businesses who will give you credit right away, so you can quickly establish credit in the name of your new business. Perhaps you need office supplies, a business credit card, or some other service; this kind of credit builder can hook you up with companies who will fulfill these basic business needs while allowing you to build a credit history. All you need is that first opportunity to build credit and the rest takes off from there.

Dream Big

Maybe the idea of having your own corporation never entered your mind until reading it here. Let the idea settle in. Don't automatically think that it is too complicated. It is not. The methods that are part of the *Debt Cures* solutions have, at their core, the underlying fact that you are in control. By taking control of your debt, and taking on the big credit card companies, you should feel a sense of power and an "I can do it" attitude.

That same attitude carries over into building wealth. You learn the secrets that they don't want you to know and not only do you get out of debt, you have the ability to leverage credit, the bank's money, to build your wealth.

Every corporation started from scratch with no credit, no history. And virtually every strong corporation built a strong credit profile by doing the methods you have learned. Easy methods like paying your bills on time, not using up all your available credit, and all the other tips that apply to individuals as well. The beauty of having a corporation is that it has more potential than you as an individual.

> A corporation with a strong credit profile gets rewarded with huge credit lines.

A corporation with a strong credit profile gets rewarded with huge credit lines. It is no exaggeration that someone who creates a new credit record through a corporation can get $1 million in credit, or even much, much more!

More Benefits

In general, the interest rates on business credit cards are lower than the interest rates you pay on your personal credit cards. The corporation also gets the benefit of being able to deduct the interest as a business expense on their tax return. Also, when a business uses credit to buy something, it is usually something that will make the company money and in doing so, it pays itself off.

Sue decided to start a dog grooming business. Using a corporate credit card or line of credit, she purchased a new sink and sprayer for her basement business. By having better equipment, she gets the job done more efficiently and is able to groom more dogs. She makes more money and can pay off the sink very quickly.

Starting Out

Get a business bank account. Many people want to mix their business funds with their personal funds. Bad idea. Maintain separate accounts. You are probably wondering how the nuts and bolts of getting started actually happens. In the words of a famous shoe company, you just do it.

A little effort can grow into the ability to have $1 million at your disposal. I hear you ask: Where do I begin? First check under the couch cushions and in your jacket pockets for lost coins and bills. Cash in the penny jar on the kitchen counter. Then open your mind and get creative.

$10,000 IN 24 HOURS!

Borrow

Borrow from yourself. If you've got it, use it. Any cash in the bank, in stocks, or any investments will serve you well by helping to start your corporation.

Borrow from friends and family. Quite often, there is a trusted friend who sees the possibilities when others sometimes choose to feel the fear instead. If this person believes in you, enough to loan you some money, you need to believe in them! As we mentioned earlier, money borrowed from friends and family does not hit the credit report, and they don't hit you with outrageous interest.

Borrow against something you own. If you have something of value, you can take out a loan using that item as collateral. You can take a personal loan, using your car as collateral. If you don't pay the loan, the bank takes your car.

Home Equity

Borrow against your house. Your home is usually your biggest investment and your largest asset. You can take out a home equity loan or line of credit and use that cash to build equity in your business. Often the interest rates are good, and again, the interest would be tax deductible.

Using your home equity is quick and easy, and can add up to a sizeable amount of cash. Most lenders let you borrow against the equity you have in your home. To figure out your equity, you need to know what your home is worth currently, not what you paid for it. Take the fair market value of your house and subtract whatever you still owe on your mortgage. If you have a second mortgage or other loans against your house, subtract those too. If your mortgage was completely paid off, you would have 100% equity in your house, but most of us are not there yet.

Ed and Sue's house is now worth $350,000. They have a mortgage balance of $225,000. Their equity is $125,000. The bank will let them take an equity loan for 75% of the appraised value, less what they still owe. Some banks will allow you to use 100% of the value of your house, less the mortgage balance.

Home's current value	$350,000 x 75% =	$262,500
Balance still owed on their mortgage		$225,000
Home equity loan allowed		$ 37,500

That is a nice amount to put into a new business!

Other Options

If you have a certificate of deposit (CD) in the bank, you may be able to borrow the money back and repay it at a very good interest rate. If you own stocks, you do not have to sell them. You may be able to borrow 50% of the value you have in your stocks. If you have life insurance policies, you may be able to borrow against the cash value of the policy.

There are other options as well – venture capital, the Small Business Administration, and "angels." I will get to these in the Free Money chapter!

Get Creative

Don't tell me that you are not creative. I know better. You have a creative streak in you or you would not still be reading this book. You're interested. You know you can do it. Sometimes all it takes is a little encouragement.

Co-signers

As was discussed in dealing with personal credit, you can use many of the same techniques to get liquid money right now. Get a co-signer on a loan! It is immediate cash. With the help of a co-signer who has good credit, you can get a good interest rate and better terms and fees. You can have $10,000 today!

Uncollected Funds

An obscure way to raise quick cash is to find uncollected funds you never knew you had. There are databases on the internet that list refunds owed to people. Oprah covered this on her show once, and it is estimated that nine out of ten people are owed some money. The websites state that there is $400 billion in unclaimed money that belongs to the American people.

These internet sites profess that the state of New York has unclaimed bank accounts and security deposits that total over five billion dollars, and California is sitting on over three billion dollars of other people's money. The United States Treasury has unredeemed savings bonds, old ones, that amount to $1.3 billion. American Express has an extra $3.8 billion, due to all the traveler's checks that have been issued and not cashed. The Internal Revenue Service issued tax refunds over the years, totaling $25.6 million, and these people have not cashed their refund checks!

There may be money out there with your name on it. Many times, it is small rebates from manufacturers that never made its way into your hands, but it is your money just the same. There is free money waiting to be collected. Perhaps some of it belongs to you.

Sue went on the internet and searched for uncollected funds. She discovered that she was owed $230 from Bed, Bath and Beyond. She collected the cash and put it toward her dog grooming business. Little checks all add up.

Entrepreneur

Too many people put the cart before the horse. They put the product or service out there without understanding if there is actually a need or a want for that product or service. Supply and demand makes sense, so use it to your advantage. Whatever people are demanding, that is what you want to supply. Far too often, folks think they have the greatest gadget and then they have to spend their energy trying to get people to want it, to create the demand. It needs to work the other way around.

There is an ancient tale of a Russian archer. He was a small man who didn't talk much, but he was known throughout the village as the best marksman. His bow and arrow were amazingly accurate, nothing but bull's-eyes. The trees of the forest were marked with target circles, and his arrows were found dead center in the middle of the circle every time. The czar of Russia was passing through their tiny hamlet and witnessed all the clean targets with the arrows perfectly landed. He demanded to speak to this amazing archer.

> You can conquer debt AND create weatlth!

"How can it be that you hit your target perfectly every time?"

"It is simple," the archer replied. "I shoot the arrow and then I draw the target."

Bull's-eye

Today the world is full of people trying to make big bucks quickly off of eBay. They often have the wrong approach. Most people scour their homes and garages and attics and basements, trying to find stuff that they can unload, and they have visions of huge dollars dancing in their heads. People don't want your junk.

Or some folks buy up worthless stuff in bulk and hope to peddle it for a profit. Then they are stuck with 2,000 pink plastic back scratchers when they realize that there is no demand for them.

Don't fall into that trap. First, you must determine what the demand is, and then you be the one to supply it. What are purchasers searching for on eBay? That is what you want to sell. Find the items that people are looking for. Find it for them and you will make a profit.

You might have the entire Bee Gees collection on vinyl, in mint condition, but if there is no demand, your supply will just sit. If the hot search is for Joan Baez records, find them fast and cheap, and sell them to the demanding public.

Successful

That is how successful people operate. They see where there is a need or a want, and they fill it. I might enjoy making wool scarves, but if I live in Miami, there is not going to be much demand for what I can supply. But if there is an influx of people with their little dogs, then I can be smart like Sue and start a dog grooming business.

Ed's hobby of fixing old clocks can become a booming business, because few people have the expertise. There is a need, a demand Ed can supply. In order to be successful, you need to target what people are looking for, instead of trying to convince them that what they really need is a yarn potholder that you learned to make after you bought a bunch of discount yarn, hoping, and failing, to sell on eBay.

Can Do

When you first started reading this book, you may have been feeling a little down. You may have been interested in *Debt Cures* because of debt issues in your life that needed to be addressed. Now you can see that your debt became such a nightmare because the federal government allowed the banks and credit card industries to play games. The troubling matter is not just that they are allowed to mess with our money, but that they are allowed to mess with our lives.

We don't have to let that be the case. The industry secrets that they have literally banked on are now exposed. When the truth is out, we can take advantage of it and no longer be the pawns in their big money games.

It is freeing. No longer in bondage to the banks! No longer a slave to your debt! Using the concepts outlined in *Debt Cures,* you have the upper hand. You can rid yourself completely of debt, and you can build wealth.

I bet when you started reading Page One, you never dreamed that it was possible. Now you know that debt collectors cannot control you. You can start fresh with perfect credit. By using your knowledge and your power, you can access money and achieve dreams that you never dared to let yourself dream.

You can do it. I want to hear about it. Contact success@debtcures. com – and I know you have already peeked at the last chapter, so without further adieu, I want to tell you about FREE MONEY!

CHAPTER 24

FREE MONEY!

"I would not exchange my leisure hours for all the wealth in the world."

~ Comte de Mirabeau

Why do we desire wealth? Just to be rich? No.

Think about it.

We want to be free from the strain of the daily struggle where all we do is get out of bed, go to work, pay the bills, and get up the next day and do it all over again. We want the freedom to not worry about money more than we want money. Does that make sense?

If you have money to pay for the basics of life, plus you have a nest egg and can save for retirement and can pay for your kids' education and can take a vacation and have a little left over to invest, you are wealthy! The dollar signs and the number of zeros don't matter. You don't have to set a goal of how much money you want; the goal is to live your life free from the stress of money.

Curing your debt is the best thing you can do for your life as a whole. To be able to wake up each day and not have a feeling of dread wash over you is a sign of being wealthy. And that is also healthy. When you are free to make decisions based upon your dreams, and not what you owe to the banks or credit card companies, you are wealthy. When you indeed have leisure hours to spend with your family and your friends, pursuing the desires of your heart, you are indeed wealthy.

Getting out of debt and on to creating wealth is the goal of this book. The concepts that have been outlined are easy to follow. Thousands of people have gotten out of their rut and are now living the life of their dreams. You can too.

Free Money

You need to know that there is money out there and available for you to use; *free* money. What do I mean by free? You do not have to repay.

> What do I mean by free? You do not have to repay.

No, it does not grow on trees; and I am not telling you to put on a black mask and rob a convenience store. Don't snatch purses either. Gifts are great, and an inheritance would be wonderful, but most of us don't have an old rich uncle who will leave us set for life. However, there are programs and grants out there, right under our noses, which could give us money to pay living expenses or start a business or pay credit card bills. You just have to know where to find them.

Where to Begin

The government has billions of dollars in grants, and most people don't know that they even exist. It is not something they advertise on billboards or tell you about when they send your tax bill. Big business knows about this money. You need to as well.

The beauty of grants is that they are not loans, and they are not federal aid. A grant is money given to you, money that you do not have to repay. There are also low cost loans with low interest, but free money sounds a heck of a lot more fun.

The money can go to anyone who qualifies and asks for it. There may be income limits for some programs, but not all. A number of millionaires and even huge corporations have taken advantage of these programs, so you should too.

There are hundreds and thousands of programs out there. Some have specific restrictions as to how you must spend the money; some do not. Getting the money could even be easier than you would expect. Phone calls and filling out applications is usually all it takes. Some require lots of paperwork, but you can find grants that merely require an easy-to-complete form with information you already know. Whatever office is giving the grant can answer any of your questions.

I hear your question: There is more than one office that gives out free money? Yes. The government is a huge network of offices. You cannot find one that has "Free Money" in big block letters on the door. If there were such an office, I would like the job of being the guy to hand out the checks. It may take a little bit of searching to find the programs that meet your needs, but a small investment of your time is worth the opportunity of receiving money that never needs to be paid back.

Take It!

The big corporations and their lobbyists know all about government money and how to get these grants. They know the system because they work the system; they basically created the system. What you need to know is that government grants are not just for their pals and contributors. It may not be widely known, but it is true: Grants are available to non-profit organizations, small businesses, and you, the individual! These programs are in place and you need to tap into them! The government and the corporate big guys know how to take advantage of you; you need to be aware that you can take advantage of government money that is available to you!

Maybe you've gotten frustrated in the past searching out these free money opportunities? Stop banging your head against the wall and keep reading. You no longer have to apply for loans, only to agonize over whether or not you'll be able to repay once you qualify. I'm not writing about loans; I'm writing about *grants*. Grants that are available to you *right now,* whether you want to pay your bills, fill your children's lunchboxes, start your own business, pay your property taxes, or put food on the table.

Yes, there are a variety of free money programs you can qualify for! I list some of them in this book, but I don't even come close to naming each and every single one; there are just too many!

As you look over these pages, keep in mind that some of this information may be out of date. Changes may have occurred after this book was printed. Websites are constantly going down, and agencies are constantly amending their programs, so do the research and adjust your actions accordingly. All that said, let's move forward…

The Hardest Part Is Done for You Right Here

Some people don't know that free money exists. Others may have been aware, but quickly became overwhelmed trying to find it. One of the greatest pleasures for me in this entire book is helping you find these sources that can get you on your way to wealth creation. I don't know how they did it before the internet, but the technology that we now take for granted is your new best friend. Even if you do not have a home computer, you can use one for free at the public library or go over to a friend's house. With this information, your friends will want to do their own searching too!

The saying goes, "The best things in life are free." To that, I would like to also add, "The best sites in life are free." Don't pay for access to online databases. You can learn where to find the same sources yourself; I will tell you how. Right here, right now.

One site that is fantastic, one I find really incredible, is www.govbenefits.gov. This site has information on thousands of programs. It is easy to navigate, which I appreciate. Some websites can seem so confusing. I like it when they make it easy for me!

There are two ways to maneuver this site. Let's assume you have no idea what you might qualify for or what you are looking for specifically. Click on the "Start Here" button. It will take you to an easy-to-answer questionnaire. There are some questions to go through and depending upon how fast you read, it will take you 5 to 10 minutes to complete. The questions are simple and straightforward, and completely anonymous. You do not give your name or social security number. The only personal questions are age, gender, and income level.

After you answer the questions, a list of possible grant or benefit programs pops up that you could be eligible for. Nothing could be easier! (Except maybe Uncle Sam knocking at your door with a fistful of twenties.)

You then can review the list of agencies and programs that you have pre-qualified for based upon the answers to your questions. This feature alone can save you days and weeks, if not months and years, of time searching for possible free money sources.

If you already know where your interest lies, for example, "utilities" or "education," you can also use the Quick Search feature on govbenefits.gov. Select the topic, which include: Awards; Counseling; Disaster Relief; Financial Assistance; Grants, Scholarships, Fellowships; Housing; Loans; Social Security/Pension; Child Care; Disability Assistance; Education; Food; Health Care; Insurance; Medicare; and Utilities. A list of all the programs in that category appears.

Click each one that interests you or that is in your state. Then you can view the details of each, or click to see if you could be eligible. You answer a few questions, and what you may be eligible for is narrowed down. The results appear on your screen before you can say, "Wow, this site is amazing." It does the work for you. Some of the free money sources are limited to your income level, but even if you have a high income, there are still low-cost loan opportunities on this site. My hat is off to the creators of www.govbenefits.gov. Instead of searching forever, or wondering if a grant applies to you, you can get to the nitty gritty right away. That is a beautiful thing.

Free??

Yes, the best things in life sometimes really are free. Another fantastic resource available at your fingertips, another resource that is not widely known or publicized, is www.grants.gov.

Most federal agencies who offer grants post them here. You can read about the grant, see if you qualify, and download and submit your application, all online. Instead of having to search through hundreds of different agency programs, this site allows you to look for what you may be able to apply for, in one location. There are over 1000 grant programs from 26 agencies on this site; over $400 billion to be awarded!

The government has looked the other way while the credit card companies and banks have pilfered money out of your pocket, and no one is going to knock on your door to tell you that this money is available. But now you know. It is up to you to make the effort to get it.

Found Money

With www.grants.gov, the search process through the maze of federal grants out there has been connected into one big site where you have to enter your information just once. One congressman commented, "I'm often asked where people can go to get the necessary federal grant money. The resource I always mention first is Grants.gov." You can look at grants by agency name or by category. It is amazing how much government money is out there and available, and very few people know it.

> The government has looked the other way while the credit card companies and banks have pilfered money out of your pocket...

You can become aware of grants and sources that you would not have known about. If you just want to browse through the grants, you do not have to register. If you want to apply for a grant, you will need to register. Follow the instructions on the website. They also provide a user guide for you at www.grants.gov/assets/GDG_AppUserGuide_0207.pdf.

There are also many programs through the Small Business Administration that you should not overlook. These are not all grants, but loans with very good interest rates and easy terms. Probably one of the best loans you could ever get.

Don't overlook all the foundations and private sources that provide various funds. See: www.foundationcenter.org/getstarted/individuals/ or www.fundsnetservices.com or www.kn.pacbell.com/products/grants/locate.html. Hundreds of possibilities are at your fingertips.

More Great Sites

Besides the wonder power of www.grants.gov and www.govbenefits. gov, there are more terrific, valuable, and useful websites that can help you find fantastic grant and low cost loan opportunities. There is so much information out there, for FREE, and no one knows about it. Most people think it doesn't exist or that they have to pay for it. Now I hope you can see what I am so excited about. Free money and amazing loan opportunities are out there, and I want you to know about them!

The official website of the federal government, USA.gov (http:// www.usa.gov), contains valuable information about all US government agencies. The first topic listed is Benefits and Grants. This link gives you lots of official information on grants, loans, financial aid and other benefits from the US government. You can even sign up to be notified when the benefit page is updated. Outstanding!

Look for yourself and see if among the thousands of available grants the government is giving away, maybe one, two, or more just might be right for you. Look, find a grant, check your eligibility. So simple, so easy, so quick! Start now! Or maybe you will want to finish the book since you are in the homestretch, and then you can jump on the computer!

Govloans.gov (http://www.govloans.gov) is your gateway to government loan information. This site directs you to the loan information that best meets your needs and is an excellent source for locating loans for children, agriculture, business, disaster relief, education, housing, veterans, or just about anything for which you might need a loan.

$$$

Lots of people – a million every year – are getting free money and cheap loans from the government! These entrepreneurs are finding the grants that they don't have to pay back, and they are taking out low interest loans to build their wealth. They talk to the Small Business Administration and they seek venture capital – private investors willing to invest in their business. They also know that there are "angels" all around us. Sometimes these angel investors are more than willing to donate to your business.

So why wait around when you can take advantage today? The Small Business Administration has implemented programs that have drastically changed the futures of the individuals and the companies that have qualified for them. You can qualify too.

There's the Small Business Innovation Research program, also known as the SBIR. In an effort to stimulate the forward-thinking aspects of qualifying small businesses, the SBIR offers a host of monetary awards, some totaling as much as $100,000. Yes, you read that right: $100,000.

For the last 25 years, the SBIR has been awarding all kinds of money to all kinds of small business owners! And you deserve to get in on the action too.

There are eleven agencies and federal governments who, each year, set aside funds to give away to people just like you! And it's simple. It's there for the taking. Once you check the site (www.sba.gov/SBIR/indexsbir-sttr.html) to make sure you meet all eligibility requirements, you're halfway there. Then it's on to putting together an excellent proposal that'll catch their attention.

When reviewing proposals, agencies look for small businesses that can demonstrate an exceptional degree of development and technical prowess. If a company can successfully exhibit these things, then it has a great chance of qualifying! If you meet all eligibility requirements, it's worth putting the time into applying. When we're talking about free money in amounts of up to $100,000, you might as well give it a go!

The SBA Office of Technology also has the Small Business Technology Transfer Program (STTR). Five federal departments award $2 billion to small high-tech businesses in this program. If that is your business and you have less than 500 employees, you can apply to get a piece of that $2 billion pie. It's very exciting to learn that the Department of Energy, Department of Defense, Department of Health & Human Services, National Science Foundation, and NASA have a percentage of their R&D budget allocated for this program. The SBA is the coordinator between those that apply for the grants and these agencies. The dollars are big, the work is important; very heady stuff.

The Small Business Administration offers other great free money programs, and you can learn more about them here: www.sba.gov. I cannot begin to list everything, but I hope you get the idea that the money is there, and I hope you see that finding it is not as hard as you may have thought.

Federal money programs, grants and loans, for everything you could ever dream of:

- ✔ $25,000 "micro-loan" to start a business – www.sba.gov
- ✔ $200,000 to run a ranch or a farm – www.fsa.usda.gov
- ✔ $200,000 credit line for small businesses – www.sba.gov/financing/loanprog/caplines.tml
- ✔ $500,000 to start a business – www.sba.gov
- ✔ $300,000 to help you get government contracts! – www.dla.mil/db
- ✔ $500,000 for females and minorities to get government contracts – http://osdbuweb.dot.gov
- ✔ $3,000,000 in venture capital! – www.sba.gov/INV/venture.html

WOW!

I think you get the idea. There are an amazing amount of offers sitting there. I have only given you a small sampling.

> Need some start-up money to get things going?

In addition to grants, there are many loans available that are quick, and guaranteed by the Small Business Administration. You fill out one page and can get $150,000. That is worth the time it takes to fill out a single sheet of paper! Find out about the Low Documentation Loan Program at www.sba.gov/financing/lendinvest/lowdoc.html. There are Small Business Development Centers in every state as well. Contact www.sba.gov/services.

As I mentioned before, many big businesses got their start with government venture capital. There is another great program that the Small Business Association offers, and it has been around for years. Since 1958, The Small Business Investment Company (SBIC) has been offering programs that provide venture capital to small businesses that are intent upon growing! Yes, this program has been around for nearly 50 years, and hardly anyone knows about it.

The great news is that the program doesn't cater to any specific facet of business. So, regardless of what your company does, you may be eligible to take advantage!

Need some start-up money to get things going? Not a problem. How about some expert management assistance to take you to the next level? You got it. The SBIC can cover you, so don't waste any time in applying. Go to www.sba.gov/aboutsba/sbaprograms/inv/index.html. The potential dollars are encouraging. The SBIC funding for small businesses includes $10 billion from the government and private funding of over $12 billion.

The SBIC site likes to share their success stories and reading them is very inspirational. Check out http://www.sba.gov/aboutsba/sbaprograms/inv/INV_SUCCESS_STORIES.html and see if you are in awe, as I was. They state it perfectly: "The most exciting potential of an SBIC investment is how it can turn one small company into a great success story." Your company could join the ranks of big names (who once were small) like America Online, Apple Computer, Federal Express, Gymboree, Jenny Craig Inc, Staples, and many, many more. There is free money for your business. Who knows, you could be "small potatoes" today, and in the future, you could join the list that contains the likes of Outback Steakhouse, Restoration Hardware, and Costco.

There are hundreds of state agencies with money to help your business. All you have to do is reach out to them. Also available to you are local programs. Your city, county, and even local organizations all offer assistance in the way of grants and low-interest loans, and venture capital as well.

Let's take a state like New York. Growing a business in New York can be tough – especially when it's technology-based. With all the fierce competition out there, it can be daunting for a business owner who hopes to transform the market with cutting-edge technologies. That is exactly why the Small Business Technology Investment Fund Program (SBTIF) exists.

Free money can change everything. Watch your business soar to heights you never imagined – all because of the venture capital you gained from the SBTIF. New York's economic development agency, Empire State Development, started this fund in the hopes to nurture all businesses based in technology. Read about this and other venture capital opportunities in New York here: www.nylovessmallbiz.com/growing_a_business/venture_capital.asp.

In a place like Rhode Island, Workforce Development is of great value. The Governor's Workforce Board knows just how important it is for employees of any business to possess the best skills and techniques. Great employees build great companies; it's a fact.

That is why the Governor's Workforce offers a series of grants to develop and train a team that will yield your business the best possible results. These Comprehensive Worker Training Grants can get you up to $50,000 of free money! If a stronger workforce is what your company needs, then this grant will be of tremendous benefit. Learn more about it here: www.rihric.com/awards.htm.

Also, in case you didn't know, the agencies out there have tailored all kinds of programs to suit all kinds of people. If you are a woman, a minority, a veteran, or disabled, you have even more chances to get your hands on the free money!

If you have questions, and most new business owners do, you have free help waiting there as well. Many communities have agencies that offer free legal services. The Small Business Administration also offers legal advice.

Women Entrepreneurs

There are many terrific grant opportunities if you are of the female persuasion. The entire purpose of the Small Business Association's Office of Women's Business Ownership is to help women achieve their dreams and improve their communities by providing assistance for starting a business. They provide training on how to get started and how to maintain a successful business, and they offer plenty of help along the way. Check out the SBA's website for all the details (http://www.sba.gov/aboutsba/sbaprograms/onlinewbc/index.html).

Among the wonderful resources for women is SBA's Women Business Centers (WBC). Available for guidance every step of the way, this SBA program provides resource centers all across the nation to help women get their businesses launched. Grants are available to these WBCs for five years, and there is even an option to renew for another five years. The program's mission is to "level the playing field." The WBC provides assistance to new businesses and existing businesses looking to expand.

For a complete list of the addresses, websites and email contacts for each state, see http://www.sba.gov/idc/groups/public/documents/ sba_program_office/sba_pr_wbc_ed.pdf.

Teachers, Principals, Listen Up!

Move to the head of the class or at least the head of the line when it comes to getting money for your school or your programs. This site – http://www.schoolgrants.org – which they dub as "your one stop site for PK -12 school grant opportunities" is an A+ site for educators. They offer grant writing tips and workshops focused solely on how to write successful grants in the area of education. In addition to help in writing grant applications, they provide a list of grants and where to find more information and opportunities. If education is your field, this is your site.

Variety Is the Spice of Life

If you are of a certain age, like me or older, you'll remember ads that said, "Let your fingers do the walking." The phone book and the yellow pages were how we found information in the olden days. Today it's all online and at http://www.foundations.org, someone else has done the searching for you. This great site has compiled a directory of charitable foundations.

They've gathered the information; you simply click away. Select "Directories" and choose either "community foundations" or "corpo- rate/private foundations." A long list of people/organizations giving away free money pops up for you to peruse. You can then select from your area of interest/locale or a certain corporation. For example, I clicked on the Eddie Bauer corporation and learned all the charitable activities of that company, including providing scholarships through the Hispanic College Fund, which assists students attending schools all around the country. If you are a Hispanic college student, you've just found another source of money to apply for that you didn't know existed two minutes ago.

Simply finding what is available is more than half the battle in the search for free money. Sites like this get you on your way quicker, and it is so easy! Especially if you are looking for scholarships, check out all the community foundations in your state, county, and city. They usually have many private donors offering a wide variety of private scholarships. Ten minutes spent searching these sites could land you $10,000 – a very wise investment of time and a wonderful investment in your future or the future of your student.

Another site to add to your favorites: http://www.grantsolutions.gov. This is the web address for the Grants Center of Excellence (COE). It is a partnership between agencies within Health and Human Services, Department of Agriculture, the Denali Commission, and Department of Treasury. The COE states that these partner agencies distribute over $250 billion in grants each year. Did I just say $250 billion? Yes, I did. That's a lot of grants. The COE serviced over $58 billion of those grants in fiscal year 2006, which is about 13% of all US grants. This is another site worth checking out.

The CFDA, Catalog of Federal Domestic Assistance, is also a great resource. This site gives access to a database of all federal programs that are available to state and local governments. You can search and find what you are eligible for and then contact the agency or program to apply. The site is updated biweekly as new programs are posted by federal agencies. See http://12.46.245.173/pls/portal30/CATALOG. FIRST_TIME_USER_DYN.show.

There is so much information available! Are you feeling empowered and motivated? I hope so.

Now, turn the page – we're not quite done yet.

(The sequel? Part 2? Who cares – It's more free money!)

More Free Money!

"Lack of money is no obstacle. Lack of an idea is an obstacle."
~ Ken Hakuta

I need to keep telling you about free money, but I have learned that people like shorter chapters. So I decided to pause, to give you time to catch your breath and scratch your head in amazement. I bet you've already told somebody at least one thing that you have read about in Chapter 24, Free Money. Well, there's more. This is Chapter 24 continued. The rest of the story. This is filled with more places in which you can find free money.

Other Grants

Besides the government (federal, state, county, city – check them all), there are many grant opportunities available through private foundations. Private funds and community groups often like to focus their grants on non-profit agencies (there are many grants out there for you if you are a non-profit organization!) and minorities and women.

There are business grants available through the Women's Financial Fund (http://www.womensbusinessgrants.com/who.shtml), and they state right on their website that since they are giving you a grant, not a loan, your repayment ability is not an issue. They won't even take a

> There are many grants out there for you if you are a non-profit organization!

peek at your credit report, and they pass out up to $5000.

Another opportunity is a loan program of up to $10,000 for women in business (www.count-me-in.org). Also see: www.lib.msu.edu/harris23/grants/3women.htm; www.fundsnetservices.com/women.htm; or www.womensnet.net; plus a host of others. Another helpful resource, www.ehome-basedbusiness.com/articles, provides a list of 25 important telephone numbers for those launching a business.

Pay the Bills...and Other Expenses

I know what you're thinking. You initially picked up this book because you wanted answers on how to cure your debt. Maybe you don't need money to grow a business. Maybe you need money for more immediate things, like paying some of your bills. If you have debt, it's probably holding you back from the things you'd like to do in the future. Perhaps the will to succeed in starting your own business is hindered due to the mounting debt that is crushing you. Well, worry no more! There's a good chance that there is some "free money" out there for you. The only thing is, you have to really look for it to find it, and I'm going to help you do that. There are programs to help with paying utility bills, child care, and even food expenses! There are organizations out there who give out money that they like to call "emergency money." You can use this money to keep debts and monthly expenses under control.

Those Everyday Expenses. Paid.

If you are disabled or if you are a senior, the Supplemental Security Income (SSI) can help you. Funded by general tax revenues, it exists to aid seniors, the blind, and the disabled in paying off their everyday expenses. Blind and disabled children can apply as well. The less income you have, the more you can qualify for. All it takes is an application, and you can be one step closer to paying off your bills. The SSI sends out checks *every month* to help people pay off their expenses. You can receive up to thousands of dollars a year.

To apply, you must be a U.S. citizen. If you're a non-citizen, you can still be eligible, as long as you are in alignment with the alien eligibility criteria under the 1996 legislation and the amendments that followed it.

All your resources are counted by the SSI, and what you own must not exceed $2000 for an individual, and $3000 for a couple. Keep in mind, the SSI is fair when it comes to determining which of your resources to count. It won't count the home that you own or the wedding ring you're wearing on your finger. Your personal items and fancy household appliances will remain off the tally as well. However, it will count any cash, bank accounts, stocks, or bonds that you may have. Also, if you've recently received any type of grant or scholarship, all you have to do is wait nine months to be eligible for SSI. Seems like a pretty fair deal to me. Aside from all that, you must currently be bringing in little to no income to qualify. Call Social Security at 1-800-772-1213 to see if you meet the current income requirements. You can also learn more and apply at www.socialsecurity.gov/ssi/text-understanding-ssi.htm.

Though it does change each year, the monthly benefit rate for an individual is $623, while couples can receive $934. There are even some states out there that will take it a step further and actually *add* to the benefits that SSI is already giving! So what you initially receive may increase even more. Not only that, but if you qualify for SSI, you may also qualify for certain services within your state. It just gets better and better, doesn't it? If you need help paying for Medicare, your state may just foot the bill. Maybe you need some assistance with job training? Your state may just take care of all that for you! Contact Social Security for questions.

The Utilities. Paid.

How about getting those utility bills paid? They make it easy in Phoenix, Arizona. There's an organization known as the Arizona Public Service (APS), and they have a program that helps low-income residents to pay their energy bills. That's right – you can get a discount of up to 40% off if you qualify for it! Factoring in how much income your household makes each month, along with how much energy you use, the program makes paying your energy bills an absolute breeze. With those huge savings, you can use your money toward other things, like paying off credit card bills. Take a look at the APS site, which can be found at www.aps.com. You can also call 1-800-582-5706 to find out more about eligibility requirements.

And don't start pouting just because you reside outside of Arizona…

The Low Income Home Energy Assistance Program (LIHEAP) is a great place to go if you're looking for some funds to pay your energy bills. Run by the Division of Energy Assistance, the program is federally-funded. The best part is that every year, money is distributed among all fifty states! That means that you should check to see what you can qualify for within your state. Get more information here: www.acf.hhs.gov/programs/liheap.

Got other utilities, aside from energy bills, that need to be paid? Your state may offer a program that will cure your financial woes. How are you going to know if you don't pick up the phone and ask? Asking never hurt anybody. The worst thing that can come from it is a simple "no." And if that happens, all you have to do is move on to the next organization or agency. There are plenty out there. So grab your phone book and get in touch with the utility office in your state. You never know – you may be one step away from receiving significant discounts on all your utilities.

> Lucky for you, there are countless programs for children out there.

Expenses Toward Your Children. Paid.

Maybe you have kids and you're struggling to make ends meet. Lucky for you, there are countless programs for children out there. Child Care can really wipe you out by the time the end of the month comes along. Many families would experience a tremendous boost in income if they suddenly didn't have to pay Child Care expenses. It doesn't seem fair that we have to struggle to pay such high Child Care costs while we're fighting to put food on the table, among other things. That is why places like the Office of Family Assistance (OFA) are around. The OFA runs the Temporary Assistance for Needy Families (TANF) program, which has been up and running since 1997. Not only does the program provide free job training and education, but it helps with locating grants that pay for Child Care. By contacting state agencies, it can find a program that is right for you. You can learn more at www.acf.hhs.gov/programs/ofa/. Also, be sure to check out some other opportunities at www.childcareaware.org or www.workfamily.org.

The Child Care and Development Block Grant (CCDBG) provides funds to assist with Child Care costs as well. The U.S. Department of Health and Human Services is responsible for heading this terrific organization. Every year, financial burden is eased, as families receive up to thousands of dollars to pay their Child Care costs. Parents are allowed to choose their own Child Care provider, as long as it is legally operating and it meets all state health and safety requirements. More information can be found at www.naeyc.org/policy/federal/ccdbg.asp or www.nccic.org.

Does dread fill your chest when you hear the words *Internal Revenue Service*? When I tell you about the amazing Child Care benefits they offer, you might want to change your tune. Just take a look at their Publication 503, which is entitled *Child and Dependent Care Expenses*. You may be eligible to receive hundreds, even thousands, toward paying off Child Care. To learn more about this, go to www.irs.gov. You can also call them directly at: 1-800-829-1040.

There are many employers out there that offer a plan where you can pay your Child Care with pre-tax money – that means big savings at the end of the year. So don't waste any time in contacting your employer to find out if this benefit is available to you. Remember, you never know until you ask.

Aside from Child Care, raising a child brings about a number of other considerations. Education is a fundamental piece of the puzzle, and it's something that we should never skimp on. Head Start exists to provide your child with free Pre-School! Geared toward providing low-income families with the tools to successfully enhance the development of their children, the program offers a variety of educational, social, and health services. Armed with the skills to go into kindergarten with confidence, children get a "head start" on the path toward success. You can't go wrong with this program. Go here to get more information: www2.acf.dhhs.gov/programs/hsb.

Did you know about the Adoption Tax Credit?

There is also a program run by the Federal Transit Administration that can be of great benefit to you if you're having trouble transporting your child to a specific location. The program is actually geared toward providing free transport to seniors and those with disabilities. Within the FTA's "guidance document" (C9070) on the topic, there is language that plainly states that free transportation can be used by other parties if they can demonstrate that an unplanned event has left them in a bind. So, if your child is suddenly left with no way to get to school or to the doctor's office, and there's nowhere else to turn, you should try to take advantage of the free transportation available. The FTA hands out millions of dollars a year to local groups in order to fund this free service. That's a lot of money, and if you need the assistance, you shouldn't hesitate in seizing the opportunity. Learn more at www.fta.dot.gov. You can also call them at: 202-366-4020.

And how about adopting? Do you plan on adopting children in the future? If so, you probably already know that adoption can be costly and that you might need a little extra help. Organizations like the National Adoption Foundation can give you the financial assistance that you're looking for. It provides grants, not only to be used toward adopting a child, but toward raising a child as well! Learn more at www.nafadopt.org.

Did you know about the Adoption Tax Credit? You can get up to $10,960 in tax breaks! That's a big chunk of change! There are a variety of adoption expenses that qualify, and you can get all your information here: www.irs.gov/taxtopics/tc607.html.

More and more companies today are offering adoption benefits to their employees. They're realizing how adoption is becoming more common with each passing year, and they want to help you ease the burden of your costs. Check with your employer to find out what your company is offering, and if they aren't offering anything, talk to them about implementing some adoption benefits! It may just take someone speaking up to get the ball rolling.

Transportation. Paid.

As an employee, you can receive transportation fringe benefits. Taking advantage of these benefits can lead to big savings. Every single month, you may be eligible to receive $110 for transportation costs, or $215 for parking costs! The money is yours tax free, and at the end of the year, you'll have more in your pockets. To get more information on this Qualification Transportation Fringe Benefit, go to www.irs.gov/publications/p15b/ar02.html#d0e2081. Once you've checked that out, talk to your employer to find out how you can start receiving these benefits.

Health Insurance. Paid.

Health insurance can be costly; that is why more and more people are opting to go without it. But it doesn't have to be that way. Why endure the risk of being left unprotected in the face of some unforeseen emergency that could, in the end, wipe you out completely? If you're over the age of 65, then there is no getting around the fact that you need a health insurance program that you can rely on. And if you're one of the many people who struggle to pay for Medicare coverage, I've got some great news for you...

Qualified Medicare Beneficiary (QMB) is a program aimed toward easing the burden of Medicare payments, and it's simple to apply for. If you qualify, the benefits are hefty; payments toward Medicare Part A and Medicare Part B, along with co-insurance and deductibles, can take the pressure off your pocketbook.

If you apply as an individual, your monthly income cannot exceed $837, and for couples, you can't go past the $1120 mark. Also, as an individual, your assets can't total up to more than $4000; for a couple, it's $6000. But don't worry – QMB doesn't count things like your home or car. Not only that, there are some states out there that don't set any limits on assets.

You can get in touch with Medicare by calling 1-800-MEDICARE (1-800-633-4227). Or simply visit their site at www.medicare.gov.

And Even More Free Money!

Need cash? In Arizona, your local Family Assistance Administration Office (FAA) may be able to help. The FAA administers the Arizona Cash Assistance Program, which gives cash for services to kids, families and individuals. This program issues debit cards you can use at ATMs and in most stores. Talk about convenient! Be sure to check out http://www.govbenefits.gov (type in the name of the program in the search box) to see if you are eligible and to get more information on program requirements and program contact information. To download an application, visit http://www.de.state.az.us/faa/appcenter.asp. For questions about this program, call FAA Customer Services at 800-325-8401. If you want to locate the FAA office closest to home, go to http://www.de.state.az.us/faa/contact.asp. It doesn't hurt to look! It's quick, it's easy, and best of all, it's FREE money!

California's CalWORKs welfare program gives cash aid and services to California families in need. Families that apply and qualify for ongoing assistance receive money each month to help pay for housing, food, and other necessary expenses. There are offices located in each of the 58 counties and you can apply at any one. For your convenience, the county welfare department is even listed under the County Government Section of the telephone book. Or you can visit the counties' websites here: http://www.dss.cahwnet.gov/cdssweb/CountyWebS_296.htm. For eligibility requirements and other details, visit http://www.govbenefits.gov!

Free House Repair!

I'm not making this up. It's absolutely true! Want to fix up that kitchen? What about those pesky repairs in the bathroom you need to get around to? Well, now's the time to do it all! The Rural Housing Repair Loans and Grants can give you the free money or a low cost loan to help you with improving your home. Through their program, you can potentially receive over $7000 in free money! That's a lot of cash that you can put into your home, without having to worry about paying it back. This is a US Department of Agriculture program and you can get all the details, including more information about the application process, at http://www.govbenefits.gov and http://www.rurdev.usda.gov/rhs/.

Free Eats!

The Emergency Food Assistance Program (TEFAP), commonly known as the food stamp program, is a great program to get help with emergency food assistance at no cost. The TEFAP is a federal program that helps supplement the diets of individuals and families. For information you can check out their website at http://www.fns.usda.gov/fdd/programs/tefap. Managed by the US Department of Agriculture, the program contact information is: Headquarters Office, Food Distribution Division, FNS, USDA, Room 502, Park Office Center, 3101 Park Center Drive, Alexandria VA 22302. For eligibility details and information on the application process, don't forget to check out http://www.govbenefits.gov.

How About Cutting Your Rent?

Is it a constant battle to make payments to your landlord on time? Even if you do make those payments in a timely fashion, you're probably turning over the couch cushions, rounding up whatever you can to pay the rest of your bills. Paying the rent can dry us out, making it difficult to put money into other expenses.

The Section 8 Rental Assistance Program is in place for such situations. Through it, the Public Housing Authority (PHA) steps in and makes payments to your landlord. In doing so, you could end up only paying 30% of your income toward the rent! The unit must adhere to Section 8's quality standards, and households must be low-income to qualify for the program.

The U.S. Department of Housing and Urban Development can point you in the right direction. For more information, go to www.hud.gov.

And What if You're Out of Work?

When you're out of a job, it's time to take advantage of unemployment insurance. Every state has it. If, through no fault of your own, you find yourself jobless, you have every right to reap the benefits of free money. Why shouldn't you? We all know how stressful job hunting can be while you're trying desperately to pay the bills. Not a fun scenario. Take that weight off your shoulders and apply with your state. In places like California, you can get up to $450 a week! That's $450 every week that you *don't have to ever pay back*. In the state of New York, you can collect up to $405 a week. How much you receive is determined by past wages, along with the maximum amount that your state allows. Not only that, but in most states, you have a right to keep receiving that free money for 26 weeks! That's almost seven months of checks in your mailbox! And those checks come with no strings attached!

So get in touch with your state and you can start collecting too! Get more information here workforcesecurity.doleta.gov/unemploy/uifactsheet.asp.

How About Emergencies?

Sometimes the unexpected occurs, catching us off guard, forcing us to pick up the pieces and, in some cases, start all over again. But how to go about this? If you're like most Americans, you probably don't have a sufficient cushion set aside for those rainy days. If you're living paycheck to paycheck, you definitely don't have the funds to put into those last-minute emergencies that pop up from time to time. But at least there are places to turn to. If you look, you will discover that there are a number of agencies and organizations that have funds set aside to help individuals like you. If you need money for bills, for rent, for job training, for car maintenance – these places can help you!

The U.S. Department of Health and Human Services (DHHS) is a great place to start if you're looking for some extra funds. Operating in ten regions all over the country, the DHHS strives to look after the health and well-being of our nation. Being there in times of emergency is one of them. Of course, every DHHS office varies from region to region, so be sure to check what is available where you live. In the Seattle region, I know that DHHS offers three different kinds of emergency grants for an assortment of circumstances. They work with the Welfare Rights Organizing Coalition to meet needs of housing, medical care, food, and clothing, among other things. You can look into this further at www.wroc.org/factsheets/emergencygrant.htm. And, of course, if you're outside the Seattle region, simply go to the main DHHS site at www.dhhs.gov.

The Community Action Partnership is another great place to go. It heads a network of Community Action Agencies, which exist all over the country. These nonprofit organizations exist to provide support and financial assistance to low-income families. They are intent upon attacking poverty in our country, and for years, they have demonstrated that through community outreach, job training, counseling, food donations, and on-demand transportation programs. Learn more about them at www.communityactionpartnership.com.

You can also go to www.govbenefits.gov to learn more about a variety of emergency grants. And if you want to pick up your phone book and call a local charity organization, you'll be surprised to find that there are ways in which they can help with things like food, shelter, and education. Calling your local Salvation Army can make all the difference, if you're in need of financial assistance. To learn more, you can go to www.salvationarmy.org.

> If you look, you will discover that there are a number of agencies and organizations that have funds set aside to help individuals like you.

Finally, you can always go to your local Public Assistance office to apply for the funds that you need. In some states, they offer free money to people who are still waiting for other grants to pan out. The amount varies from state to state, but it's worth a call to check and see what's available!

When an emergency situation disrupts your way of living, there are always resources that you can rely upon. Take advantage of them when you need them!

Free Vacation Anyone?

The USDA Forest Service (FS) offers a great volunteer program that involves traveling to various sites throughout the year. All you need to bring with you is a sense of adventure, as you will find yourself engaged in various archaeological and historical preservation projects.

The program is called Passport in Time, and there is no fee required to join. All you have to do is find your own way to get to the site, and in some cases, Passport in Time might provide you with food and a place to stay. If you have a curious spirit and a hunger to explore, this may just be the vacation you're looking for. You can find out about current projects at www.passportintime.com.

Study Abroad – Free of Charge

Ever fantasize about pursuing your education in some exotic overseas locale? The U.S. Department of Education has all kinds of programs designed for current students to travel abroad. They're handing out free money to encourage students and educational institutions to become more involved in foreign language and area studies. If you're a student looking to experience another country, or if you're a teacher interested in leading a group to study abroad, contact the Department of Education. They give free money to fund traveling and living expenses! You can learn more at www.ed.gov/programs/iegpsflasf/index.html.

In addition, see http://www.worldstudy.gov/overview2.html for scholarships and fellowships that provide significant funding for study abroad, in amounts of up to $20,000 and even $30,000 for study in both the United States and abroad.

The National Security Education Programs funds Boren Fellowships, which provide grad students the opportunity to study languages and cultures that are deemed important to US national security. Students who desire a career in the federal government and wish to take course-work abroad should consider this opportunity. Fellowships are up to $30,000. Applications must be completed online. See http://www.iie.org/programs/nsep/graduate/award.htm.

That Exists??

There are programs out there that all of us can qualify for. Of course, all of us can't qualify for every single one of them, but if we make the calls and do the research, we will find the free money that we're looking for. There are programs for everything. I repeat: everything. There are programs for things that you could never even imagine.

The Senior Farmers' Market Nutrition Program (SFMNP) is a great one. Through it, seniors receive money to buy fresh, locally-grown fruits and vegetables from farmers' markets and roadside stands. It's a fantastic way to not only keep low-income seniors fed, but to also keep them healthy and in support of local independent farmers. The SFMNP has given money to hundreds of thousands of seniors, and you can be one of them. Congress has set aside $15 million for the SFMNP to use through 2007 alone, and I'm sure there's more where that came from for next year! You can learn more and see how much you qualify for here: www.fns.usda.gov/wic/SeniorFMNP/SFMNPmenu.htm.

What if you are looking for a job and need an outfit to wear to the interview, but don't have the money to buy new clothes? Instant savings happens when you get clothes for free! It may help you get the job, and the clothes are yours to keep. Most every state has such a program. Contact www.dressforsuccess.org and www.bottomlesscloset.org.

Don't be hesitant or ashamed to take advantage of the assistance that the government provides. You have paid your taxes and there are billions of dollars in programs to help if you need it. If you are having a tough time right now, don't hesitate to use the aid that is there for you. Things will get better, but for the time being, if the government can provide free or reduced cost lunches for your kids at school, let them. That adds up to big savings for you to pay off your bills. Contact www.fns.usda.gov/cnd/lunch/.

> You have paid your taxes and there are billions of dollars in programs to help if you need it.

If you are an older person having trouble making ends meet, you can get meal assistance and apply the money saved to other pressing debt, like your credit cards. Contact your local Center for the Aging or www.fns.usda.gov/fdd/programs/nsip.

If you are what we call a "senior" – and I don't mean high school – there are endless easy money tips for you. Ask for your discount at the restaurant, at the hotel, on your airline tickets. You can get a cheaper camping rate at the state parks, and a discount on your eyeglasses based on your age. If you are 100 years old, you get 100% discount at Pearle Vision Centers! You can get a free fishing license in many states. The chances to save a buck are everywhere and they add up to big free money!

They Never End

There are countless programs available to you. Open an Individual Development Account, a special kind of savings account. For every dollar you put in, the government puts in a dollar, and a private group puts in a dollar. It triples your investment! The money can be used to buy a house, go to school, or start a business; whatever you want! Contact www.idanetwork.org.

If you live near a university or medical college, you can often get your health check-ups, eye exams, and dental visits for free! If not free, they will be at a much cheaper rate. To find a dental college, contact: www.adea.org; to find an eye doctor school, contact www.aoa.org.

Your local community may have programs to help you with after school care, or taking care of your elderly parents, or even substance abuse. For free care and information, contact www.salvationarmyusa.org or www.catholiccharitiesusa.org.

One of the most crippling expenses facing many people today is prescription medicines. There are assistance programs available that can save you hundreds, perhaps thousands, of dollars! Usually you will need your doctor's involvement. Contact www.helpingpatients.org.

That's Not All, Folks

Many county government offices offer programs for first-time home buyers. You can literally save thousands. Programs vary widely, so contact your local office. There are also programs for homeowners who get caught in a temporary situation and cannot make their house payment. To see if your area gives aid to get you through a bind, contact www.hud.gov/offices/. If you live in a rural area, there are programs to help you fix up your house, pay your rent, or even purchase a house. Contact www.rurdev.usda.gov.

It may be the American dream to own a home; the government launched a grant program in 2004 called the American Dream Downpayment Act. This is not a reduced loan; this is your actual down payment. You have to be a first-time buyer to qualify and there is an income limitation. See http://www.hud.gov/offices/cpd/affordablehousing/programs/home/addi/ for more information.

If you own a home and are at least 62 years old, you can take out a reverse mortgage on your house. Instead of making house payments, your house pays you every month! There usually is no interest, and you can use the money for whatever you want. Pay off your credit cards! Start a business! Travel the world! Contact your banker or go to www.ftc.gov.

Students

College students who qualify may be able to get a grant of up to $4000 per year to pay their bills. Contact www.ed.gov/about/offices/list/fsa/index. html. Want to learn a foreign language? Get a fellowship grant to pay your tuition. Contact www.ed.gov/about/offices/list/ope/iegps/index.html. You can get a grant for $28,000 to get your doctorate degree overseas and not have to repay it! Contact www.ed.gov/programs/iegpsirs/index.html. There are hundreds of grants to help you go to school! Contact your school or state aid office or go to www.studentaid.ed.gov.

Maybe you never thought you could go to college. Even if you are no longer a 20-something, if getting a college education is your dream, it still can happen. There are programs to help you succeed. One foundation provides scholarships for lower income women who are over 35. If you have such a dream for yourself, check out www. rankinfoundation.org.

Have you finished your degree and want to continue? Many grants and fellowships are available. See http://www.aauw.org/fga/fellowships_ grants/; www.grants.gov.; or look up grants in your field. Opportunities abound. For example, the National Institute of Health offers programs for medical and dental students (http://grants.nih.gov/grants/index. cfm). You can also check out the Department of Education at http:// www.ed.gov/about/offices/list/ocfo/grants/grants.html. There are also many private funding sources out there. One such program offers fellowships and grants for education research (http://www.spencer. org/programs/grants/research_grants.htm). Private foundations are a wonderful source for dollars that you do not have to pay back.

Tax Credits

Aside from all the free money programs out there, you also have to think about *keeping* money in your pockets. To me, this is just as valuable as being handed a free check each month! Receiving money is always great, but making it last is another topic all together. Knowing how to hold on to what you've got is everything. That is why I believe it's important to educate yourselves on tax credits. There are tax credits out there that some of you don't know about, and this is a case where what you don't know *will* hurt you. It is wasteful to put dollars and dollars of your hard-earned money into something that isn't necessary. You could be using that money to pay off all your debt!

This is a gold mine that no one talks about. You can hold onto significant sums of money by way of these tax credits. A tax credit is not an expense that lowers your taxable income. A tax credit is actually tax dollars that you do not pay – tax dollars that stay in your pocket and do not get mailed off to Uncle Sam.

> There are tax credits out there that some of you don't know about...

It is easy, yet so many people assume that a tax credit is only for somebody else, somebody with "connections." Not true. Want $500? You can get money for making improvements to your house. By becoming more energy efficient – replacing old windows, updating your furnace, or putting new insulation in your home – you can get up to $500. Not a bad deal. Saving energy is good for the planet and your pocketbook.

If you convert to a solar energy system to heat your water, you can get a tax credit of up to $2000! That is $2000 in taxes that you do not have to pay – that equals free money! If you buy a new hybrid kind of car – a part gas/part electric, or one that runs on an alternative fuel like ethanol, or even a diesel car – you can get a tax credit, up to $4000! There is a formula that is used to compute the credit for energy efficient cars; the IRS or your car dealer can help you determine what the exact credit would be for your car.

For more information on all these energy credits, go to www.energystar.gov.

There are many tax credits that people do not know exist, and therefore they do not claim them. If you claim all the credits you are entitled to, you may be able to wipe out up to 80% of your tax bill!

You can use a company to help you find and take advantage of these hidden tax credits. You can simply search on the web for "enterprise zones" or "tax credits" and find one of those companies that fits your needs. I'll give you more information on enterprise zones in just a bit. Most of them help corporations of all sizes claim the benefit of all available state and federal tax credits. In fact, one small one that I am familiar with, over the last ten years, has helped businesses document over $100 million in tax credits.

You can also cut back on federal income taxes by taking advantage of the Child Tax Credit. You can knock off $1,000 for each of your children! You're eligible for this credit as long as your child is...

... a U.S. citizen or resident alien.

...under the age of 17 at the end of the tax year.

...your son or daughter, whether he or she is a stepchild, adopted child, eligible foster child, sibling, or stepsibling.

There are some other eligibility requirements involved as well. If your modified adjusted gross income gets too high, you may not be able to collect as much as the maximum allows. The phase-out of benefits starts occurring once these income targets are hit:

...Married Filing Jointly	$110,000
...Married Filing Separately	$55,000
...Others	$75,000

The amount of income tax you owe also plays some part in dictating your credit. If the income tax you owe is less than your Child Tax Credit, that could work out to be a great thing for you! You can possibly take that difference and claim it as well! It would be an "additional" Child Tax Credit. That means that you would be able to collect a refund, without owing any taxes at all! More money for you. Now that you're informed, you no longer have to blindly dish funds out to the government each year; you can seize the financial control and mold it to your liking. After all, it is *your* money.

Take a look at Form 1040 or 1040A to take advantage in claiming your Child Tax Credit. If you need a little extra help, you can always grab a copy of Publication 972 from the IRS. It will provide complete details on how to fill out your paperwork and get the ball rolling. If you need any additional assistance, you can always go to www.irs.gov. And if you'd like to receive these forms by mail, call 1-800-TAX-FORM (1-800-829-3676).

Now, let me direct your attention toward another excellent credit that many people don't know about. It's known as the Earned Income Tax Credit (EITC), and it was designed for working low-income people who don't have a lot of money to spare when it comes to income taxes. If you qualify for the EITC, you might be surprised to see how substantially your income taxes are reduced. Not only that, but in some cases, you might even receive a refund! Not only does the amount of credit you receive have to do with your income, but it is also determined by the size of your family. If you are married, filing jointly, with two or more qualifying children, you can receive up to $4,716 in credit!

To find out if you qualify, go to www.irs.gov. From there, download Form W-5 and Publication 96. You can call 1-800-TAX-FORM (1-800-829-3676) to request that these items be sent by mail as well.

EZ

Ever heard of enterprise zones? Some states use the name "empowerment zone" or "renewal communities." Basically, by operating your business in a prescribed location and hiring employees from a target area or population, you could get big tax breaks! By working with your community to develop the local economy, you are helping to revitalize your area, and you may be eligible for tremendous tax dollar savings. These programs offer billions of dollars in tax savings!

Almost all 50 states offer these programs! For example, California has 42 enterprise zones across the state. Florida has 56, and Colorado has 18 with ten different tax credits for doing business in those zones. By hiring your workers from the specified zone or population, or starting or expanding your business in certain rural or urban areas, you can reap the reward of huge dollars that stay with you and your business instead of being paid in state taxes.

Do a computer search for your state's enterprise zones to get information regarding what areas are included, what paperwork you need to fill out, and what tax credits are available to you. Creating jobs and investing in the community is a win-win deal.

The federal government may also have tax incentives for doing business in certain zones. For further information, and to see if your address qualifies, go to http://www.hud.gov/economicdevelopment/index.cfm.

You don't have to be in an enterprise zone to take advantage of other tax credits – there are many available. The federal Work Opportunity tax credit allows any company in the U.S. to take tax breaks if certain employees are hired, and it can be $2400 per new employee. There is the Welfare to Work credit, which allows a credit of up to $8500 if you hire someone who receives federal assistance. You may be able to receive a $4000 credit for hiring certain Native Americans.

> States offer many credits as well.

States offer many credits as well. Wages to qualified employees can save you up to $10,000 in taxes. There generally are property tax credits and sales tax and use tax credits available as well. It is to your advantage to check out the web pages for your county and state, and to check out companies that specialize in tax credits (for example, www.taxcreditcompany.com or www.ntcgtax.com).

The list of tax credits is long. Really long. Odds are you are eligible for something. You can take a look at www.irs.gov or talk to the person who does your taxes or look for a tax credit company to help you ferret out everything you've got coming. Tax credits are free money, and can be big money, and you deserve what is rightfully yours. If you qualify, take that tax credit!

It Works

It is smart to take advantage of every opportunity that comes your way, and if the government programs can help out the likes of well-known millionaires and billionaires, and huge companies like Chrysler, you should feel free to take what is there. It was not all that long ago that Chrysler was facing financial ruin. Chrysler did not want to file bankruptcy and lay off thousands of workers. They borrowed a tidy sum in government-guaranteed loans, and they got back on their feet. If Chrysler can borrow over one billion dollars from the feds, you can get your piece of the pie too. It is a huge buffet. There is plenty for everyone.

Now, Go and Do

You can contact the websites, the agencies; you can do your own research. You are now able to see that the possibilities are endless. There are generic programs offering money to train your employees, and there are specific grants, for example, like ones for libraries that serve Native Hawaiians.

I have gotten you started here on where to look. Don't be intimidated. Finding the grants is the time consuming part and *Debt Cures* has helped you on your way. When you find a grant, you'll see that many grant applications are done online. Follow the instructions, step by step. Different grants ask for different things. If you have questions, contact that agency directly. Most have help sections on their websites to guide you through the process.

For the federal government agency directory, you can contact www.firstgov.gov or www.pueblo.gsa.gov/call or 1-880-FED-INFO. There is also a giant book if you want paper to read, during a period of hibernation perhaps. It's 2400 pages. Detailed grant information is printed in the Catalog of Federal Domestic Assistance and is available for $75. You can order it from the US Government Bookstore at http://bookstore.gpo.gov/actions/GeneralSearch.do.

If you have a question for a state agency or department, the state information office can direct you. The contact information for each state is listed as follows:

ALASKA
www.state.ak.us
907-465-2111

ARKANSAS
www.state.ar.us
501-682-3000

COLORADO
www.colorado.gov
303-866-5000

ARIZONA
http://az.gov
602-542-4900

CALIFORNIA
www.ca.gov
916-322-9900

CONNECTICUT
www.ct.gov
860-240-0222

DELAWARE
http://delaware.gov
302-739-4000

FLORIDA
www.myflorida.com
850-488-1234

GEORGIA
www.georgia.gov
404-656-2000

HAWAII
www.state.hi.us
808-548-5796

IDAHO
www.state.id.us
208-334-2411

ILLINOIS
www.illinois.gov
217-782-2000

INDIANA
www.state.in.us
317-232-1000

IOWA
www.iowa.gov
515-281-5011

KANSAS
www.kansas.gov
785-296-0111

KENTUCKY
www.kentucky.gov
502-564-3130

LOUISIANA
www.louisiana.gov
225-342-6600

MAINE
www.state.me.us
207-624-9494

MARYLAND
www.maryland.gov
800-811-8336

MASSACHUSETTS
www.mass.gov
617-722-2000

MICHIGAN
www.michigan.gov
517-373-1837

MINNESOTA
www.state.mn.us
651-296-3391

MISSISSIPPI
www.state.ms.us
601-359-1000

MISSOURI
www.state.mo.us
573-751-2000

MONTANA
www.state.mt.us
406-444-2511

NEBRASKA
www.state.ne.us
402-471-2311

NEVADA
www.nv.gov
775-687-5000

NEW HAMPSHIRE
www.state.nh.us
603-271-1110

NEW JERSEY
www.state.nj.us
609-292-2121

NEW MEXICO
www.state.nm.us
800-825-6639

NEW YORK
www.state.ny.us
518-474-2121

NORTH CAROLINA
www.ncgov.com
919-733-1110

NORTH DAKOTA
http://discovernd.com
701-328-2200

OHIO
http://ohio.gov
614-466-2000

OKLAHOMA
www.state.ok.us
405-521-2011

OREGON
www.oregon.gov
503-378-3111

PENNSYLVANIA
www.state.pa.us
717-787-2121

RHODE ISLAND
www.state.ri.us
401-222-2000

SOUTH CAROLINA
www.sc.gov
803-896-0000

SOUTH DAKOTA
www.state.sd.us
605-773-3011

VERMONT
http://vermont.gov
802-828-1110

WEST VIRGINIA
www.wv.gov
304-558-3456

TENNESSEE
www.state.tn.us
615-741-3011

VIRGINIA
www.virginia.gov
804-786-0000

WISCONSIN
www.wisconsin.gov
608-266-2211

TEXAS
www.state.tx.us
512-463-4630

WASHINGTON
http://access.wa.gov
360-753-5000

WYOMING
http://wyoming.gov
307-777-7011

UTAH
www.utah.gov
801-538-1000

WASHINGTON DC
www.dc.gov
202-727-1000

Applying: Easy Peasy

Once you've determined which grants are right for you, it's time to start applying for them. There's no need to drag your feet because you're worried that the process will be time-consuming and difficult. *It's not.* Don't let anything deter you from getting the free money that you need. You've come so close already. Why not take some extra time to sit down and apply? Think about it: an afternoon (could be more, could be much less, depending on the grant) of filling out grant applications could lead to major amounts of free money in the near future! If that's not time well spent, I don't know what is.

All grants are different, so be sure to carefully read through the qualifications and instructions for applying. If there's anything you don't understand, you can always call the agency or foundation that you're applying to.

Applying for many of the grants is an easy process. And actually, I've made it even easier by coming up with some great tips that'll help you along the way…

Know It

Make it your mission to really understand what it is you want. This especially comes into play if you're thinking of putting together an organization or business.

Sit down and take all kinds of notes. Become familiar with your objectives. Write about your qualifications. If there are any other people involved in your venture, write about their qualifications too. Special sells, so let them know what is so unique about you and your goals. Let them know that what you have to offer is unlike anything else. Be honest about the challenges that you foresee in the future, and let them know of the ways in which you will meet those challenges. Get all the details down on paper, and don't worry about making it sound brilliant yet. For now, just get everything out on paper. Once you do, you'll feel really good going forward. You know what they say: knowledge is power.

Show It

The guys reading these applications want to know why they should be cutting you a check. Make it easy for them. When you sit down to write, make a decision. Make a decision to infuse your application with energy and enthusiasm. Be passionate about what you want, whether it's money for child care services or money to start your very own business. Passion is an exciting thing – it gets people interested in you!

Write It

Now comes the easy part: the writing. Since you know what you're talking about, and you're prepared to enthusiastically show it, the writing should be a breeze. Don't worry about getting it perfect the first time around. You can always go back and edit later. I know there are some people who are intimidated by facing a blank page, but think about it this way: nothing is ever set in stone until you're ready for it to be. You know what it is you want. Just go for it. Write it. Worry about the other stuff later. These foundations and agencies make it so easy too, because their applications guide you through every step. Take each step one at a time, and get it done!

Edit It

Once you're done with the writing, then comes the editing. Sometimes it's hard to be objective about your own writing, so grab a friend or the guy sitting next to you in the cafe, and ask them if they'll read your grant proposal for you. Tell them to look out for typos and grammatical issues. Also, tell them to be honest about what they think. If you can, show it to a few other people, and get a consensus going. It will help you in the long run. These foundations and agencies like to see well-written applications, so hit your friends up for some favors and get some opinions.

Send It

Once you've worked any kinks out, and you're happy with your application, it's time to send it out! Be sure to know what the deadline is in advance, so you're not disappointed if you suddenly find out you're too late. If that's the case, you'll have to wait until next year. However, there's no need to worry – there are so many grants out there, and they're all going on at different times. You can always find something to apply for. You just have to look. Since I've already pointed you in the right direction, that shouldn't be too difficult!

Celebrate It

Your application's out there, and that's a reason to celebrate. The potential for free money is now closer than it ever was before. Some grants will get back to you within weeks, others will take months. Whatever the timeframe is, be patient. Put it out of your mind, and if there are other grant applications you'd like to apply for, go for it. You might as well. The process is so utterly simple; what have you got to lose?

If you want to know more about how to write grant proposals, there's a great amount of information here too: www.nonprofit.about. com/od/fundraising/ht/proposals.htm.

CHAPTER 25

O Canada

O Canada, we stand on guard for thee.
~ from Canadian national anthem

Most of what has been covered in *Debt Cures They Don't Want You to Know About* applies to residents of Canada as well. Many of the methods and techniques are universal and can be used to reduce or eliminate debt and get on the path to wealth. No matter where you live, interest is a killer. The less interest you can pay, life is better all around. Avoiding fees is wise, no matter what state or province you live in. This chapter will address the information that is different for Canadian residents.

Credit Reporting Agencies

Residents of Canada are also allowed a free credit report each year, but the agency to contact depends upon province of residence. The annualcreditreport.com only works for the United States. And the word free is a misnomer. It is free if requested by mail, but there is a small fee if requested immediately online. Don't ask me why. I'm just the messenger.

✔ TRANSUNION: *For Quebec Residents*

TransUnion
1 Place Laval Ouest
Suite 370
Laval, Quebec
H7N 1A1
1.877.713.3393
www.transunion.ca

✔ TRANSUNION: *For Provinces Other than Quebec*

TransUnion
P.O. Box 338, LCD1
Hamilton, Ontario
L8L 7W2
1.800.663.9980
www.transunion.ca

✔ EQUIFAX

Equifax Canada Inc.
Consumer Relations Department
Box 190 Jean Talon Station
Montreal, Quebec
H1S 2Z2
1.800.465.7166
www.equifax.ca

✔ NORTHERN CREDIT BUREAUS, INC

Northern Credit Bureaus, Inc
336 Rideau Boulevard
Rouyn – Noranda
No phone # given
www.creditbureau.ca

Northern Credit Bureaus, Inc. is an Experian company, so you can see the big three credit reporting agencies of America are in Canada as well. The same advice applies. Get your credit report and review it for accuracy. If there are errors, fix them immediately. If you have questions or disputes, use the contact information above.

As it is in the US, it is in Canada: if you want your FICO score, you have to pay the small fee. FICO does not give freebies. Canada uses the FICO score as well, and it is important to know what your score is since that is the number that determines your credit fate.

The same guidelines apply to getting and reviewing the credit report and disputing any errors or erroneous information. There could be out-dated items, incorrect items, or items that simply are not yours. The credit reporting agency has 30 days to verify the accuracy of the item you are questioning or it must be removed from the credit report. You can also contact the creditor directly to clean up the item and they can forward the correction to the credit reporting agency. You also have the right to add a "consumer statement" to your credit report to explain an accurate yet negative item. Also the credit reporting agency should forward the corrected report to anyone who has requested it in the last six months.

Credit Scores

The methods and techniques to lower the credit score apply the same no matter where you live. What you have read in these chapters works for you in Canada as well. The same tips to improving the credit score apply. For example, getting a secured credit card from a Canadian financial institution that reports to the credit reporting agencies is a quick way to up the credit score. Canadian lenders also like to see that you have a checking account and a savings account, so make sure that you open those two accounts. Canadian credit unions are easy to work with and a good place to start building credit. Follow all the other tips previously outlined in the earlier chapters and the credit score will head north!

One thing to note, some credit reporting agencies also use a credit rating. Each item on the credit report is rated on a scale of 1 to 9. In this case, the higher number is not better. A nine indicates that you don't pay your bills on time to that creditor or that you are negotiating a debt repayment plan. The lower rating is best; one means you pay each month on time.

The rating also includes a letter that indicates the type of credit of that item. R stands for revolving, which is all your credit cards. I is for installment loans, like a car loan or a personal loan. O indicates open, for example, a line of credit. You are approved for up to so much and can borrow from it at any time. This could also include student loans, which you do not have to repay until graduation.

The ratings are:

R1 = Pays within 30 days
R2 = Pays 30–60 days; or one late payment
R3 = Pays 60–90 days; or two late payments
R4 = Pays 90–120 days; or three or more late payments
R5 = Account is 120 days past due
R7 = Paid through a credit counseling or debt management program
R8 = Repossessed
R9 = Collection or bankruptcy or bad debt

There is a rating of R0 that indicates an account is new and not yet used. There is not an R6 rating.

Out with the Old

One thing that is different in Canada versus the United States is the length of time that an item stays on the credit report. In the US, the length of reporting is consistent across the nation and the credit reporting agencies. In Canada, it depends upon who your credit reporting agency is and that depends upon where you live.

If you think an old negative item should have dropped off your credit report, and it is still hanging on, check the chart first. The length of time is different depending upon the type of item and your territory. For example, bankruptcy will stay on your credit report for six years if you live in British Columbia, but seven years if you live in Ontario. No one ever said life was fair, or that money matters made sense. If the time has in fact expired and the item should be removed, then you should contact your credit reporting agency.

The chart on the following page is from the Financial Consumer Agency of Canada:

TransUnion	BC	AB	SK	MB	ON	QC	NB	NS	PEI	NL	Terr.
						(Years)					
Credit transactions (trades) (from the date of last activity or the date opened)	6	6	6	6	6	6	6	6	6	6	6
Judgments (from the reporting date)	6	6	6	6	7	7	7	6	10	7	6
Collections (from the reporting date)	6	6	6	6	6	6	6	6	6	6	6
Secured loans (registered items) (from the date opened)	5	5	5	5	5	5	5	5	5	5	5
Bankruptcy (from the discharge or reporting date)	6	6	6	6	7	7	7	6	7	7	6
Registered consumer proposal, Orderly payment of debts (from the date satisfied or reported, whichever comes first)	3	3	3	3	3	3	3	3	3	3	3
Credit counseling (from the date satisfied or reported, whichever comes first)	2	2	2	2	2	2	2	2	2	2	2
	BC	AB	SK	MB	ON	QC	NB	NS	PEI	NL	Terr.

Equifax	BC	AB	SK	MB	ON	QC	NB	NS	PEI	NL	Terr.
						(Years)					
Credit transactions (trades) (from the date of last activity)	6	6	6	6	6	6	6	6	6	6	6
Judgments (from the date satisfied or deposit)	6	6	6	6	6	6	6	6	7 to 10	6	6
Collection (from the date of last activity)	6	6	6	6	6	6	6	6	6	6	6
Secured loans (registered items) (from the filing date)	6	6	6	6	6	6	6	6	6	6	6
Bankruptcy (from the discharge date)	6	6	6	6	6	6	6	6	6	6	6
Registered consumer proposal, orderly payment of debts (from the date paid)	3	3	3	3	3	3	3	3	3	3	3
Credit counseling (from the date paid)	3	3	3	3	3	3	3	3	3	3	3
	BC	AB	SK	MB	ON	QC	NB	NS	PEI	NL	Terr.

Source: http://www.freecreditfixes.com/index.php/creditrepair/articles/length_of_reporting_canada/

Identity Theft

It is sad to say, but identity theft is the way of the world. No matter where you live, you have to be cautious at all times. The bad guys are everywhere and getting craftier everyday. Take all the steps previously discussed to safeguard your financial information. Review your credit report. Credit monitoring is a good idea as well, and is available through the credit reporting agencies in Canada also.

If you are a Canadian resident and you find a suspicious item on your credit report, or if you know that you have been the victim of identity theft, contact the fraud department of your credit bureau immediately.

TransUnion	
All provinces except Quebec: Fraud Victim Assistance Department P.O. Box 338, LCD 1 Hamilton, Ontario L8L 7W2	Phone: 800-663-9980
Residents of Quebec: Centre De Relations Aux Consommateurs TransUnion 1 Place Laval, Suite 370 Laval, PQ H7N 1A1	Phone: 877-713-3393 514-335-0374 (in Montreal)
Equifax	
Consumer Fraud Division P.O. Box 190 Jean Talon Montreal, PQ H1S 2Z2	Phone: 800-465-7166 514-493-2314
Experian	
P.O. Box 727 Rouyn-Noranda, PQ J9X 5C6	Phone 888-826-1718
Supportive Agencies	
PhoneBusters P.O. Box 686 North Bay, Ontario P1B 8J8	Phone 888-495-8501 705-494-3624

Source: http://www.transunion.ca/ca/personal/fraudidentitytheft/restoring/contacts_en.page

Guard It

In Canada, the equivalent to the Social Security Number in America is the Social Insurance Number. If you suspect that your SIN is being used by another person, to get a job or in any way, contact Human Resources Development Canada right away.

> Social Insurance Registration
> P.O. Box 7000
> Bathurst, NB E2A 4T1
> E-mail: sin-nas@hrdc-drhc.gc.ca

Everyone Values Privacy

Canada has privacy protection laws, as does the United States. The Personal Information Protection and Electronic Documents Act (PIPEDA) is the privacy law to protect the personal information of Canadian citizens.

If you feel an organization is not properly handling your private information or you want to file a complaint, do so at the following address. The website address is for information purposes. Complaints or any private information should not be e-mailed.

Also if you contact the credit reporting agency and they do not respond within 30 days, it is considered a "denial of request" and you can write the Privacy Commissioner a formal complaint.

> **The Office of the Privacy Commissioner of Canada**
> 112 Kent Street
> Ottawa, ON K1A 1H3
> Telephone: (613) 995-8210
> Toll-free: 1-800-282-1376
> Fax: (613) 947-6850
> Website: www.privcom.gc.ca

Canadians get their share of junk mail too. If you want to "opt out" of marketing offers, contact the Canadian Marketing Service. They are the keepers of the Canadian version of the "do not call" list, but they are not a government organization. They are a private trade association, funded by members, and they offer the Do Not Contact Service free of charge to Canadian consumers. By registering with them, you will significantly reduce the number of mail offers and telephone calls. By registering, you are removing your name from marketing lists. Follow the online registration instructions at https://cornerstonewebmedia. com/cma/submit.asp.

The Dreaded Debt Collector

Debt collectors exist in Canada too of course. Canadian law has the Collection Agencies Act, which states what debt collectors can and cannot do. They are not supposed to contact you on a holiday or a Sunday, except between 1 and 5 pm. They are not supposed to contact you other than by ordinary mail more than three times in a seven day period. Some things never change, no matter what country we are talking about. The most complaints received by the Ontario Ministry of Government and Consumer Affairs have to do with collection agencies. If you need more information, contact the Consumer Protection Branch at 1-800-889-9768.

If you have issues specific to your province or a consumer affairs question, the contact information is provided here for you.

Directory of Organizations – Consumer Affairs Offices

Staff in these offices can help you with consumer problems.

Federal Government

Office of Consumer Affairs
Industry Canada
235 Queen Street
Ottawa ON K1A 0H5
Fax: (613) 952-6927
Email: consumer.information@ic.gc.ca
Website: www.consumer.ic.gc.ca

Competition Bureau
50 Victoria Street
Gatineau QC K1A 0C9
Tel.: (819) 997-4282
Toll Free: 1-800-348-5358
TDD: 1-800-642-3844
Fax: (819) 997-0324
Email: compbureau@cb-bc.gc.ca
Website: www.competitionbureau.gc.ca

Financial Consumer Agency of Canada (FCAC)
427 Laurier Avenue West, 6th floor
Ottawa ON K1R 1B9
Tel.: (613) 996-5454 or 1-866-461-FCAC (3222)
Fax: (613) 941-1436 or 1-866-814-2224
Website: www.fcac-acfc.gc.ca

Provincial and Territorial Governments

Alberta Service Alberta Consumer Contact Centre 17th Flr., TD Tower, 10888 – 102 Avenue Edmonton AB T5J 2Z1 Tel.: (780) 427-4088 (Edmonton and area) Toll Free: 1-877-427-4088 (Alberta only) Email: governmentservices@gov.ab.ca Website: www.servicealberta.gov.ab.ca	**British Columbia** Business Practices & Consumer Protection Authority (BPCPA) PO Box 9244 Victoria BC V8W 9J2 Tel.: 1-888-564-9963 Fax: (250) 920-7181 Email: info@bpcpa.ca Website: http://www.bpcpa.ca
Manitoba Manitoba Finance Consumer and Corporate Affairs Consumers' Bureau Suite 302, 258 Portage Avenue Winnipeg MB R3C 0B6 Tel.: (204) 945-3800 Toll Free: 1-800-782-0067 Fax: (204) 945-0728 Email: consumersbureau@gov.mb.ca Website: www.gov.mb.ca/finance/cca/consumb	**New Brunswick** Rentalsman and Consumer Affairs Department of Justice Centennial Building P.O. Box 6000 Fredericton NB E3B 5H1 Tel.: (506) 453-2682 Fax: (506) 444-4494 Website: www.gnb.ca/justice
Newfoundland and Labrador Trade Practices Division Department of Government Services 5 Mews Place P.O. Box 8700 St. John's NL A1B 4J6 Tel.: (709) 729-2600 Fax: (709) 729-6998 Email: gslinfo@gov.nl.ca Website: www.gs.gov.nl.ca/cca/tpl/	**Northwest Territories** Consumer Affairs Municipal and Community Affairs Suite 600, 5201 - 50th Avenue Yellowknife NT X1A 3S9 Tel.: (867) 873-7125 Fax: (867) 873-0609 Email: michael-gagnon@gov.nt.ca Website: www.maca.gov.nt.ca
Nova Scotia Service Nova Scotia and Municipal Relations P.O. Box 1003 Halifax NS B3J 2X1 Tel.: (902) 424-5200 Toll Free: 1-800-670-4357 Fax: (902) 424-0720 Email: askus@gov.ns.ca Website: www.gov.ns.ca/snsmr	**Nunavut** Consumer Affairs Community and Government Services P.O. Box 440 Baker Lake NU X0C 0A0 Tel.: (867) 793-3303 Toll Free: 1-866-223-8139 Fax: (867) 793-3321 Website: www.gov.nu.ca/Nunavut/ English/departments/CGT/

Ontario	Prince Edward Island
Ministry of Government Services Consumer Protection Branch 5775 Yonge Street, Suite 1500 Toronto ON M7A 2E5 Tel.: (416) 326-6414 Toll Free: 1-800-889-9768 Fax: (416) 326-8665 TTY: (416) 325-3408 TTY Toll free: 1-800-268-7095 Email: info.MGS@ontario.ca Website: www.ontario.ca/consumerprotection	Consumer, Corporate and Insurance Division Office of the Attorney General 4th Floor, 95 Rochford Street P.O. Box 2000 Charlottetown PEI C1A 7N8 Tel.: (902) 368-4550 Toll Free: 1-800-658-1799 Fax: (902) 368-5283 Website: www.gov.pe.ca/oag/ccaid-info/index.php3
Quebec	**Saskatchewan**
Office de la protection du consommateur Suite 450, 400 Jean-Lesage Boulevard Quebec QC G1K 8W4 Toll free: 1-888-OPC-ALLO (1-888-672-2556) Fax: (418) 528-0976 Website: www.opc.gouv.qc.ca	Consumer Protection Branch Saskatchewan Department of Justice Suite 500, 1919 Saskatchewan Drive Regina SK S4P 4H2 Tel.: (306) 787-5550 Toll Free: 1-888-374-4636 (Saskatchewan only) Fax: (306) 787-9779 Email: consumerprotection@justice.gov.sk.ca Website: www.saskjustice.gov.sk.ca
Yukon	
Department of Community Services Consumer and Safety Services P.O. Box 2703 Whitehorse YK Y1A 2C6 Tel.: (867) 667-5111 Fax: (867) 667-3609 Email: consumer@gov.yk.ca Website: www.community.gov.yk.ca The Andrew Philipson Law Centre 2130 - 2nd Avenue Whitehorse YT Y1A 5H6 Tel.: (867) 667-5111	

Source: Canada's Office of Consumer Affairs (OCA), www.ic.gc.ca/epic/site/oca-bc.nsf/en/ca01506e.html

CHAPTER 26

It's a Wrap!

You have taken in a large amount of information in these chapters. There is knowledge and power on these pages. Use it and use it wisely. Share what you have learned with your family and your friends. The more people who know what the banks and credit card companies are up to, the more power we have to fight back against their outrageous practices.

You have learned simple steps that can help you get your debt under control and help you take your life back. That is true freedom. Ridding yourself of debt is the first step to creating wealth.

You can apply these concepts and enjoy a debt free life. You can live the life of your dreams! It is possible – don't ever think it is beyond your reach! Lots of folks are buried in debt and being eaten up by all the interest and fees. These folks are stressed and anxious and frustrated. They could not see a way out. Now they can!

There is a way out! The methods that you have learned about here – the *Debt Cures* they don't want you to know about! – are already helping people just like you, and these methods can help you too! Don't ever think that you have to remain stuck in a life of debt and anxiety.

I hear from people every single day and they tell me how much their lives have improved. I want to hear from you. Join the thousands of others who have found relief and have moved on to victory over their creditors. You can triumph as well! Send your success story to success@ debtcures.com!

Don't forget that the *Debt Cures* newsletter provides continuing updated information of the credit lending industry, and all the latest opportunities for free money as soon as they become available!

Thank you for investing the time to read this book. You are making an investment in yourself, and there is no better way to spend your time. My sincere wish for you: happiness, health, and wealth. I look forward to hearing your success stories.

Kevin Trudeau

Cited Sources

(Current online as of July 24, 2007, certain sites updated as of February 14, 2008)

Chapter 1

"The California District attorney involved in the case stated…"
www.commondreams.org/headlines02/0713-02.htm

"The *San Francisco Chronicle* reported that Providian founder Andrew Kahr wrote…" www.commondreams.org/headlines02/0713-02.htm

"The man President Bush…" www.commondreams.org/headlines02/0713-02.htm

"…a story that was printed in the *Houston Chronicle*…" Steffy, Loren. *Houston Chronicle* 19 Oct. 2005. http://consumersdefense.com/news.html#agg

"They allegedly even told one nine-year-old girl…"
www.consumeraffairs.com/news04/2007/06/debt_horror.html

Chapter 2

"…first paragraph of the disclosure statement…" Disclosure Statement, Capital One, 2007.

Chapter 3

"In 1995, the government launched…" Morgenson, Gretchen. "Home Loans: A Nightmare Grows Darker." New York Times 8 Apr. 2007.l

"The financial aid director at Johns Hopkins University is alleged to…"
www.washingtonpost.com/wp-dyn/content/article/2007/05/21/
AR2007052101622.html

"According to a May 7, 2007, article in the *New York Times*…"
http://select.nytimes.com/gst/abstract.html?res=F30E17F73F550C728DDD
AC0894DF404482

"The April 2007 News Blog of the *Chronicle of Higher Education*…"
http://chronicle.com/news/article/1954/education-dept-puts-student-loan-
official-on-leave-as-controversy-widens

Chapter 4

"…words of Dr. Seuss, "Congratulations!…" Dr. Seuss. *Oh, the Places You'll Go!* New York: Random House, 1990. 1–2.

Chapter 5

Chapter 6

"When the president of a major credit card company…" www.opensecrets.org/2000elect/contrib/P00003335.htm

"In an interview for the PBS documentary *Secret History of Credit Cards*, Harvard law professor, Elizabeth Warren…" FRONTLINE's *Secret History of Credit Cards*. Dir. David Rummel. 2004. www.pbs.org/wgbh/pages/frontline/shows/credit/interviews/warren.html

Chapter 7

"The lender allegedly convinced them to sign the papers…" *Maxed Out*. Dir. James Scurlock. DVD. 2006.

"Duncan McDonald, former Citibank General Counsel…" FRONTLINE's *Secret History of Credit Cards*. Dir. David Rummel. 2004. www.pbs.org/wgbh/pages/frontline/shows/credit/etc/script.html

"According to TransUnion, an individual's credit score…" https://www.transunioncs.com/TCSWeb/help/terminologyFAQ.do;jsessionid=Gm9QyPxDRb14lbJqJ1LvxRZTCbsQKDNNqLQdBhd1V7m06LQy9NYF!463976471

Chapter 8

"In a documentary that aired on PBS called *Secret History of the Credit Card*, author and actor, and former host of *Win Ben Stein's Money*, Ben Stein…" FRONTLINE's *Secret History of Credit Cards*. Dir. David Rummel. 2004. www.pbs.org/wgbh/pages/frontline/shows/credit/etc/script.html

"Edward Yingling, president of the American Bankers Association, called the revolvers…" FRONTLINE's *Secret History of Credit Cards*. Dir. David Rummel. 2004. www.pbs.org/wgbh/pages/frontline/shows/credit/interviews/yingling.html

"According to a July 2003 survey by the Consumer Federation of America…" www.consumerfed.org/releases2.cfm?filename=072803 creditscores.txt

Chapter 9

"You can view one at …" www.debtcures.com/samplecreditreport

Chapter 10

"According to About.com: Home buying, the breakdown is as follows…" http://homebuying.about.com/cs/yourcreditrating/a/credit_score.htm

"A FICO credit expert, Hazel Valera,…"
http://vids.myspace.com/index.cfm?fuseaction=vids.
individual&videoid=10579847

Chapter 11

"According to credit expert Hazel Valera of Clear Credit Exchange, in her remarks to
the Millionaire Real Estate Club of Las Vegas…"
http://vids.myspace.com/index.cfm?fuseaction=vids.
individual&videoid=10579847

Chapter 12

"…the secondary market in bankruptcy paper."
www.businessweek.com/magazine/content/07_46/b4058001.htm

"Prisoners of Debt: Big lenders keep squeezing money out of consumers whose debts
were canceled by the courts."
www.businessweek.com/magazine/content/07_46/b4058001.htm

Chapter 13

"As of April 2007, six major universities (St. John's, Syracuse, Fordham, New York
University, University of Pennsylvania, and Long Island University) agreed to
over $3 million in reimbursements to students because of the revenue sharing
agreements they had with the private student loan agencies. Obviously these
students were not getting the best deal…"
www.msnbc.msn.com/id/18040824/: April. 10, 2007 Associated Press
"College loan scandal 'like peeling an onion'"

"Over 6 million federal student aid applications are processed online each year to get
a piece of the $67 billion…" http://usgovinfo.about.com/blstudentaid.htm

"Both types are Stafford loans and carry a fixed interest rate (currently 6.8 %)…"
www.finaid.org/loans/studentloan.phtml

"As we have talked about, the best interest rate is so important…"
www.finaid.org/loans/studentloan.phtml

"However, it is a little known fact that your loan can be discharged in the event of a
permanent disability." http://studentaid.ed.gov/PORTALSWebApp/students/
english/discharges.jsp?tab=repaying#content

"Once you have fulfilled this trial period, your loan will be returned to the regular
student loan servicing center, and the fact that it was in default status will
be DELETED from your credit report." www.ed.gov/offices/OSFAP/DCS/
repaying.html

"Monitor your credit report regularly and always review each monthly credit card
statement." www.debtcures/monitoring

"That's over 60 million people affected by this new change."
www.credit.com/credit_information/credit_report/Consumer-Alert-FICO-
Formula-Changes.jsp

Chapter 14

"You have a 30-year, $136,000 mortgage at 5.25%. If you paid each month…"
www.unitedfirstfinancial.com

Chapter 15

"In the film *Maxed Out*, a bankruptcy judge was asked…" *Maxed Out*. Dir. James
Scurlock. DVD. 2006.

"'We started robbing Peter to pay Paul…'" FRONTLINE's *Secret History of Credit
Cards*. Dir. David Rummel. 2004.
www.pbs.org/wgbh/pages/frontline/shows/credit/etc/script.html

"As Jim said, 'Forget the fact…'" FRONTLINE's *Secret History of Credit Cards*. Dir.
David Rummel. 2004.
www.pbs.org/wgbh/pages/frontline/shows/credit/etc/script.html

Chapter 16

"but according to www.bcsalliance.com and attorney Robert Hinsley of
www.consumersdefense.com…"
http://consumersdefense.com/bank-offenses.html &
http://bcsalliance.com/x_creditcardtricks2.html

"According to Houston attorney Robert Hinsley of consumersdefense.com…"
http://consumersdefense.com/bank-offenses.html

"MSNBC.com's Bob Sullivan reported…" Sullivan, Bob. "Capital One Sued Over
Marketing Practices." MSNBC.Com. 3 Jan. 2005.
www.msnbc.msn.com/id/6781155/

"According to Texas attorney Robert Hinsley…"
http://consumersdefense.com/bank-offenses.html

"In a 2007 article for reuters.com, Harvard Law School professor and bankruptcy
expert Elizabeth Warren…" Nicolaci Da Costa, Pedro. "U.S. Film Shows
Despair Under Mountain of Debt." *Reuters*. 21 Feb. 2007.
www.reuters.com/article/idUSN1535741120070220

"According to Gabriel Stein, an economist…" "U.S. Film Shows Despair Under
Mountain of Debt." *Reuters*. 20 Feb. 2007.
www.reuters.com/article/entertainmentNews/idUSN1535741120070220?
pageNumber=3

"According to a 2005 survey, the latest data…" Loeb, Marshall. "One late payment and
rates can skyrocket." *Market Watch*. 6 March 2007.
www.marketwatch.com/news/story/how-one-late-credit-card-payment/story.
aspx?guid=%7BA5BC6C3F-257F-4CB2-8839-FB193D263173%7D

"In the 2006 documentary film *Maxed Out*, director James Scurlock…" Bennett,
Jessica. "Q&A: The Hidden Dangers of Credit Card Debt." MSNBC.com
Newsweek. 14 April 2006. www.msnbc.msn.com/id/12306509/site/newsweek/

"In an April 2007 Market Watch article posted on Yahoo Finance..." Openshaw, Jennifer. "Getting Back in the Black." *Market Watch.* 13 April 2007. www.marketwatch.com/News/Story/Story.aspx?guid=%7BAE50CE51-44F2-4CEA-B4C2-71A01645C7BA%7D

"According to the CNNMoney..." Laurier, Joanne. "US consumer debt reaches record levels." *World Socialist Web Site.* 15 January 2004. www.wsws.org/articles/2004/jan2004/debt-j15_prn.shtml

"David Wyss, a chief economist..." Laurier, Joanne. "US consumer debt reaches record levels." *World Socialist Web Site.* 15 January 2004. www.wsws.org/articles/2004/jan2004/debt-j15_prn.shtml

Chapter 17

"The *Wall Street Journal* front page story on..." Malkin, Michelle. "Bank of Illegal Aliens in America." 13 February 2007. http://michellemalkin.com/2007/02/13/bank-of-illegal-aliens-in-america/

"An article on BusinessWeek.com..." "Embracing Illegals." 18 July 2005. www.businessweek.com/magazine/content/05_29/b3943001_mz001.htm

"James Scurlock, the maker of the documentary feature-length film, *Maxed Out,* states..."

Bennett, Jessica. "Q&A: The Hidden Dangers of Credit Card Debt." MSNBC.com *Newsweek.* 14 April 2006. www.msnbc.msn.com/id/12306509/site/newsweek/

"In an MSNBC.com article..." Bennett, Jessica. "Q&A: The Hidden Dangers of Credit Card Debt." MSNBC.com *Newsweek.* 14 April 2006. www.msnbc.msn.com/id/12306509/site/newsweek/

"In the movie Maxed Out, two mothers told..." *Maxed Out.* Dir. James Scurlock. DVD. 2006.

"Elizabeth Warren..." FRONTLINE's Secret History of Credit Cards. Dir. David Rummel. 2004. www.pbs.org/wgbh/pages/frontline/shows/credit/interviews/warren.html

"In the feature film documentary, *Maxed Out*..." *Maxed Out.* Dir. James Scurlock. DVD. 2006.

"In *Secret History of Credit Cards*, Harvard Law professor Elizabeth Warren..." FRONTLINE's *Secret History of Credit Cards.* Dir. David Rummel. 2004. www.pbs.org/wgbh/pages/frontline/shows/credit/etc/script.html

Chapter 18

"In the documentary *Secret History of Credit Cards,* the president of the American Bankers Association, Edward Yingling,..." FRONTLINE's *Secret History of Credit Cards.* Dir. David Rummel. 2004. www.pbs.org/wgbh/pages/frontline/shows/credit/interviews/yingling.html

"When Yingling talked about..." FRONTLINE's *Secret History of Credit Cards.* Dir. David Rummel. 2004. www.pbs.org/wgbh/pages/frontline/shows/credit/etc/script.html

"Elizabeth Warren argues..." FRONTLINE's *Secret History of Credit Cards*. Dir. David Rummel. 2004.
www.pbs.org/wgbh/pages/frontline/shows/credit/etc/script.html

"Let's return to the interview..." FRONTLINE's *Secret History of Credit Cards*. Dir. David Rummel. 2004.
www.pbs.org/wgbh/pages/frontline/shows/credit/interviews/yingling.html

Chapter 19

Chapter 20

"...in the movie *Maxed Out,*..." *Maxed Out*. Dir. James Scurlock. DVD. 2006.

"Attorney Richard DiMaggio states..." DiMaggio, Richard L. *Collection Agency Harassment,* Archimedes Press, Inc., 2002. 21.

"You want to push them..." Nicolaci Da Costa, Pedro. "U.S. Film Shows Despair Under Mountain of Debt." *Reuters*. 21 Feb. 2007. www.reuters.com/article/idUSN1535741120070220.

"Another collector told a woman..." DiMaggio, Richard L. *Collection Agency Harassment,* Archimedes Press, Inc., 2002. 10.

"A collection agent from San Diego was sent to prison..." Yuravich, Albie. "Keeping your debt collectors in check." *Register Citizen*. 23 May 2007. www.registercitizen.com/site/news.cfm?newsid=18374513&BRD=1652&PAG=461&dept_id=12530&rfi=6

"The New York attorney general..." AND "The Federal Trade Commission..." Chan, Sewell. "An outcry rises as debt collectors play rough." *New York Times*. 5 July 2006. http://consumersdefense.com/news.html#Outcry

"An article ran in the *New York Times*..." Chan, Sewell. "An outcry rises as debt collectors play rough." *New York Times*. 5 July 2006. http://consumersdefense.com/news.html#Outcry

Chapter 21

Chapter 22

"According to credit expert Hazel Valera..."
http://vids.myspace.com/index.cfm?fuseaction=vids.individual&videoid=10579847.

"Ms. Valera also said..." http://vids.myspace.com/index.cfm?fuseaction=vids.individual&videoid=10579847

Chapter 23

"The author of *Rich Dad, Poor Dad*, Richard Kiyosaki..." "Debt Free." *The Millionaire Inside*. CNBC.

Chapter 24

"One congressman commented..." www.grants.gov/aboutgrants/testimonials.jsp

"The SBIC site likes to share their success stories and reading them is very inspirational." www.sba.gov/aboutsba/sbaprograms/inv/INV_SUCCESS_STORIES.html

"The program's mission is to 'level the playing field.'" www.sba.gov/idc/groups/public/documents/sba_homepage/wbc.pdf

"Your one stop site for PK -12 school grant opportunities." www.schoolgrants.org

Chapter 24.5

Chapter 25

Chapter 26

Samples

Sample Letter of Net Worth

Date

Your Name
Your Address

Collector's Name
Collector's Address

Dear (name of collector or creditor):

Our firm has represented [your name] for the last several years. To the best of my knowledge, as of today's date, [insert date], [your name] is insolvent.

[Your name] does not have any material assets. [He/she] [*leases a car* and is *renting an apartment.*] According to the [Experian] credit report for [your name] as of [insert date of credit report], there is approximately [$xx,xxx] due to credit card companies. We are also aware of personal loans in excess of [$x,xxx].

As previously stated, [your name] is insolvent.

If you need any further information, please contact me.

Sincerely,

Name of Accountant

{**Note to Reader:** Send letter with return receipt requested and keep a copy for your records. Insert your appropriate information. If you own your home and/or car, of course, change or omit that sentence. Customize the letter to your situation. Use your credit report to your benefit. State your liabilities. Keep the letter brief. The key is to simply state that you are insolvent.}

Sample Letter to Debt Collector

Date

Your Name
Your Address

Collector's Name
Collector's Address

Dear (name of collector or creditor):

I'm writing in response to your [phone call/letter] of [insert date]. To the best of my knowledge, I do not owe that debt.

I have not been contacted by anyone about this alleged debt, and I ask you that you send me any and all information that you have on this debt: the amount, the creditor, and proof that you are licensed to collect debts in my state.

I am disputing this alleged debt. If you are not the party who owns this debt, please send my letter to the creditor who does, so that they are notified that I dispute this debt.

Sincerely,

Your Name

{**Note to Reader:** Send letter with return receipt requested and keep a copy for your records. Insert your appropriate information. Keep detailed records of all communications (telephone and letters) with debt collectors.}

BALANCE SHEET

Assets	Liabilities
Savings:	Home Mortgage:
Stocks/Mutual Funds/CDs:	Car Loans:
	Credit Cards:
	Student Loans:
Real Estate:	Other Bank Loans:
	Investment Property Mortgage:
Business:	Business Loans:
Autos:	Other Bank Loans:

INCOME STATEMENT

Monthly Income	Monthly Expenses
Salary:	Taxes:
Interest:	Home Mortgage:
Stock Dividends:	Car Payment:
	Credit Card Payment:
Real Estate:	School Loan Payment:
	Other Loan Payment:
	Child Expenses:
	Insurance (Home/Auto/Health):
Businesses:	Utilities:
Other:	Other Expenses:

Total Monthly Income _____

(minus) Total Monthly Expenses (_____)

Monthly Cash Flow _____